# James
## Faith Without Works is Dead

*An Urgent Call to Practical Christianity*

**Moses C. Onwubiko**
*Foreword by Dr. Tom Holland*

Essence
PUBLISHING

Belleville, Ontario, Canada

# JAMES
## Faith Without Works is Dead
Copyright © 2011, Moses C. Onwubiko

All Scripture quotations, unless otherwise specified, are from the *New American Standard Bible*, copyright © The Lockman Foundation 1960, 1962, 1963, 1968, 1971, 1972, 1973. All rights reserved. • Scripture quotations marked RSV are from the *New Revised Standard Version* of the Bible, copyright 1989, by the Division of Christian Education of the National Council of the Churches of Christ in the United States of America, and are used by permission. All rights reserved. • Scripture quotations marked NKJV are taken from the New King James Version. Copyright © 1979, 1980, 1982. Thomas Nelson Inc., Publishers. • Scripture quotations marked KJV are from *The Holy Bible, King James Version*. Copyright © 1977, 1984, Thomas Nelson Inc., Publishers. • Scripture taken from the HOLY BIBLE, NEW INTERNATIONAL VERSION ®. Copyright © 1973, 1978, 1984 by International Bible Society. Used by permission of Zondervan Publishing House. All rights reserved.

ISBN: 978-1-55452-651-2

Cataloguing data available from Library and Archives Canada

**To order additional copies, visit:**
www.essencebookstore.com

**For more information or
to order additional copies, please contact:**

Grace Evangelistic Ministries
P.O. Box 111999 Nashville, TN 37222-1999
www.gemworldwide.org

*Essence Publishing* is a Christian Book Publisher dedicated to furthering the work of Christ through the written word. For more information, contact: 20 Hanna Court, Belleville, Ontario, Canada K8P 5J2.
Phone: 1-800-238-6376. Fax: (613) 962-3055.
Email: info@essence-publishing.com
Web site: www.essence-publishing.com

## Dedicated to

My beloved Mother, Mrs. Abigail Onwubiko: Words are inadequate to express my gratitude to her for the role she played in my life. In ignorance of the truth, she carried me on her back as a child, or held me in her hand and walked thousands of miles in Africa often barefoot to occult services, far and near, one worship center to another. Then she found the truth she had been missing. She found Christ, the Savior! She is one of a kind; and for that I am immensely grateful to my Awesome God that He elected to bring me into this world through her, the finest mother I have ever known!

## In Memory of

John W. Brunner, for his fatherly love and role, in imparting to his son, the message of James' epistle. Undoubtedly, the indelible mark of James motivated his son, John G. Brunner, to both challenge and persuade me tirelessly to write this book for the benefit of everyone. Simply put, what this book in your hand means to my bosom friend, John G. Brunner cannot be expressed in words!

# Advance Reviews

"Moses Onwubiko is a first class communicator and he is correct to stress the security of the believer. He also helpfully stresses the importance of recognizing that justification language has a semantic domain (a range of meanings) and that it is important to choose the correct meaning by closely considering the context in which the word is used. Many will be helped by the way Moses unpacks the letter for his readers."

—**Dr. Tom Holland**, Head of Biblical Research, Wales Evangelical School of Theology, U.K.

"This book will move mountains."

—**John G. Brunner**, Chairman, ViJon, Inc. St. Louis, MO, U.S.A.

"This study of James epistle answers several thorny theological questions and provides timeless and indisputable insights. It settles an age old running battle between interpreters of the New Testament writings of the Apostle Paul and James the half brother of Jesus. This book is most refreshing and a must read by all who wish to divide the Word of TRUTH accurately."

—**Dr. Darlington E. Elekwa**, M. Div., National Facilitator for Haggai Institute, Nigeria

# Financial Policy

Grace Evangelistic Ministries does not solicit funding. We believe that God in His infinite grace will continue to meet our financial needs as they arise.

We do not charge for publications. No money is ever requested. When gratitude for the Word of God and realization of the need to reach unsaved souls with the simple grace gospel and sound Bible teaching motivates you to contribute, you have the privilege of giving and sharing in the dissemination of the Word of God. This is a grace ministry.

Grace Evangelistic Ministries
P. O. Box 111999,
Nashville, TN 37222-1999
www.gemworldwide.org

# Contents

# Foreword

In an age when much Christian publishing focuses on the stories of celebrities or those who aspire to be such, it is a pleasure to commend a book that focuses in the church's experience of God and the discipleship of her members.

Moses C. Onwubiko is a man who knows the importance of Christian experience and discipleship. His evangelistic and teaching ministries have touched the lives of countless thousands of people for the good of their souls and the glorification of Christ. Sadly, such teachers are not in abundance in the Christian church today and, therefore, this book is an even more valuable resource.

Commendably, Moses does not point to his own experiences but to a crucial New Testament letter that deals with Christian behavior. He takes his responsibility to understand the great teachings of Scripture very seriously, marking him out as a true servant of Christ. It is because of this that I warmly recommend this book to you as a valuable guide to a more mature faith in Jesus Christ.

Dr. Tom Holland
Head of Biblical Research
Wales Evangelical School of Theology
United Kingdom

# Acknowledgments

My profound gratitude goes to Dr. Tom Holland for taking his time to read through our first draft of James. To Pastor Andy Paterson for providing Kingston Baptist Church in the UK as a platform to address and discuss the Epistle of James and to his Assistant Pastor, Tayo Arikawe, of the Gambia who introduced us all. To Rev. Bruce Bumgardner for his ongoing friendship and candid review and to John Brunner a driving force behind this book.

Often the work of editors is not recognized and appreciated. But they should be! They are the eagle eyes of a well written book. With this in mind, I owe my deepest gratitude to Debby Hagar for her passion and the time she spent collecting everyone's input, questions, and her editorial and proofreading contributions! The same gratitude goes to Karen Frantzen, and Richard Hays.

Others who played a vital role in getting this book to you are Kevin and Patti Banker, Debbie Bendy, Paula Bowers, Elaine Brokaw and Perry Hartman. Last but not least Sherrill Brunton, chief editor (Essence Publishing) and her editorial team. Working behind the scene is my God-given wife, Gloria. Her effort can only be rewarded by Him who holds our future.

To top off my overflowing gratitude, I pour it all on the alter of praise to my Lord and Master, my Savior Jesus Christ, the Epicenter of Christianity, thanking Him for His unsurpassed sacrifice on the cross 2,000 years ago!

# Word of Hope

*But a natural [unsaved] man does not accept the things of the Spirit of God; for they are foolishness to him; and he cannot understand them, because they are spiritually apprai*sed (1 Corinthians 2:14).

This is the fact of God's Word! Based on this truth, the information in this book cannot benefit you unless you are a believer in the Lord Jesus Christ. The good news is that you can trust the Lord Jesus Christ for your salvation right this minute, right where you are, and be eternally saved! How good can such good news be? The news even gets better: salvation is a free gift! It is the epitome of God's grace! What's more, it is very simple to obtain. It's as easy as ABC! In Acts of the Apostles 16:30, a man desperate for his eternal destiny asked this urgent question to Paul and Silas: "*Sirs, what must I do to be saved?*" The Scriptures alone provide the one and only answer: "*They [Paul and Silas] said, 'Believe in the Lord Jesus, and you will be saved, you and your household [if they would also believe]'*" (Acts 16:31).

It's that simple! Faith alone in Christ alone!

Elsewhere the apostle John declared, "*But these [facts, including unique miracles that Jesus Christ performed] have been written [recorded] so that you may [have the evidence to] believe that Jesus is the Christ, the Son of God; and that believing [in Christ alone] you may have [eternal] life in IIis name*" (John 20:31).

Later, the same apostle affirmed, "*Whoever believes that Jesus is the Christ [the Savior] is born of God*" (1 John 5:1).

*"For God so loved the world, that He gave His only begotten Son, that whoever [including you—whoever] believes in Him [will] not perish, but [will] have eternal life"* (John 3:16).

Contrary to public opinion, salvation is not based on morality or good works. It's a free gift (Romans 6:23). The apostle Paul vividly stated, *"For by grace you have been saved through faith; and that not of yourselves, it is the gift of God; not as a result of works [i.e., good works], so that no one may boast"* (Ephesians 2:8-9).

It's faith alone in Christ alone! That's grace! That's God's way! The only way! No other way! Believe on Him and be eternally saved. Right now, you may wish to pause and heed the exhortation of the Holy Spirit: *"For He says, 'AT THE ACCEPTABLE TIME I LISTENED TO YOU, AND ON THE DAY OF SALVATION I HELPED YOU'…behold, now is 'THE DAY OF SALVATION'"* (2 Corinthians 6:2 emphasis added).

You can receive this great and awesome gift of salvation and be forever saved by simply telling God the Father, "God, I am placing my trust entirely on Your Son Jesus Christ as my Savior." The Bible gives the only assurance you need: *"He who believes in the Son has eternal life; but he who does not obey [the command to believe in] the Son will not see life, but the wrath of God abides on him"* (John 3:36).

The moment you believe, you will, for the first time, be indwelt and filled with the Holy Spirit, who in turn enlightens you as you read on!

# Restoration to Fellowship

Sin ruptures our fellowship with God and robs us of the filling of the Holy Spirit, the Greatest Teacher of all time. If you are already a believer in the Lord Jesus Christ, you need to ensure that you are filled with the Holy Spirit, so that He will open your eyes to the truth communicated herein; so you may comprehend and appreciate *"with all the saints what is the breadth and length and height and depth"* (Ephesians 3:18) of His unchanging Word! In preparation, you may pause, search your soul, and acknowledge all known sins to God the Father. The Bible is crystal clear: *"If we confess our [known] sins, He is faithful and righteous to forgive us our [known] sins and to cleanse us from all unrighteousness [unknown or forgotten sins]"* (1 John 1:9).

Dear Heavenly Father,

We approach Your throne of grace with an offering of thanksgiving and petition for all who will be reading this book. We pray that its doctrinal content will be a tremendous source of a challenge and blessing to all of us.

Father, we humbly ask that You revive us in Your truth so that the impact of Your infallible Word will reverberate and reign supreme in our souls. May the content thereof cause people everywhere to take a fresh look at both personal and national disasters. Please challenge us to turn to You in every sense of the word. We lift our prayer in the name of our Savior, Jesus Christ. Amen.

# Introduction

Beloved of God, we are indebted to God's matchless grace for James' epistle, one of the most unique and most practical in the New Testament. It is a short epistle, only five chapters. But it's packed with words of admonition and rebuke for believers who had drifted from their spiritual life as well as words of exhortation and encouragement to the remnant who remained spiritually on course. Our task is a simple one: to accurately interpret James' epistle and clarify its message, through the empowerment of the Holy Spirit, for the edification of the saints.

Many scholars believe that James, the half brother of our Lord Jesus Christ, was the author of the epistle that bears his name. We do not know the exact date of its authorship, although Zane C. Hodges, the Late Greek professor at Dallas Theological Seminary, suggests dates of A.D. 34-35.[1] Most scholars hold the view that the epistle was written very early and may possibly be the first recorded epistle of the New Testament. Its intended audience was Jewish Christians, which is clear from the text itself.

*"James, a bond-servant of God and of the Lord Jesus Christ, To the twelve [Jewish] tribes who are dispersed abroad: Greetings"* (James 1:1). Why did James address his epistle in this manner? Because at the time of his writing, the Gentiles as a group of people had not yet been included in the Church Age, which began on the Day of Pentecost. Present on that day *were [only] Jews living in Jerusalem, devout men from every nation under heaven"* (Acts 2:5). Robinson concurs:

James is addressing all who form the true, spiritual Israel [i.e., Jews who, like Abraham, had been born again by faith alone in Christ alone in the second Person of the God-head (Yahweh or LORD in the OT, and Christ in the NT)], wherever they are. And he can address them in such completely Jewish terms not because he is singling them out from Gentile Christians but because, as far as his purview is concerned, there are no other Christians [at this time].[2]

Gentiles were added to the Church at a later date, Cornelius and his household being the first (Acts 10). This inclusion began with a dialogue between the Lord and the apostle Peter while he was in a trance. The Lord introduced forbidden animals to Peter and told him to "*kill and eat*" (Acts 10:13). God used the occasion to assure Peter that the Gentiles were now part of the royal family of God through faith alone in Christ alone. Later the apostle Peter used the incident to convince his fellow apostles of this. Luke highlights,

> "*Therefore if God gave to them [the Gentiles] the same gift as He gave to us also after believing in the Lord Jesus Christ, who was I that I could stand in God's way?" When they [the Jewish disciples] heard this, they quieted down and glorified God, saying, "Well then, God has granted to the Gentiles also the repentance that leads to life*" (Acts 11:17-18).

This epistle was written out of James' abiding love and passion for his fellow believers. How do we know this? Think of it; James called them "my brethren" or "my beloved brethren" at least fifteen times. No other author of Scripture, in a single epistle, has addressed his audience this many times. He employed those brotherly phrases because of the bond they shared by means of their "*faith in our glorious Lord Jesus Christ*" (James 2:1; cf. Hebrews 2:11).

We can presume that some recipients of James' epistle had been members of the Jerusalem Christian church where he was a leader, before persecution drove them out (Galatians 2:9; cf. Acts 8:1-4). We know that, in God's plan, persecution or suffering often brings awesome results. That's Good News!

When my team and I visited China in 2010, we had the privilege of meeting Samuel Lamb, a founder of the house church movement in China—a 21st century hero of the faith! He told us that the more the Chinese government persecuted him, the more his church grew both spiritually and in number. How true! His church membership grew, under governmental pressure and twenty years imprisonment, from less than a dozen to over 400 and now has grown to over 4,000, with his outreach and influence going far beyond!

The early church had the same experience. Persecution caused Christianity to spread like wildfire. Believers formed new churches as persecution drove them from one place to another. The sad news for James' audience was that under prolonged persecution and suffering they grew lukewarm. Finally, they became cold and apathetic, and as a result many committed spiritual adultery (James 4:4; cf. 1 John 2:15). What's more, a great number of them completely lost touch with their first love: their Savior, Jesus Christ (cf. Revelation 2:5).

Beloved, words are inadequate to describe their spiritual failures as true believers. The bottom line is that they had immersed themselves in a quagmire of perpetual carnality. Their state of spiritual degeneracy prompted James' admonition in the strongest terms. He challenged them to put aside *"all filthiness and all that remains of wickedness"* (James 1:21; cf. 1 Peter 2:1). Because of their indifference to the Word, he exhorted, *"Receive the word implanted, which is able to save your souls"* (James 1:21; cf. 1 Peter 2:2). That's not all; many of them had abandoned their spiritual life and were behaving like unbelievers. For example, church leaders were mistreating the poor *"with an attitude of personal favoritism"* (James 2:1).

The list of their spiritual failures grew even larger. They developed a heart of coldness to the needs of their fellow brethren. They addressed the needy with spiritual phrases, such as *"Go in peace, be warmed and be filled"* (2:16). They knew the correct verses to quote but many times came short of actually allowing the Lord to use them to meet those needs. This inclination can be seen in Christians today.

James rebuts such a merciless attitude: "*If a brother or a sister is without clothing and in need of daily food, and one of you [my brethren] says to them, 'Go in peace, be warmed and be filled,' and yet you [a believer] do not give them what is necessary for their body, what use is that?*" (James 2:15-16).

In other words, what kind of application of biblical truth is that? Later, the apostle John painted more graphically this picture of false application of biblical truth in regard to love: "*But whoever has the world's goods, and sees his brother in need and closes his heart against him, how does the love of God abide in him? Little children, let us not love with word or with tongue, but in deed and truth*" (1 John 3:17-18).

What's more, the little truth they knew stalled in application. This begged a rhetorical question from James, their spiritual father: "*What use it, my brethren, if a man says he has acquired biblical truth, but he has no application? Can that biblical truth without application deliver him from divine punishment?*" (James 2:14).[3]

Of course the answer is *no*! Heartbreakingly, the poor spiritual condition of the recipients of James' epistle doesn't end in their indifference to the needs of their fellow believers. They had become busybodies. They began maligning and judging others. They developed an appetite for approbation in the area of teaching, which drew a stern warning from their spiritual father: "*Let not many of you become teachers*" (James 3:1). Their misuse of the tongue had become so hurtful to self and others that James devoted an entire chapter to dealing with this issue (James 3). They had sunk so low spiritually that James had no choice but to label them spiritual "*adulteresses*" (James 4:4). Even then, they were still his "*beloved brethren.*" That's grace!

We are not yet finished. Cheating, defrauding and withholding the poor man's wages had become a way of life for many of these born-again believers! Chilling is the right word for this heartless and unjust practice.

James, as a spiritual doctor, took time to carefully diagnose the spiritual problems of his Christian audience and their ramifications. He was aware of the Old Testament quotation "*For whom the LORD loves [including James' readers] He reproves [disciplines severely]*" (Proverbs

3:12; cf. Hebrews 12:6; Psalm 119:67, 71). Realizing that much of their suffering came from their spiritual condition, James admonished, "*The prayer offered in faith will restore the one who is sick...and if he has committed sins, they will be forgiven him*" (James 5:15).

James knew the majority of his readers were heading to a point of crisis where maximum divine discipline would result in premature physical death. "*A man who wanders from the way of understanding Will rest in the assembly of the dead*" (Proverbs 21:16; cf. 10:27; 1 Corinthians 11:30). Aware of these truths, he made a heart-wrenching appeal: "*My brethren, if any among you [Jewish Christians] strays from the truth and one turns him back, let him know that he who turns a sinner [believer in prolonged carnality] from the error of his way will save his soul [life] from [premature physical] death*" (James 5:19-20).

My beloved, here is the dramatic testimony of James' love and compassion, as well as the bedrock of our introduction. The next two chapters are important to prepare us to understand the background necessary for the correct examination and interpretation of this magnificent epistle.

Part 1

# Preparation for the Study of James

## ONE

# James and Paul in Perfect Harmony

Debates have raged for centuries over apparent contradictions in James' and Paul's epistles. The debate was so heated that Martin Luther called James' work "the epistle of straw"[4] and suggested that it be placed in an appendix. What we seek in our work here is not only to identify and clear up some misconstrued words, phrases and terminologies, but also to demonstrate that both Paul and James were in perfect harmony.

The harmony between James' and Paul's thinking is fascinating. Their approaches and messages are so similar that one is forced to conclude that this is the work of the Holy Spirit! We know the word of God cannot contradict itself, because God is not the author of confusion (1 Corinthians 14:33).

To set the stage we observe two groups of believers; both had been in a prolonged state of carnality—James' audience and Paul's Corinthian congregation. See how these men expressed a sense of maturity in the way they defused the time bomb of spiritual maladjustment with gentleness (Galatians 6:1), sensitivity, great poise and grace. Both had traits of humility and hearts that glowed with compassion.

They began helping their Christian audiences recall their position in Christ. James emphasizes that every good thing, which would include salvation, is a *"perfect gift"* (James 1:17). The apostle Paul couldn't have agreed more: *"The free gift of God is eternal life"* (Romans 6:23; cf. 1 Corinthians 1:7). James underscores that their salvation is the work of God: *"In the exercise of His will He brought us forth [i.e., new birth]"* (James 1: 18). The apostle Paul tells the Corinthians the same thing: *"By His doing you are in Christ Jesus"* (1 Corinthians 1:30).

## Assurance of Salvation by Grace

So both believe salvation is a matter of God's grace. This, however, does not negate our responsibility. Man is solely responsible in accepting God's ultimate "free gift" by an act of trust (confidence), faith alone, in Christ alone.

Despite the colossal failures of their audiences, both James and Paul addressed them as God's children, *"brethren"* (James 1:2; cf. 1 Corinthians 3:1). Both reminded them that the Holy Spirit indwelled them (James 4:5; cf. 1 Corinthians 3:16). James never had a doubt about the eternal salvation of his audience.

The apostle Paul didn't doubt the salvation of his audience either. He said to them, *"[You are] men of flesh, as to infants in [union with] Christ"* (1 Corinthians 3:1). Both James and Paul, as spiritual shepherds, were concerned for their flocks. Out of love they wanted to warn their congregations about the danger of premature physical death and lack of eternal reward. James makes it clear: *"When sin is accomplished, it brings forth death"* (James 1:15). Likewise, Paul warned, *"For this reason many among you are weak and sick, and a number sleep [have already died]"* (1 Corinthians 11:30). Concerning the sin issue, both Paul and James begin with gentleness and build up to strong castigation.

To the Corinthians, the apostle Paul appealed, *"Now I exhort you, brethren, by the name of our Lord Jesus Christ, that you all agree and that there be no divisions among you, but that you be made complete in the same mind and in the same judgment"* (1 Corinthians 1:10).

What about James? *"My brethren, do not hold [stop the habit of holding] your faith [confidence] in our [James' plus his readers'] glorious Lord Jesus Christ with an attitude of personal favorit*ism" (James 2:1).

Having gained their attention, James sharply chastises his audience, *"You adulteresses"* (4:4). While this is spiritual adultery as we shall see when we get to James 4, Paul's sharp rebuke was literal: *"Shall I then take away the members of Christ and make them members of a prostitute? May it never be [God forbid]!"* (1 Corinthians 6:15). You see some of these believers who have been *"washed," "justified,"* and *"sanctified"* (1 Corinthians 6:11) were returning to their old lives of pleasure in the pagan temple that, according to Dr. Spiros Zodhiates, was offering "a thousand sacred prostitutes."[5] He added that at Corinth, "Pleasure was worshipped more than principles."[6]

These believers were actually involved in sexual misconduct with prostitutes. So Paul admonished, *"Or do you not know that the one who joins himself to a prostitute is one body with her?"* (1 Corinthians 6:16). One can speculate, as did Dr. Zodhiates, that since the apostle Paul could not spend more time with them before he left, perhaps some were having a hard time breaking away from old habits.

This could also be true of James' audience. They had little time to become rooted in God's plan before persecution began and forced them out of Jerusalem during the formation of the early church. Though they were already saved (James 2:1), James' indictment sticks: *"You adulteresses, do you not know that friendship with the world is hostility toward God? Therefore whoever wishes to be a friend of the world makes himself an enemy of God"* (James 4:4).

What's more, in application of God's word, James was emphatic. *"What use it, my brethren, if a man says he has acquired biblical truth, but he has no application? Can that biblical truth without application deliver him from divine punishment?"* (James 2:14).[7]

Similarly, the apostle Paul reminded his readers, *"If I have all faith, so as to remove mountains, but do not have love, I am nothing"* (1 Corinthians 13:2). He is nothing, or useless, not unsaved or an immaterial object. Paul implies that any claim by these carnal Corinthians of super-duper miraculous faith is useless if they do not demonstrate agape[8] love.

More than this, James and Paul each emphasize rewards. The apostle Paul maintained that a believer who failed to execute God's plan would lose every reward, *"but he himself will be saved, yet so as through fire"* (1 Corinthians 3:11-15). James, on the other hand, uses Abraham and Rahab to illustrate that one is justified by faith (confidence) alone for his eternal salvation and by application for his reward. Believers are justified for rewards based on works—the maximum execution of

God's plan for the individual's life (James 2:21-26). Beloved, the comparisons are endless.

Another issue we need to address before we launch into James is the idea that one who is saved *must* produce good works. Keep in mind that Scripture must harmonize with Scripture. We discover that many interpreters fall short in their effort to reconcile obscure passages such as James 2:14-26 with the rest of the Bible. An example is Millard J. Erickson. In his work *Christian Theology* he states "works do not produce salvation. Yet the biblical witness also indicates that while it is faith that leads to justification, justification must and will invariably produce works appropriate to the nature of the new creature that has come into being."[9]

This statement sounds appealing. The problem is that his commentary cannot be reconciled with the rest of Scripture. He, and others who take this position, imply that every genuine believer must produce good works. However, this clearly conflicts with other passages of Scripture, such as,

> And I, brethren [a reference to those who are united with Christ], could not speak to you as to spiritual men [those who bear fruit in Christ], but as to men of flesh [lack of spiritual production, carnal], as to infants in Christ. I gave you milk to drink, not solid food; for you were not yet able to receive it. Indeed, even now you are not yet able, for you are still fleshly [carnal, after about 18 months since their conversion and face-to-face teaching with the great apostle, Paul. Yet there was no sign of fruit (Acts 18:11)]. For since there is jealousy and strife among you, are you not fleshly [carnal], and are you not walking [living] like mere men [unbelievers]? (1 Corinthians 3:1-3).

Despite his rebuke, he added, "*For we [Paul and his colleagues] are God's fellow workers; you [the carnal Corinthians] are God's field [no matter your status quo],…you belong to Christ [no matter the state of the believer, carnal or spiritual]; and Christ belongs to God*" (1 Corinthians 3:9, 23).

This is amazing indeed!

Of course, a good student of God's Word would never ever argue that the Corinthian believers were not genuinely saved, for Paul affirmed their salvation. For example, the word *sanctified* in 1 Corinthians 1:2 is a perfect tense participle and also in the passive voice. The perfect tense underscores the fact that their sanctification was once and for all (cf. Hebrews 10:10). The passive voice highlights the fact that their salvation was solely God's business from start to finish—from the onset of their confidence alone, in Christ alone to the end (1 Corinthians 1:7-9, 30). James also believed this (James 1:18). But again, anyone who examined 1 Corinthians through the lens of so-called saving faith would wonder if they were truly saved. But they were! Their salvation was a gift (Romans 6:23), not according to their deeds (2 Timothy 1:9)! It's grace from start to finish! It's arrogance to think that a believer who fails in his spiritual life is not truly saved.

What about the Exodus generation? Should we doubt their salvation? Over two million of them were eternally saved on the "Passover night" prior to their deliverance from slavery in Egypt. But suffice it to say, *"they believed in the LORD [Yahweh]"* (Exodus 14:31), the same way their father Abraham *"believed in the LORD; and He reckoned it to him as righteousness"* (Genesis 15:6).

However, from that moment on, spiritual failure marked their journey. Many times, the Lord punished them severely. For instance, on one occasion *"twenty-three thousand fell in one day"* (1 Corinthians 10:8; cf. Numbers 25:9). Because of their accumulated spiritual failures the Israelites eventually used up their last extension of grace, and the Lord, according to His justice, had no recourse but to administer judgment: *"So the LORD'S anger burned against Israel, and He made them wander in the wilderness forty years, until the entire generation of those who had done evil in the sight of the LORD was destroyed"* (Numbers 32:13).

Two questions are in order. Were they believers? What was their spiritual failure?

The Bible states they were believers: *"All ate the same spiritual food; and all drank the same spiritual drink, for they were drinking from a spiritual rock which followed them; and the rock was Christ"* (1 Corinthians 10:3-4).

But nothing in their behavior could point anyone who observed them to the life of Christ. They had been delivered from slavery by the true God, yet they returned wholeheartedly to idolatry. Over and over they complained about God and Moses. God called them "*an obstinate people*" (Exodus 32:9). At one point, God wanted to wipe them out completely. They were spared only because of Moses' intercessory prayer (Exodus 32:10-14). Afterward, they continued in obstinate carnality until God destroyed that generation because of their "*unfaithfulness*" (Numbers 14:33). Moses failed also, and his failure cost him entry into the promised land. Clearly the promised land was a reward. **Loss of that reward did *not* mean loss of salvation.** Remember, that same Moses was with the Lord at His transfiguration (Matthew 17:2-3).

In light of this truth, take notice: it is false to believe that those who are truly saved must produce good works. To believe this is to believe that the spiritual life is automatic, that it is a natural thing. On the contrary, it requires self-discipline, personal responsibility and perseverance, utilizing the power of the Holy Spirit (Philippians 2:13). To insist that regeneration *must* evidence itself in good works is to downplay the enormous magnitude that the sin nature exerts on us upon new birth (Galatians 5:16, 17).

## Commanded to Bear Fruit

An observant student of the Word may ask, "Why does passage upon passage of Scripture use the imperative mood, commanding us to bear fruit, if bearing fruit is automatic based on regeneration?" Good question! Why command something that happens naturally? For instance, "Why command a pregnant woman to deliver her baby on her delivery date?" That sounds ludicrous.

Scriptural mandates abound commanding us to do things that are totally unnatural to our human nature: "*Therefore bring forth fruit in keeping with repentance*" (Matthew 3:8). John the Baptist commanded those who had accepted his message to bear fruit. There was no guarantee that all would respond to his mandate. Similarly, the apostle Paul wrote the believers in Ephesus, "*For you were formerly darkness [unregenerate people], but now you are light in the Lord; walk [present imperative = Keep on walking] as children of light…Do not participate [present imperative = stop participating] in the unfruitful deeds of darkness, but instead expose them*" (Ephesians 5:8, 11; cf. Romans 13:12-14).

The Lord Himself explicitly mandated, "*Abide in Me [a command],... As the branch [born-again believer] cannot bear fruit of itself unless it abides in the vine, so neither can you unless you abide in Me. I am the vine, you are the branches [all believers]; he who abides in Me and I in him, he bears much fruit, for apart from Me you can do nothing*" (John 15:4-5).

Then comes the warning: "*If [indicating possibility] anyone [any believer] does not abide in Me, he is thrown away as a branch [unfruitful believer] and dries up; and they gather them, and cast them into the fire and they are burned [metaphor for intensive divine discipline and premature death]*" (John 15:6).

What's more, these proponents ignore, or fail to take into account, that believers who take their spiritual life carelessly may end up in perpetual carnality and consequently suffer premature death. That's the heart of James' epistle, and he addresses it head-on (James 1:13-15; 1:21; 5:19-20). We shall develop this as our study progresses.

But before we do, we need to further consider the issue of fruit-bearing: "*So then, you will know them by their fruits*" (Matthew 7:20). Someone can be truly saved and not manifest the life of Christ (1 Corinthians 3:1-3). If the believer chooses to perpetually live in carnality it can result in premature death (John 15:4-6; 1 Corinthians 11:30). We can hardly conclude whether one is saved or not based on one's lifestyle.

But what about Matthew 7:20, "*So then, you will know them by their fruits*"? Good question! Many lift this verse out of context and in conjunction with James 2:20, "*Faith without works is useless,*" hold the position that if there is no manifestation of good works in life, the believer is not "really" saved. Time and again we forget that the Church is the Lord's and that He alone is responsible for its upkeep (Ephesians 5:25-27). This, every believer ought to hold securely in their mind.

Dr. Arnold Fruchtenbaum in his commentary on James states that "Lordship salvation"

> Insists that good works inevitably accompany saving faith. Thus, in that sense, works are a condition of obtaining salvation; but

33

neither...James nor any other biblical writer teaches this. The good works are a result of and not a cause or condition of salvation. Even so, not all believers will consistently build with gold, silver, and precious stones. Many will build, even primarily so, with wood, hay, and stubble. Yet, even those are said to be saved (1 Corinthians 3:11-15).[10]

He adds,

Lordship salvation claims that while a true believer may fall into deep sin, because of its interpretation of perseverance of the saints, such a believer will eventually repent. While that was true with David, there is no evidence that Solomon ever repented for falling into idolatry. Solomon was, indeed, eternally saved; but he did not persevere to the end. Hence the term eternal security is much more fitting than the term perseverance of the saints. If perseverance is the issue, then it is better expressed as the perseverance of God, since it is God Who keeps the believer saved.[11]

We saw from our earlier examination that one can be saved and not manifest any good works. One of our examples was the Corinthian believers. Despite Paul's rebuke, he assured them, *"For we are God's fellow workers; you are God's field [no matter your status quo], God's building...you belong to Christ [no matter what]; and Christ belongs to God"* (1 Corinthians 3:9, 23; cf. 5:1-5).

The apostle Paul voiced his frustration to the Corinthians because of their lack of spiritual production. They were not living the spiritual life and were hindering the manifestation of the fruit of the Spirit (Galatians 5:19; cf. Ephesians 4:30). Think of it; Paul's epistle came to them after about 18 months of his face-to-face teaching of truth!

Let's assume you were a fruit inspector for the Corinthians. Based on the premise that those who are saved *must* show evidence by good works, is there one iota of spiritual fruit among the Corinthian believers that would compel you to conclude that they were saved? Outwardly no, but inwardly these have been *"circumcised [once and for all] with a circumcision made without hands…[but] by the circumcision of Christ"* (Colossians 2:11)! They were already in Christ by God's doing! *"But by His doing you are in Christ Jesus"* (1 Corinthians 1:30) (You may want to pause here and read the entire epistle.)

*"So then, you will know them by their fruits"* (Matthew 7:20). But what fruits? Are the fruits in question the outward manifestation of one's life? Not according to the context, as we shall see.

In the Old Testament, we notice that King Saul was saved. He had an enduement[12] of the Holy Spirit (1 Samuel 10:9-10). Which of the fruit-inspectors in Saul's day would, after observing his life as a believer in Yahweh, conclude that he was ever saved? Did Saul bear fruit? Yes, he did, but what kind of fruit did he bear? Was not the fruit that marked his life that of intense anger, hatred, jealousy and many attempts of premeditated murder against David (1 Samuel 18:6-11)? Obviously, the outward manifestation of Saul's life was anything but pleasing to God; yet he was truly saved. But hold it!

> *So Saul died [premature death] for his trespass which he committed against the LORD, because of the word of the LORD which he did not keep; and also because he asked counsel of a medium, making inquiry of it, [and as a believer] did not inquire of the LORD. Therefore He [God] killed him and turned the kingdom to David the son of Jesse* (1 Chronicles 10:13-14).

We can see that Saul paid dearly. A believer does not turn their back on God without severe consequences. The question then is: What is the accurate interpretation of Matthew 7:20, *"So then, you will know them by their fruits"*? Let us turn to the context.

In Matthew, the Lord's warning is worthy of our attention: *"Beware of the false prophets, who come to you in sheep's clothing, but inwardly are ravenous wolves. You will know them by their fruits"* (Matthew 7:15-16). Ravenous wolves in sheep's clothing! What a camouflage! My friend, how can you recognize a wolf in sheep's clothing? Can you identify him as a wolf by observation? Not at all! That's exactly the point the Lord seeks to make (cf. 2 Corinthians 11:12-15). Likewise, we cannot pinpoint those who are truly saved by observation or "fruit-inspection."

And even then, *"The Lord knows those who are His"* (2 Timothy 2:19). What a true statement! While we are to love everyone unconditionally; treat everyone who claims to be a Christian, without any suspicion of whether the individual is born again or not, ultimately, the Lord is the only One, who knows, and can accurately identify *"false prophets, who come to you in sheep's clothing"* (Matthew 7:15-21). No one else can with certainty! This is because man's heart is so deceitful (Jeremiah 17:9); and often its content is not always registered on one's forehead where it can be read and deciphered! God is the only One, who can read us inside-out! Thank Him for that!

To drive His point home, the Lord used the example of false prophets:

> *"Not everyone who says to Me, 'Lord, Lord,' will enter the kingdom of heaven, but he who does the will of My Father who is in heaven will enter. Many will say to Me on that day, 'Lord, Lord, did we not prophesy in Your name, and in Your name cast out demons, and in Your name perform many miracles? And then I will declare to them, 'I never knew you; DEPART FROM ME, YOU WHO PRACTICE LAWLESSNESS'"* (Matthew 7:21-23).

Take notice! These false prophets laid hold of their works for salvation. Their claims were undeniable! They did spectacular works! But were they saved? No. They depended on their good works and rejected God's grace offer (eternal life appropriated by means of confidence alone in Christ alone, Ephesians 2:8, 9). They did not do the will of the Father.

We ask, "What exactly is the will of the Father for the unbelievers?" Scripture has the answer: *"For this is the will of My Father, that everyone who beholds the Son and believes in Him [confidence alone] will have eternal life, and I Myself will raise him up on the last day [guaranteed]"* (John 6:40). God's will for an unsaved person is simply to trust (have confidence) in Christ alone (Acts 16:31).

The answer to the meaning of *"So then, you will know them by their fruits"* (Matthew 7:20) is found in another passage. Remember, we use Scripture to interpret Scripture. We all concurred, according to

Scripture, that a wolf in sheep's clothing can hardly be detected as a wolf. So in Matthew 12:33-37, what the Lord meant came to light. *"Either make the tree good and its fruit good, or make the tree bad and its fruit bad; for the tree is known by its fruit. You brood of vipers, how can you, being evil, speak what is good? For the mouth speaks out of that which fills the heart...For by your words you will be justified."*

The issue is "words," and not outward manifestation. We all run into people who outwardly are sweet as pie and honeycomb but inwardly are not regenerated. This hidden side often manifests itself when there's a conversation regarding Christ, the Savior. It is possible to differentiate a wolf in sheep's clothing from a true sheep, not by his actions, but by his words. Only when the wolf in disguise barks does he reveal himself, for sheep cannot bark!

The writer remembers vividly a heartbreaking circumstance that happened to a young lady in a church where he was once a member. A young man, though a ravenous wolf in a sheep's clothing, came into the church as a true sheep of our Lord. His purpose was crystal clear, namely, to marry this lady. He did everything to associate with the church. He was baptized. He participated in all church activities. Outwardly, he appeared to be one of us. He eventually married this lady and went on a honeymoon and never came back to church. Later he told her that he wasn't interested in a church, and he hadn't made up his mind to trust in Christ. There you have it! A great example of our verse (Matthew 7:20).

In case you are still unconvinced, consider Judas Iscariot. He is a perfect example to illustrate that *"you will know them by their fruits"* has no bearing on overt manifestation. Was he saved?

Let's back up a bit. He was called and chosen by the Lord (Matthew 3:13-19). He was among those sent to evangelize (Luke 9:1-2). He was the ministry's treasurer (John 12:6). He ate with the Lord, served with the Lord; he did everything all the other disciples did. But, he was a wolf in sheep's clothing. His co-disciples didn't even know that he was a wolf. They were exceedingly disturbed when our Lord said, *"One of you will betray Me. Being deeply grieved, they each one began to say to Him, 'Surely not I, Lord?'"* (Matthew 26:21-22). In other words, "Who would do such a thing among us?" They did not know!

Only the Lord knows who are His! Only He knew that Judas wasn't His; although Judas was one of the chosen ones, Jesus knew that one of them "*is a devil*" (John 6:70). He knew that Judas was one of those "*who do not believe*" (John 6:64). That's why our Lord could say to His disciples, "*You are clean [metaphor for spiritual purification], but not all of you*" (John 13:10). Judas was not clean (John 13:11). Only the Lord knew that he was "*the son of perdition*" (John 17:12), the lost one. My beloved, herein is our Lord's word exemplified!

"*So then, you will know them by their fruits*" (Matthew 7:20) is more or less inward, expressed in words rather than actions. It is possible to be a fruitless believer, but that status comes with a great price, discipline in time and lack of reward in eternity (2 Peter 1:5-9; cf. Proverbs 21:16; 14:27; 10:27)!

Beloved, with the problem of what seemed to be an apparent contradiction between these great men of God, the apostle Paul and James, resolved, we are now ready to till the ground in order to lay a solid foundation for the studying of James' epistle. To this end, we must give the next chapter our undivided attention. It holds the keys that unlock the entire epistle of James.

# TWO

# Understanding Key Words in James

James' epistle is like a two sided-coin. One side is a revelation of God's justice regarding spiritual failure. The other side is a treasury of information about how a Holy God justifies a believer to receive superabundant blessing, both in time and eternity.

For centuries many of the words in James have been misinterpreted, making the book of James the most misunderstood, misapplied and distorted epistle in all of Scripture. Sadly, its misinterpretations have neutralized many believers in the Lord Jesus Christ, causing them to live less effectively as Christians.

We ask, "Why has this fine epistle become an object of distortion and false teaching?" The answer is straightforward: Satan. Scripture casts light on his craftiness and manner of operation; he is a master schemer. He targets unbelievers and believers alike.

- In the case of unbelievers, he works tirelessly to blindfold the "*minds of the unbelievers, to keep them from seeing the light of the gospel of the glory of Christ*" (2 Corinthians 4:4 RSV).

- He targets believers in Christ on two fronts, distortion and spiritual life, in order to neutralize them. Let's examine these in detail.

First, Satan launches an attack on believers using distortions of the Word of God as his weapon. He used this tactic in the Garden, where he successfully twisted God's prohibition to Adam and Eve (Genesis 2:16-17; cf. 3:1-6). He tried the same scheme with the Lord, but was unsuccessful (Matthew 4:6; cf. Psalm 91:11-12). He searches Scripture for any possible ambiguity in an interpretation of a passage. When he finds one, he concentrates on that passage to ensure that believers spend their time disputing and arguing over its meaning, leaving little or no time to master and digest its truth. In that way, he slows them down, or totally neutralizes them from actually learning and applying God's Word to their lives, so they cannot fulfill God's plan (2 Timothy 2:14).

Satan realizes that if he can distract scholars and Bible teachers—particularly those who think they can interpret any passage without total reliance on the Holy Spirit—by engaging them in endless debates, then his plot is victorious.

On the second front he assaults the believer's spiritual life. While Satan is not omnipresent, his demons are everywhere. They concentrate their time and energy on distracting believers from living a life worthy of their calling (Ephesians 4:1). Satan knows that he can render believers' testimony ineffective by making their lifestyles depict the opposite of what they profess. This is clearly why the apostle Paul cautions the Philippian brethren "*Only conduct yourselves in a manner worthy of the gospel of Christ*" (Philippians 1:27). In other words, let your lifestyle accurately reinforce and reflect your testimony concerning Christ.

In James' epistle, we come face-to-face with the reality that Satan is indeed at work to obscure its meaning. He has succeeded, tempting so many scholars and Bible teachers to spend their time in disputes over biblical matters.

Satan has also succeeded in persuading many to view James' work as one that is meant to question the genuineness of believers' faith. Rather it was meant to challenge believers of James' day to get right with God and advance with their spiritual life. Obviously, many Bible teachers, because of oversight and inaccurate interpretation of the Epistle of James arrived at a conclusion that, according to James, salvation must show itself in works. In the following chapters we will clearly show that an individual can be truly saved by faith alone in Christ alone and still fail to live up to his new life.

James explains, "*You see then that a man is [also] justified [experientially] by works [for reward], and not by faith only [confidence in Christ for salvation]*" (James 2:24 NKJV). With this verse James sets the tone for a double justification, which we shall discuss later.

Here, we underscore our primary purpose in this chapter: to draw the attention of teachers and believers to Satan's scheme and the passages that he has attempted to obscure. With careful scrutiny, we discover that many passionate and honest Bible communicators err in their interpretation of James' epistle by misuse of words.

My beloved, make no mistake, words are important! Our misunderstanding of words inevitably leads to misinterpretation. To this effect, we need to pay special attention to words and their context. To highlight this truth, consider the word *lead*. According to Webster's New World Dictionary, *lead* has several meanings based on context. It means "guide," "to be at the head or be first," "lead on:—to guide further." But it can also mean "a heavy, soft, gray metal that is a chemical element."[13]

---

**My beloved, make no mistake, words are important!**
**Our misunderstanding of words inevitably leads**
**to misinterpretation.**

---

Armed with this knowledge, we list eight key words in the epistle of James and their contextual use. We must understand the meaning of these words **in context** if we are to understand James' message. If we fail to do this properly, we shall fall short of accurately interpreting James' epistle.

## Overview of the Key Problematic Words in James

• *Faith*: Greek *pistis*, has at least four meanings:
1) Trust/confidence (Hebrews 2:13; Psalm 56:3)
2) Believe (Acts 16:31; Deuteronomy 1:32)
3) Faithful/faithfulness/reliability/trustworthy (1 Corinthians 1:9; Lamentations 3:23)
4) Biblical truth/beliefs/doctrine (James 2:14; Jude 1:3)

• *Believe*: Greek *pisteuo*, a cognate of the Greek word *pistis,* has two meanings:

1) Trust (John 3:16; Acts 16:31)
2) Biblical truth/doctrine/beliefs (James 2:19; 2 Timothy 2:13)

• *Save*: Greek *sozo*, has at least four meanings:
1) Salvation/Save: saved from eternal lake of fire (Acts 16:31; Ephesians 2:8)
2) Rescue: saved from physical danger (Acts 27:31; Psalm 56:13)
3) Deliverance: saved from premature physical death (James 1:21; 5:19-20)
4) Restore: bring back, reinstate (James 5:15)

• *Soul*: Greek *psuche*, means one of four concepts:
1) Man: (Ezekiel 18:4)
2) Spirit: (1 Thessalonians 5:17)
3) Life: (James 1:21; 5:20)
4) Soul: (Ezekiel 18:4)

• *Works*: There are at least six Greek words in the Bible for works:
1) *Ergazomai*: used intransitively in Matthew 21:28; John 5:17, and transitively "to work something, produce, perform, e.g., Matt 26:10."[14]
2) *Katergazomai*: "to work out, achieve, effect by toil" (Romans 1:27)
3) *Energeo*, "work in" used in passive to denote God's energizing power in the believer to accomplish His purpose, "*It is God who is at work in you, both to will and to work [energeo] for His good pleasure*" (Philippians 2:13). Used of the Holy Spirit (1 Corinthians 12:11; of God's Word (1 Thessalonians 2:13).
4) *Poieo*: "to do", is rendered to work in Matt. 20:12, A.V."[15]
5) *Sunergeo*: "to work with or together" (Romans 8:28).
6) *Ergon*: among other things denotes
    i. Works of morality as in Galatians 2:16, "*since by the works of the Law [morality] no flesh will be justified*."
    ii. Works of sensitizing, thinking and applying principles of biblical truth to every exigency of life. For example, Abraham's works in offering Isaac on the altar (James 2:21; cf. Hebrews 11:17-19) is not a work of morality.

iii. divine deeds done by believers through the power of the Holy Spirit (Hebrews 6:10)

• *Dead*: Greek *nekros,* there are at least eight types of death in Scripture:
1) Pre-salvation spiritual death (Romans 5:12)
2) Post-salvation temporary spiritual death (Romans 8:6)
3) Physical death—separation of human spirit and soul from the body (John 11:14)
4) Second death—eternal separation from God (Revelation 20:14)
5) The death of Christ on the cross (John 19:33)
6) Abraham's sexual death (Romans 4:19)
7) Dead womb (Romans 4:19)
8) Dead faith—metaphorically inactive—"*You are dead*" (Revelation 3:1)

• *Fruit*: Greek *karpos,* fruit has at least seven meanings in the Bible:
1) Natural fruit (Genesis 3:2)
2) Fruit of the womb (Psalm 127:3)
3) "*Fruitful labor for me [believers]*" (Philippians 1:22)
4) "*First fruit*"—a reference to the "first produce" (Numbers 18:12), and Christ's resurrection (1 Corinthians 15:20,23), the first group of believers in the Church Age, namely Jewish believers (James 1:18) etc.
5) Winning of souls (John 15:16-17)
6) Words (Matthew 12:33-37)
7) Fruit of the Holy Spirit (Galatians 5:22)

• *Anointing*: translated from two Greek words:
a) *Aleipho*: ordinary rubbing with oil as in the case of the Good Samaritan (Luke 10:34; cf. James 5:14)
b) *Chrio*: use of anointing oil in a sacramental sense (1 John 2:20)

With our list completed, we are now ready to begin identifying these eight key words contextually in James' epistle.

## Summary of Contextual Use of 8 Key Words

Beloved of God, we cannot over emphasize the importance of interpreting words based on their contexts. This is the hallmark of *"rightly dividing the word of truth"* (2 Timothy 2:15 NKJV). Context is not limited to one verse. Often, to interpret a word, the chapter or the entire book in which the word occurs must be carefully considered as part of its context. This helps eliminate the chance of misinterpretation.

---

**Context is not limited to one verse; often the chapter or the entire book must be carefully considered.**

---

We have listed eight key words. Misinterpretation of these words seem to be the primary source of confusion in James' epistle. With this in mind, let's scrutinize these words carefully, one by one.

## Faith

The word *faith*, like the word *lead*, has multiple meanings, as we just noted. This fact makes it difficult to determine one specific definition. The Bible defines *faith* as *"the assurance of things hoped for, the conviction of things not seen"* (Hebrews 11:1). Lewis Sperry Chafer expounded, "faith is a personal confidence in God."[16] These definitions still leave room for other definitions. For instance, *faith* also means "faithfulness," "trustworthiness," "reliability," "doctrine," "creed," "beliefs" and "biblical truth." Because of these various meanings, each definition of faith is strictly based on its context.

The use of *faith* in Romans 5:1, *"having been justified by faith [trust in Christ], we have peace with God,"* fits perfectly with the Hebrews 11:1 definition. But that is not true of 1 Corinthians 1:9, *"God is faithful."* The emphasis here is on God's reliability! But when faith denotes the body of truth, as in Jude 1:3, *"contend earnestly for the faith,"* the definition becomes "doctrine," "biblical truth," "beliefs," or "creed."

As a student of God's Word, a careful scrutiny of Scripture reveals that Jude and the apostle Paul, among other New Testament writers, used *pistis* to refer to biblical truth as well as trust.

Referencing salvation from the lake of fire, the apostle Paul affirmed, *"For by grace you have been saved [from the lake of fire] through faith [trust in Christ]"* (Ephesians 2:8). Referring to doctrine or biblical truth, he warned, *"But the Spirit explicitly says that in later times some will fall away from the faith [sound biblical truth], paying attention to deceitful spirits and doctrines of demons [falsehoods]"* (1 Timothy 4:1; cf. v. 6).

There Paul warned of apostasy, whereby many believers would abandon sound biblical truth in exchange for falsehood, namely, *"doctrines of demons."* The apostle is not alone; Jude did the same. In his epistle, we read, *"Beloved, while I was making every effort to write to you about our common salvation [from the lake of fire], I felt the necessity to write to you appealing that you contend for the faith [biblical truth] which was once for all handed down to the saints"* (Jude 1:3).

Jude wanted to stir up his fellow believers regarding their eternal heritage in Christ, their salvation. But the Holy Spirit redirected his thought to combat heretical teaching that had infiltrated churches. Jude appealed to his audience to hold tenaciously to *"the faith [sound biblical truth]"* that was earlier handed down to them through the teachings of the apostles. Later, he brought their attention to this faith (biblical truth): *"But you, beloved, ought to remember the words [i.e., faith—biblical truth] that were spoken beforehand by the apostles of our Lord Jesus Christ"* (Jude 1:17; cf. Hebrews 2:3; Acts 2:42).

We just mentioned two men, the apostle Paul and Jude, who used the word *faith* in the sense of biblical truth. Likewise James used the word *faith* to mean "biblical truth" as well as "salvation from the lake of fire." He did this before Paul and Jude, since his epistle was possibly the earliest written.

As a master Bible communicator, James took ample time to lay the foundation of the Word of God and emphasized its importance and exhorted: *"Receive the word implanted [biblical truth]"* (James 1:21).

We know that reception is not enough in any system. Application of what's fed into the system is the key to production. For example, if a car's fuel injector receives fuel from its gas tank but it is not being converted into kinetic energy by combustion in the engine, the fuel is of no use to the automobile. Its engine won't run. That's a fact! James, aware of this phenomenal truth about application, commanded, *"Prove yourselves doers of the word"* (James 1:22). He effectively urged them to convert biblical truth into spiritual kinetic energy.

---

**We must connect all five chapters of James to its superstructure of "receive" and "prove."**

---

The words *receive* and *prove* in verse 21 and verse 22, which are the same as *learn* and *apply*, are the contextual superstructure of James' epistle. Moreover, every chapter of James' epistle is laid bare on this structure. **Failing to see the connection between the five chapters of the book of James and its superstructure of learning and applying biblical truth is to misinterpret James.**

In James chapter 2, he uses the same word, *faith*, to express two different meanings, which is easily understood when we carefully examine context.

He exhorts, *"My brethren, do not hold [literally: stop the habit of holding] your faith [trust] in our glorious Lord Jesus Christ with an attitude of personal favoritism"* (James 2:1). In other words, he is saying, "As the regenerated ones, you are a living epistle to all in your periphery, both believers and unbelievers (2 Corinthians 3:2; 2:15), so live up to your spiritual identity in Christ!"

Studying James' work is exciting! See what the Holy Spirit did through him? He used James to remind his readers of their secured position in Christ (James 2:1; cf. Hebrews 10:10); and in between 2:1 and 2:14 exposed their failure to live up to their new life. Then, and only then, did he ask, *"What use is it, my brethren, if someone says he has faith [biblical truth] but he has no works [application]? Can that faith [literally, the faith[17] (i.e., biblical truth)] save him [from premature physical death]?"* (James 2:14).

Essentially, what James is saying is this: "You have done well in obeying the first mandate, namely to *"receive the word implanted"* (James 1:21). But you have failed the second, namely, *"[Be] doers of the word"* (James 1:22). By not allowing its truth to permeate your thoughts and actions, what good is the first one to you? Can partial obedience deliver you from divine discipline?"

With an understanding of James' dual use of the word *faith* we move on to examine the passage, considered by scholars as the battleground in James' epistle. Make no mistake; it's the epicenter of James' masterpiece: James 2:14-26.

> *What use is it, my brethren, if someone says he has faith [accumulation of biblical truth] but he has no works [no application]? Can that faith [biblical truth] save him [from physical premature death]?...Even so faith [biblical truth], if it has no works [application], is dead [it's of no use], being by itself...You believe [your belief or biblical truth is] that God is one. You do well; [but just remember] the demons also believe, and shudder [misapply the truth]...faith [biblical truth] without works [application] is useless. Was not Abraham our Father justified by works [application of biblical truth in his soul], when he offered up his son Isaac on the altar?...You see that a man is justified [experientially] by works [maximum application of biblical truth for super-abundant rewards] and not by faith [trust] alone. In the same way, was not Rahab the harlot also justified [experientially for reward] by works [application of biblical truth in her soul] when she received the messengers and sent them out by another way? For just as the body without the spirit is dead, so also faith [biblical truth] without works [application] is dead [of no benefit].*

---

### James' whole epistle is about biblical truth and its application!

---

Arguably, biblical truth and the imperative resultant application of that biblical truth are the main thrust of James' epistle. This explains why in thirteen verses (2:14-26), he employs the Greek word *pistis*, "faith," and its cognate *pisteuo*, "believe," fourteen times. Intriguing, is it not? This is because of James' emphasis on the importance of God's Word. His whole epistle is about biblical truth and its application! The tragedy is that many Bible teachers, scholars, pastors, and laymen fail to clearly discern the correct definition of the word *faith* as used by James in the preceding passage.

Beloved, we need not make this same mistake. James 2:14-26 is complex. It is the heart of the epistle. Many reputable Bible teachers have grown gray hairs over this book, and a good number died before they were able to unravel James' message to the Church. The worst result is that many falsehoods have sprung up from misinterpretation of this great passage. Clearly, this is where the issue of context is very crucial. Let's consider verse 14: "*What use is it, my brethren, if someone says he has faith but he has no works? Can that faith save him?*" (James 2:14).

We are faced with two tasks: first, ascertain which definition of *faith* James had in mind. Second, answer the question "Save him from what?" People's failure to determine which *faith* best fits the context of the passage is the main source of error, confusion and major doctrinal divisions in Christianity today.

One can see how easy it is to slide onto the path of error. For instance, if one takes the view that the *faith* in this verse relates to salvation from the eternal lake of fire, he must conclude that salvation must give evidence of itself in good works. Further, such a position compels him to come up with an unbiblical phrase, such as "saving faith." Tragically, many have slid down this pathway of false premise. The truth of the matter is that one cannot insert a phrase such as "saving faith" in this text without contradicting the text and the rest of Scripture!

There is much at stake. To take this position, in essence, says that it is not possible for a believer to live or die in perpetual carnality. Therefore the erroneous conclusion is that the person who lives or dies in carnality is not a believer. Beloved, such a position cannot stand the test of Scripture at large. It will collide with the apostle Paul's indictment of the Corinthian believers over their perpetual carnal lifestyles (1 Corinthians 3:1-3). To maintain that a believer who is truly saved would necessarily remain in constant touch with the Lord makes it difficult to interpret this passage: "*For this reason many among you are weak and sick, and a number [of believers in Christ] sleep [premature physical death]*" (1 Corinthians 11:30; cf. 5:1-5). Such a position is not biblical and ought to be rejected outright!

The good news is that God in His matchless grace *always* has a remnant that stays with the truth! In the course of our research and study, we have uncovered a handful of prudent scholars and students who have harmonized Scripture with Scripture and concluded that the correct definition of *faith* in this passage is biblical truth or doctrine. James Orr states clearly that in James 2:14, "*pistis,* 'faith,' appears in the sense of creed."[18] Unger agrees: "James' epistle is aimed at Jewish believers tempted to substitute…knowledge of the Law [creed or beliefs] for a heart experience of grace manifested [biblical truth applied] in holy life."[19] Dibelius and others agree. We shall cite more scholars and documentation as our study progresses.

Our next task is to answer the question "Save him from what?" Contextually, James had already laid the foundation on the importance of perception and application of the Word: "*Receive the word implanted*" and "*[Be] doers of the word*" respectively (James 1:21-22). He underscored that God's Word, if received and obeyed, would save a believer from discipline and premature physical death (v. 21). Scriptural warnings abound: "*A man [any believer] who wanders from the way of understanding [perception and application of God's Word] Will rest in the assembly of the dead*" (Proverbs 21:16; cf. James 1:21; Hebrews 12:6; Proverbs 21:16; 14:27; 10:27).

Based on the context of James 1:13-15, "*Sin [perpetual sinning]…brings forth death,*" coupled with verse 21, "*receive the word implanted, which is able to save your souls [lives],*" it makes sense to conclude that the answer to our question is actually to "save him" from the judgment of premature physical death! In fact, it is even clearer when we factor in James' own conclusion:

> *My brethren, if any among you strays from the truth and one [of you] turns him back [helps him to recover [Galatians 6:1], let him know that he who turns a sinner from the error of his way will save his soul [life] from death and [God as a result] will cover a multitude of sins [cancelling them for further discipline]* (James 5:19-20).

Now, let's consider another word, *believe*, that led to the misinterpretation of James 2:14-26.

## Believe

We come to another problematic word. James uses believe only twice, and it's in the same verse. "*You believe [your belief or biblical truth] that God is one. You do well; [but just remember] the demons also believe [i.e., their belief/doctrine is parallel with yours], and shudder [tremble because of their misapplication of this biblical truth/doctrine]*" (James 2:19).

*Believe*, *pisteuo*, is a cognate of the Greek word *pistis*. In a layman's term, *believe* is a generic name for "faith." Because they are the same, our task is to determine which one of the various meanings for *faith* best fits our passage.

At a glance, it appears as if James might be mocking those who claimed to be saved from the lake of fire without a demonstration of their salvation through works: "*You believe that God is one. You do well; the demons also believe, and shudder*" (v. 19). But that's not what James is doing here. We run into an impassible hurdle if we take the erroneous position that James was talking about salvation from the eternal penalty of sin. We know that salvation is by faith alone in Christ alone. This has always been true, for there is "*no other name under heaven that has been given among men by which we must be saved*" (Acts 4:12).

If James meant salvation for eternal life, that would imply that he equated their faith in Yahweh (Jesus Christ) with that of the demons, "*the demons [fallen angels] also believe, and shudder.*" But that can't be the meaning, because Jesus Christ was not a true substitute for angels. Jesus Christ did not die for the sins of both men and angels. As the God-Man, He died only for the sins of the entire human race (1 John 2:2). Agreed? James was saying that "the demons agree wholeheartedly with the Jewish doctrine: God is one."

We know that salvation is not based on one's trust in the theology of the Oneness of God but rather in the person and the work of Jesus Christ. James teaches a biblical truth that only angels and born-again believers would know—the Oneness of God. No unbeliever can comprehend the mystery of this truth, let alone believe it. Some religions reject Christianity because of our claim to this phenomenal truth.

Angels knew the truth that "God is One" long before man was created. Man can grasp this truth after regeneration. Based on this revelation, we reject the interpretation that the word *believe* means "trust" in James 2:19. Rather, in this context *believe* means "biblical truth," "creed," "belief," or "doctrine." James Orr couldn't have agreed more, citing that their belief "that God is one" "is the creedal confession of the orthodox Jews."[20]

Essentially, what James was saying is simply this: "You lay hold to the biblical truth 'that God is One'; the demons also laid hold to the same truth." It was their belief/doctrine. But this biblical truth did not do them (the fallen angels) any good; for they "shuddered." In other words, despite the fact that the angels knew that the three members of the Trinity—the Father, the Son, and the Holy Spirit—are one God (with three distinct personalities and functions, co-equal, co-eternal, possessing equal sovereignty and omnipotence), they still rebelled against God and paid a grievous price. So then what James was saying is "You may know the most sophisticated biblical truth in the world, but if you are not careful to apply its principles to life, it will not do you any good."

We have settled the two most confusing words in our passage, namely *faith* and *believe*. We take up another ambiguous word, *save*.

## Save

Repeat, context is the key to unraveling the true meaning of a word in a passage. We can never stress this enough. Context can be within a verse or include verses that are before or after it. It's not limited to the passage or chapter but also considers the whole book. What's more, scriptural context is governed by the entire Bible! In other words, any interpretation of a passage must consider the whole Bible.

---

**Context is the key to unraveling the true meaning of a word in a passage.**

---

Many of us are guilty of an honest mistake: whenever we read the word *save* in Scripture, we always think of being saved from the lake of fire. Just as the word *faith*, or *pistis* in Greek, has more than one definition, so does the English word *save*. The Greek for *save* is used in several ways. It can reference salvation from the eternal penalty of sin, as in Ephesians 2:8, "*For by grace you have been save*d." It can also be used in reference to salvation from danger or physical death, as in Acts 27:31, where the apostle Paul warned the centurion, "*Unless these men remain in the ship, you yourselves cannot be saved [from physical death by drowning]*" (cf. v. 34). Or as David puts it, "*For thou hast delivered [same Greek word "sozo"] my soul from [premature physical] death*" (Psalm 56:13 RSV).

Here is the sublime truth: when the word *save* refers to a believer who has already been saved spiritually from the eternal penalty of sin "*once for all*" (Hebrews 10:10), the meaning must be a *physical* definition, as in saved from physical harm or saved from premature physical death. This is how James always used the word, with only one exception: "*There is only one Lawgiver and Judge, the One who is able to save and to destroy; but who are you who judge your neighbor?*" (James 4:12).

Here, James made a statement about God's sovereignty in general. He means that God retains the sole monopoly of saving (eternal life) those who trust in His Son, while damning those who fail to respond to His grace initiative. The other four times James used the word *save*, his audience was the object. But, aha, these believers in Christ (James 2:1) had already obtained salvation from the eternal penalty of sin. This is why James called them "my brethren" and "my beloved brethren" at least fifteen times. The meaning of the word *save* must therefore be defined as physical, as in saved from premature physical death. For example, "*In humility receive the word implanted, which is able to save your souls [life, Greek psuche]*" (James 1:21).

We know that for the believer, a lifestyle of perpetual carnality is a ticket to an early departure to heaven. Solomon reveals, "*The fear of the LORD prolongs life, But the years of the wicked [a believer in perpetual carnality] will be shortened*" (Proverbs 10:27; cf. 29:1; 14:27; 21:16; 1 Corinthians 11:30; 5:1-5; 1 John 5:16).

Knowing all this, James warned his fellow believers about premature physical death. But, if they should heed his warning and deal with their personal sins and return to the study and application of God's Word, then such action would save them from premature physical death.

We have already examined James handling of the word *save* in 1:21, 2:14, and 4:12. The remaining passages are 5:15 and 5:20. The New American Standard Version correctly translated the Greek word *psuche*, "*restored*", in 5:15: "*And the prayer offered in faith will restore [literally, save from premature physical death] the one who is sick, and the Lord will raise him up, and if he has committed sins, they will be forgiven him.*" On the one hand, James indicates the possibility of sin being the reason for some of his readers' near death experiences. On the other hand, confessing their sin and returning to the Word and its application will save the believer from severe punishment.

This brings up the final passage: "*My brethren, if any among you strays from the truth and one [of you] turns him back [helps him to recover (Galatians 6:1)], let him know that he who turns a sinner from the error of his way will save his soul [life, Greek psuche] from death and will cover a multitude of sins*" (James 5:19-20). The last passage is self-explanatory. A believer who is in perpetual carnality is in danger of premature physical death unless he changes course, either by self-motivation or by the encouragement of someone else. In summary, this is how James uses the word *save* in his epistle.

This brings up another contextual word for our scrutiny.

## Soul

*Nephesh* is the Hebrew equivalent of the Greek word *psuche*, rendered "soul" in our English Bible. However "soul" is not the only correct translation for *psuche*. Like the Greek *pistis*, for *faith* or *believe*, or the Greek *sozo*, for *save*, it too has several meanings. *Nephesh* means "a breathing creature (man or animal), breath, respiration, life, soul, spirit, mind, a living being, creature, person."[21] We shall see that James only used the definition "life" in his epistle, and our corrected translations will reflect this.

It's the tedious job of a communicator to determine, based on context, which of these meanings best suits a verse. For example, "*Behold, all souls [nephesh] are Mine; the soul [nephesh] of the father as well as the soul [nephesh] of the son is Mine. The soul [nephesh] who sins will die*" (Ezekiel 18:4). Poor translation glares at us: "*The soul [nephesh] who sins will die.*" We know that souls are immortal. They cannot die. Sadly, this kind of poor translation finds its way into the epistle of James. This passage ought to have been rendered, "Behold, all souls [*nephesh*] are Mine; the soul [life, *nephesh*] of the father as well as the soul [life, *nephesh*] of the son is mine. The soul [man, *nephesh*] who sins will die."

Consider another verse that frequently suffers from poor translation: "*[Brethren] therefore, putting aside all filthiness and all that remains of wickedness [through confession (1 John 1:9)], in humility receive the word implanted, which is able to save your souls [Greek, psuche]*" (James 1:21).

---

**When a believer is admonished regarding salvation—it is deliverance for his physical life, not his soul life.**

---

We have already established the fact that *soul* is immortal; it cannot die. The soul of a believer has already been snatched away from everlasting torment (Colossians 1:13; cf. John 5:24). When a believer is admonished regarding salvation, the salvation in question is from physical danger and the object of deliverance is the believer's physical life and not his soul life. With this clarification in mind, we can correct the poor translation of James 1:21 and 5:19-20 respectively, "Brethren, therefore putting aside all filthiness and all that remains of wickedness through confession [1 John 1:9], in humility receive the word implanted, which is able to save your life from premature physical death" (James 1:21).[22] "My brethren, if any among you strays from the truth, and one of you helps him to recover [Galatians 6:1], let him know that he who turns a sinner from the error of his way will save his *life* from premature physical death, and will cover a multitude of sins" (James 5:19-20).[23]

The illuminating light of the Holy Spirit continues to glow brightly. Very exciting! So far, we have resolved the contextual mistranslation and or misinterpretation of the Greek *pistis* for "faith" or "believe," Greek *sozo* for "save," and the Greek *psuche* for "life." We are drawing closer to the main text. But first we have a few more words worthy of our attention.

## Works

*Works!* A misunderstanding on how James used the word *works* is another source of confusion in the interpretation of his epistle. Bible students who argue that James contradicts the apostle Paul fail to draw the line between the works Paul had in mind, (works of morality for salvation), and the works James had in mind, (works of application of biblical truth for a reward).

The apostle Paul was emphatic: "*By the works of the Law [morality, human works] no flesh will be justified*" (Galatians 2:16).

But James, speaking of rewards, asked, "*Was not Abraham [a believer] justified by works [application of biblical truth for rewards] when he offered up Isaac his son on the altar?*" (James 2:21).

The difference between these two men's positions on "works" is vividly clear. When we carefully look at the context (James 2:21-24), it's obvious that Abraham's offering of his son was not works of self-righteousness or morality. Rather, it was works of maximum application of biblical truth resident in his soul.

Here is the scenario: God promised Abraham that his son Isaac would be a blessing to the world. Decades later, He asked him to offer the same son as a sacrifice to Him. My beloved, this was not an ordinary testing. But Abraham was not an ordinary believer! He was mature. Because of his maturity, he concluded "*that God is able to raise people even from the dead*" (Hebrews 11:19). Essentially, in his soul he was thinking, "God had made a promise to me to bless the entire world through my son, Isaac (v. 18). On the one hand, this promise is yet to be fulfilled. But on the other hand, I am convinced that God will fulfill His Word, even if it takes death and resuscitation!"

Beloved, under the umbrella of "*rightly dividing the word of truth*" (2 Timothy 2:15 NKJV), this is the "works" James had in mind when he wrote, "*Was not Abraham [a believer] justified by works when he offered up Isaac his son on the altar?*" This was the works of Abraham's maximum demonstration of the level of his spiritual maturity.

Similarly, Job's maturity was tested. Interestingly, throughout Job's testing he did not perform any works. Job wasn't running around doing the so-called "great things for God." He was in one place. All his works were mental, articulating God's Word in every corner of his soul, at every turn in his suffering. When his testing was over, God rewarded him doubly (Job 42:10). God, in His fairness, could not have offered such testing to a baby believer (1 Corinthians 10:13), because a baby believer has not developed the capacity to articulate and apply biblical truth.

It was the spiritual maturity of Abraham and Job that allowed their competent articulation and application of biblical truth to their respective situations (Hebrews 5:13-14).

So then, James refers to "works" as application of biblical truth, not morality. It's mental! It's allowing God's word to permeate our thinking and actions. Such works are done for His glory, not to fulfill our lust for approbation. Such divine works always attract superabundant blessing.

Note: What God rewards is not the overt work, but rather the mental attitude behind the work (1 Samuel 16:7). People can do spectacular works, even as unbelievers (Matthew 7:21-22). Some carnal believers may even witness *"from envy and strife"* (Philippians 1:15).

Here is the truth: if we agree that the works in James 2:15-26 are works of application of biblical truth instead of works of morality, we must also accept that the works of 2:14 (the main context of verses 15-26) are the works of application of biblical truth. *"What use is it, my brethren, if someone says he has faith but he has no works? Can that faith save him?"* (James 2:14).

This verse should be correctly translated, "What use it, my brethren, if a man says he has acquired biblical truth, but he has no application? Can that biblical truth without application deliver him from divine punishment?" (James 2:14, author's translation).

If we accept this clearly presented truth, that the "works" of James 2:14 are the works" of application, then we must go further to also accept that the word *faith* in the same verse is simply biblical truth. You cannot have "works" (application) without having "faith" (biblical truth); the two go hand-in-hand! This brings us to yet another important word in James' epistle.

## Dead

Studying the eight types of death in the Bible is not within our scope. Scripture does not always use the word *dead* literally, as in "*Lazarus is dead*" (John 11:14). Sometimes it uses it metaphorically, as in "*the deadness of Sarah's womb*" (Romans 4:19). We too do the same. We call a stagnant or inactive sea a "dead sea." We call a hopeless pursuit a "dead end." Beloved of God, we must learn to draw a line between literal and metaphorical uses of this word in Scripture; otherwise we will make terrible mistakes in our interpretations.

For example, when we read the word *dead* in Ephesians 2:1, "*You were dead in your trespasses and sins*," we understand the apostle was not talking literally about a corpse. Far from it! We will inaccurately interpret this passage if we interpret it literally.

---

**We must draw a line between the
literal and the metaphorical.**

---

Unfortunately, some took the word *dead* literally to mean a corpse. This false concept led to a distortion of the biblical truth of the total depravity of man. They think a spiritually dead man is a mere corpse, therefore incapable of hearing or believing the Word of God without God giving him the "gift of faith" to trust in Christ. This logic fails to pass the acid test of Scripture.

In Romans 1 we read, "*For the wrath of God is revealed from heaven against all ungodliness and unrighteousness of men who suppress the truth in unrighteousness, because that which is known about God is evident within them; for God made it evident to them*" (Romans 1:18-19).

If we agree that this passage refers to unbelievers, we must agree that total depravity does not mean incapable of logical comprehension of truth. On the contrary, the apostle Paul knew that those he indicted were capable of sound reasoning: "*men who suppress the truth.*" One cannot suppress what one does not know. Agreed? Additionally, it would be tantamount to callousness on the apostle's part to conclude that "*they are without excuse*" (v. 20) if he knew that these unbelievers were literally dead, incapable of surveying God's majestic works (the galaxies and such) and concluding that this unique design requires a Supreme Being (Psalm 19:1).

Because Paul knew that they were capable of making rational decisions, even as spiritually dead people, he could say, "*That which is known about God is evident within them; for God [the impartial One] made it evident to them.*"

Other metaphorical uses of the word *dead* abound. "*Truly, truly, I say to you, the hour is coming, and now is, when the dead [Ephesians 2:1] will hear the voice of the Son of God [through the gospel], and those who hear [and trust in Christ] will live [have eternal life]*" (John 5:25).

Craig Keener, a New Testament professor, states, "'The now is' in 5:25 is significant (cf. 4:23): the believer enters new life (3:3,5).[24] "This life is applied to those who believe."[25] More importantly though, is the fact that if the reference to the word *dead* is taken literally, then the phrase *will hear* would not apply. Agreed? A corpse cannot hear. But that's not how the Lord uses it. He knew that every unsaved person is capable of hearing. However, understanding of the truth is the dynamic work of the Holy Spirit. He illuminates our minds at the point of hearing the gospel (2 Corinthians 4:6; cf. John 16:8-9). The unsaved cannot merit God's life, namely eternal life, apart from God's grace (Ephesians 2:8-9).

This brings up another passage where *dead* was used metaphorically. "*To the angel [pastor] of the church in Sardis write... 'I know your deeds, that you have a name that you are alive, but you are dead. Wake up'*" (Revelation 3:1-2; cf. Ephesians 5:14). Here, *dead* means the church at Sardis was not living the Christian life and was spiritually inactive. What's more, the command "*Wake up*" underscores the fact that their death is metaphorical. A corpse cannot respond to the command "Wake up!"

You see our point. We must not rush to conclusions without examining every word and every passage of Scripture to ensure harmony. Scripture must harmonize with Scripture. Similarly, every word in the book of James must harmonize with the rest of his epistle!

Sadly, many Bible students fail to comprehend the difference between literal and metaphorical interpretation in James' epistle, and elsewhere. For example, many Bible teachers took the word *dead* in James 2:14-26 literally (particularly in verse 26, "*faith without works is dead*"). In so doing, they erroneously concluded that if a believer is not bearing any spiritual fruit, the individual is not truly saved. This misinterpretation became fertile ground for planting the seed of "Lordship salvation."[26]

*But James uses the word in a metaphorical sense.* Recall, James had previously exhorted, "*But prove yourselves doers of the word, and not merely hearers who delude themselves*" (James 1:22). That's the other side of "faith [biblical truth] without works [application] is dead [is of no use]."

An arsenal of biblical truth in one's soul is utterly useless (*dead*) if it's not applied. Unapplied truth cannot advance anyone spiritually. It cannot shield anyone from divine discipline or the judgment of premature physical death. The principle is clear: It's not what we know that saves us from premature physical death; it's our application of truth that delivers us.

This brings us to the second to last of the eight crucial words in James.

## Fruits

The word *fruits* occurs once in James' epistle, in 1:18, where James refers to his Jewish brethren as "*a kind of first fruits among His creatures.*" Here, there is no ambiguity over James' use of the word. But because many Bible teachers have misapplied our Lord's references to the word *fruits* in Matthew 7:20, we consider it of paramount importance to examine this word.

These Bible teachers used this passage, "*You will know them by their fruits,*" to justify their erroneous position that a born-again believer must produce divine fruits (works). We have already settled the issue of what James meant by works: application of biblical truth based on one's level of spiritual growth. We have studied Abraham's demonstration of his maturity: "*Was not Abraham our father justified by works when he offered up Isaac his son on the altar?*" (James 2:21). Similarly, Rahab applied the truth in her soul: "*In the same way, was not Rahab the harlot also justified by works when she received the messengers and sent them out by another way?*" (James 2:25). Her works demonstrate application of the truth that what God has promised, God is able to fulfill!

Just like "**faith**," "**believe**," "**save**," "**soul**," "**works**," and "**dead**" have several meanings, as we have clearly delineated, so does the word *fruits*. Scripture uses the word figuratively, as in "*the fruit of the Spirit*" (Galatians 5:22) and metaphorically, as in "*a kind of first fruits among His creatures*" (James 1:18), a reference to the first believers in the Church Age. Scripture also uses the word literally, as in "*she took from its fruit and ate*" (Genesis 3:6).

The Lord uses the word in Matthew 7:20, "*You will know them by their fruits.*" He does not mean we can know if a person is a believer by observing outward or physical manifestations. This is underscored by this warning: "*Beware of the false prophets, who come to you in sheep's clothing, but inwardly are ravenous wolves*" (Matthew 7:15, emphasis added).

Do you see what He's saying? You cannot identify a false prophet, or an unbeliever for that matter, simply by observation! My beloved, we need *more* than observation before we can call someone a believer. We need to hear the individual speak: "*For the tree is known by its fruit...For by your words you shall be [known and be] justified, and by your words you will be condemned*" (Matthew 12:33,37). And even then, only the Lord knows those who are His (2 Timothy 2:19)!

Point blank, words, not works, reveal one's character! So those who employed the word *fruits*, in their effort to interpret James 2:14-26, have done more harm than good to the rest of the text. Their error had root in their misinterpretation of the word *faith* in James 2:14 and the subsequent passages 2:18-19 and 2:26. Because of this, they were compelled to come up with the false concept of "saving faith." Let's be clear: Scripture knows nothing about this coinage. This phrase does not help the cause of Christianity; it confuses the concept of salvation.

The word *faith* in active tense simply means "trust." Anyone who exercises trust in Christ is saved instantly (1 John 5:1), and his salvation is "*once for all*" (Hebrews 10:10). Beloved, whether the saved would run a successful spiritual race like the apostle Paul, "*I have finished the course...there is laid up for me a crown of righteousness*" (2 Timothy 4:7-8), or the believer would choose to live an incestuous lifestyle like the brother at Corinth (1 Corinthians 5:1-5), the good news is that both would arrive in heaven (1 Corinthians 3:11-15), because salvation has no connotation to works, good or bad (2 Timothy 1:9). The bad news is that the latter *"will be saved, yet so as through fire"* (1 Corinthians 3:15). He would have no reward for all eternity. This every careless believer ought to seriously consider, namely, the eternal ramifications of being in heaven with no rewards (2 Corinthians 5:10). So then *fruits* does not always mean outward manifestation. Context clarifies!

This brings us to the last problematic word in our study of the book of James.

## Anointing

Anointing oil was used in a unique spiritual ceremony, a ritual limited only to the Old Testament saints. There's no record of its practice in the entire New Testament. There's no mandate for it today. We ask, "Why not?" Scripture answers: *"The anointing which you received from Him abides in you [forever]"* (1 John 2:27, cf. v. 20). The Church Age also has a unique program, but it is entirely different from the Old Testament. What's more, the rituals of the Old Testament were *"a mere shadow of what is to come; but the substance belongs to Christ"* (Colossians 2:17; cf. Hebrews 8:5; 10:1).

In the Old Testament, anointing oil was used for both medical and spiritual purposes. Regarding therapeutic application, the Lord used sarcasm when He questioned those suffering in Israel. They had turned their backs on Him and were under divine discipline as a result: *"Is there no balm [therapeutic oil] in Gilead? Is there no physician there? Why then has not the health of the daughter of my people been restored?"* (Jeremiah 8:22; cf. 46:11).

*"Where will you be stricken again, As you continue in your rebellion? The whole head is sick...From the sole of the foot even to the head There is nothing sound in it, Only bruises, welts and raw wounds, Not...bandaged, Nor softened with oil"* (Isaiah 1:5-6).

This phrase *softened with oil* will help show why James referenced anointing oil in his epistle. We find in Scripture and secular records that the use of oil as medicine was ancient in its origin. For example, when the Good Samaritan saw the robbed and wounded man, he administered first aid by bandaging him up and "*pouring oil*" on his wounds (Luke 10:34).

In the secular arena, Mitton points out, "The use of oil in the treatment of illness was very common in the ancient world."[27] Mitton says this was also the view of Mayor, who got his information "from such writers as Josephus, Philo, [and] Pliny."[28] Mitton adds that "Galen...calls oil 'The best of all remedies for paralysis.'"[29]

Anointing oil was used in a spiritual sense to commission kings in the Old Testament. For instance, the prophet Samuel anointed Saul, Israel's first king, with a holy oil (1 Samuel 10:1). It was also used to anoint David as king (1 Samuel 16:13). This holy oil was also used in the consecration of priests. This we read from Moses' account, "*You shall make of these a holy anointing oil...With it...You shall anoint Aaron and his sons...that they may minister as priests to Me...'It shall not be poured on anyone's body...Whoever shall mix any like it or whoever puts any of it on a layman shall be cut off from his people*" (Exodus 30:25-33, emphasis added).

Then the use of all anointing oil in a spiritual sense was brought to a screeching halt. Our King, the Anointed One, was anointed by God as our Great High Priest once and for all (Hebrews 7:17, 21-25). In fact, one of the two Greek words for anointing, *chrio,* is the root for the word *Christos,* Christ "The Anointed One." Because His kingship and priesthood are eternal, there was no further need for anointing oil in a spiritual sense. Remember, all those Old Testament rituals were "a shadow." They were fulfilled in Christ. Consequently, in Him, we as co-heirs share in His priesthood (1 Peter 2:9; cf. Romans 8:17) and in His spiritual anointing (Acts 10:38; cf. Romans 8:17; 1 John 2:20).

In light of this insight we ask, "Why did James still exhort the church to apply anointing oil to the sick?" Did he have in mind ceremonial or medical purposes when he exhorted his readers to do this?

---

**Understanding *Chrio* and *aleipho* is critical in deciphering James' message about anointing oil.**

---

This is where "*rightly dividing the word of truth*" (2 Timothy 2:15 NKJV) comes in. We shall see when we get to James chapter 5 that the phrase "*anointing him with oil*" (James 5:14) has a connotation of physical therapy, and that he used oil in a therapeutic sense. You ask, "How can we be so sure?" Let there be no misunderstanding; the two Greek words that are critical in deciphering James' message with regard to his reference to anointing oil are *chrio* and *aleipho*.

If James had in mind the spiritual use of anointing oil, he would have used *chrio*. Since he did not have that in mind, the Holy Spirit impressed him to use the Greek word *aleipho*, which simply means, "to rub or apply ointment."[30] He uses this word for two reasons: medical and compassion.

Medical: when we study the word *sick* from James 5:14, we see that the word there is not the usual word for sickness, but rather for incapacitation. This condition can cause a person to develop bedsores. So oil becomes necessary to soften the wounds, as in Isaiah 1:6.

Compassion: An incapacitated person can hardly move around, let alone care for his own wounds. James wanted his audience to show compassion by applying oil directly on the sick person. In this way, the sick man would experience compassion in a direct and physical way as he felt the touching hands of loving saints. *"Be kind to one another"* is the mandate of Scripture (Ephesians 4:32), which can be expressed in many ways. For example, in the care of an incapacitated, sick person as in James 5:14, where a direct application, or rubbing of therapeutic oil to the individual's bedsore, is in fact an expression of compassion and kindness.

My beloved, the grave impact on the church today because of misinterpretation of James' message regarding anointing oil is heartbreaking. The negative impact is simply immeasurable! A great number have drifted into idolatry because of false teaching in the church about the use of oil. Many look to anointing oil as a problem-solving device for healing, eradication of poverty, and keeping evil at bay, just to name a few. This practice is evil. We shall handle this subject in detail during the course of our study.

## Conclusion

Having carefully considered the key words in James' epistle, such as *faith, believe, save, soul, works, dead, fruits* and *anointing*, and having seen how people gravely misunderstand and mistranslate them, it becomes crystal clear why we have so many erroneous interpretations of this mighty epistle.

Recognizing this problem, our goal as we study the book of James is to focus on these misinterpreted words, scrutinize them according to their contexts, and provide the most accurate definitions that best fit. Only when this goal is achieved can we accurately interpret the book of James. And only when James' passages are accurately interpreted can there be a polished mirror of His infallible Word to take a close look at ourselves in and align our theology and lives according to God's divine design and purpose. When the right words are used, passages can be accurately translated and interpreted; only then can our work benefit not only our generation but generations to come.

My beloved, this is what King David's prayer is all about: "*And even when I am old and gray, O God, do not forsake me, Until I declare Your strength to this generation, Your power to all who are to come*" (Psalm 71:18).

In view of all this, it's of paramount importance that we review those major key words in James' epistle, namely *faith* or *believe*, *save*, *dead*, *works*, *soul*, *fruits* and *anointing*, keeping in mind that they have various meanings.

**Faith** or **believe:** The word *faith* or *believe* can mean faithfulness, biblical truth and trust or even confidence. James uses the word *faith* and its cognate, *believe*, at least eighteen times. Of these, he used them fifteen times alone in chapter 2 to demonstrate the relationship between faith (biblical truth) and works (application of biblical truth).

In chapter 2, as well as in the rest of his epistle, context clearly shows that only twice did James use *faith* (trust) to mean salvation from the eternal penalty of sin. We see this in 2:1, "*Do not hold your faith [trust] in our glorious Lord Jesus Christ with an attitude of personal favoritism*" and in 2:24, "*You see that a man is justified by works [application of biblical truth for a reward] and not by faith [trust] alone [for eternal salvation].*" In 2:24 *two justifications are in view!*

Then, twice, he used *faith* referring to confidence in God regarding prayer (1:6; 5:15). Outside of these four references, wherever the word *faith* or its cognate *believe* is used, it's *always* in reference to biblical truth (1:3; 2:5, 14, 17-20, 22, 24, 26).

**Save:** Similarly, the word *save* can be used in a spiritual or physical sense. In the spiritual sense, it is *always* in relation to salvation from the eternal penalty of sin. But James uses it that way only once (4:12). The rest of the times, he *always* uses it in relation to salvation from premature physical death (1:21; 2:14; 5:15, 20).

**Soul:** This word also has multiple meanings. It appears only twice in James' epistle, and in both cases, it refers to human life (James 1:21; 5:20).

**Works:** in the same way, *works* has several meanings. For example, the *"works of the law"* (Galatians 2:16) has to do with morality, and the works that has to do with application of biblical truth, *"Was not Abraham our father justified by works when he offered up Isaac his son on the altar"* (James 2:21). Here, the issue is not morality. Rather, the focus is on application of biblical truth in Abraham's soul: *"He considered that God is able to raise people even from the dead"* (Hebrews 11:19). The word *works* in James' epistle *always* refers to works of application of biblical truth (2:14, 17, 18, 20, 21, 22, 24, 25, 26; 3:13).

**Dead:** Another word in our study of ambiguous words also has multiple meanings. A careful scrutiny of context shows that James only uses it to mean uselessness or inactive and never uses it to reference a corpse.

**Fruits:** This word appears only once in the entire text, and James uses it in a metaphorical sense (James 1:18).

**Anointing:** Last but not least, the phrase *"anointing him with oil"* is used once by James and is restricted to medicinal use (never for spiritual purposes). This we know with certainty because of the Greek word he selected, *aleipho*. This puts to rest any thought that perhaps he had something else in mind.

My beloved, the pool of James' epistle has been skimmed of all debris. The ambiguity in major key words has been cleared. Armed with this knowledge, we are eager to dive into the text. But not so fast! As we proceed, let's do so with fear and trembling, knowing that God will hold us responsible if we misinterpret His Word (James 3:1)! With this in mind, we must ask for His help.

See Appendix for Key Words Quick Reference.

Our Dear Heavenly Father,
In front of us is the pool of James' epistle. We cannot correctly interpret his work apart from Your help. Please, Father-God, guide our every stroke against all currents as we swim in this mighty pool of Your Word. Please illuminate our minds so that we may interpret James' epistle accurately. Soften our hearts so we may exercise genuine humility to accept Your truth. Above all, Father, may the truth communicated by James be of a great spiritual benefit not only to this generation, but to all generations to come, for the praise of Your glory.
In Christ's name, Amen.

# Part 2

# Stability of the Soul in Suffering

## THREE

# Salutation

*"James, a bond-servant of God and of the Lord Jesus Christ, To the twelve tribes who are dispersed abroad: Greetings"* (James 1:1).

Were someone to ask how many Gospels there are, you probably would say that's easy—four: Matthew, Mark, Luke and John. But an Irish evangelist says there are indeed five: Matthew, Mark, Luke, John and you! That's right! You are the fifth Gospel; I am the fifth Gospel! *"You are a letter of Christ"* (2 Corinthians 3:3), *"read by all men"* (2 Corinthians 3:2), *"a fragrance of Christ to God among those who are being saved and among those who are perishing"* (2 Corinthians 2:15). Let this truth sink deep.

There are many around you, family members, friends, neighbors, co-workers and church members, who often find themselves so busy that they hardly take the time to open the first Gospel, Matthew, let alone Mark, Luke or John. But they cannot help but "read" you every day as a Gospel, *"a letter of Christ."*

The big question is, what is in the newspaper of your daily life? Do others "read" you, and say, "This is a copy of the life of Christ" (Acts 4:13)? Does anyone say your spiritual life is inspiring? While you ponder these questions, let's look at One whose life was so contagious that it inspired many around Him in a remarkable way.

## James: Brother of Jesus

Before the public ministry of our Lord Jesus Christ, even before He called the twelve disciples, even before the four Gospels were written, Jesus Christ, (in His human nature), was the prototype Gospel, read by all who knew Him. He is our example, and emulating Him makes us the fifth Gospel. One of those who read him completely was none other than His half brother James.

A majority of scholars, including "The church Fathers, Origen, Eusebius, Cyril of Jerusalem, Athanasius, Augustine, and many other early writers,"[31] believed James, the brother of Jesus, to be the author of the epistle of James (Galatians 1:19; Matthew 13:55). With regard to this, Dr. John F. Walvoord writes, "Though James was reared in the same home with the Lord Jesus, he apparently did not become a believer until after Christ's resurrection."[32] "For even His brothers did not believe [trust] in Him" (John 7:5)."[33] "James' encounter with the risen Lord may have brought him to…faith."[34] The apostle Paul tells us that Christ *"appeared to James, then to all the apostles"* (1 Corinthians 15:7).[35] Paul later listed James, Peter, and John as "those reputed to be pillars of the church (Gal. 2:9)."[36]

James' unique position as our Lord's half brother gave him a special opportunity to communicate Jesus' gospel as "practical Christianity." There is no substitute for understanding James, the writer, if we are to comprehend and appreciate his epistle.

The ending of his salutation demonstrated his affection toward them. Anyone can utter the word *greetings*. For some it's just a ritual, but to James it meant more than that; it meant "Peace and prosperity to you."

We must realize that James was writing about practical Christian living in light of his own Christian experience. Jesus' life made an indelible mark on James, even as an unbeliever. Growing up, he had the privilege of witnessing firsthand the prototype Gospel, as Christ exhibited the life of perfect holiness and perfect obedience to God the Father and enjoyed the rewards thereof (Philippians 2:5-11). He had the privilege of witnessing the very One whose life was consumed with compassion (Psalm 145:8; cf. Matthew 14:14), sorrow (Isaiah 53:3), grief (Matthew 26:22), and unfailing love (John 15:13). *"While being reviled,*

*He did not revile in return; while suffering, He uttered no threats, but kept entrusting Himself to Him who judges righteously"* (1 Peter 2:23). This profound impact set the tone for James' epistle.

When he became a believer after our Lord's resurrection, James must have reflected on all he had observed. He was aware of the Lord's unsurpassed suffering and saw how He handled suffering and injustice with great poise and courage. The unforgettable lessons about the power of the spiritual life and prayer impacted his own life and ministry. The life of Christ influenced and shaped James' life to the point that others regarded him as a pillar of the Jerusalem church.

The mark Christ's life left on James was manifest in both his leadership (Galatians 2:9; cf. Acts 15:1-35) and this epistle. To miss this point is to miss the overarching influence of the life of Christ on James, which guided his thoughts as he wrote. James' life had been enriched beyond measure; therefore he stood in the gap to help others. Failing to share what had so enriched his life would have been unimaginable and self-centered. By the power of the Holy Spirit (2 Peter 1:20) and with our Lord's love and compassion, he wrote a heartfelt epistle to the new Jewish believers who were dispersed outside of Jerusalem, many of whom he had known.

It's helpful to know where James came from in order to understand his impassioned plea for his brethren to *"consider it all joy...when you encounter various trials"* (James 1:2). One would have to know the content of his soul in order to understand his passionate plea for his brethren to *"prove yourselves doers of the word, and not merely hearers"* (James 1:22). One would have to be "in his shoes" to understand his fervent plea for his brethren not to hold their *"faith [trust] in our glorious Lord Jesus Christ with an attitude of personal favoritism"* (James 2:1). One would have to know James' heart in order to understand his intense exhortation for his brethren to show compassion to the needy, not just in words, but also in actions (2:14-15; cf. 1 John 3:17-18). One would have to sense James' anguish of soul in order to understand his zealous plea for his brethren to guard their tongues (James 3:5-10). Knowing where he had come from, one can understand why he heartily exhorts us all to *"submit...to God"* (James 4:7), *"Draw near to God"*

(James 4:8), *"Do not speak against one another"* (James 4:11), *"Humble yourselves in the presence of the Lord"* (James 4:10) and above all to be patient and learn not to complain against one another (James 5:9). You must have walked in his shoes, and sensed his deep concern, to have an inkling of why his last words were *"My brethren, if any one among you wanders from the truth and some one brings him back, let him know that whoever brings back a sinner [a backslider] from the error of his way will save his soul from [premature physical] death and will cover [wipe out] a multitude of sins"* (James 5:19-20 RSV).

It was as if James was saying to the recipients of his epistle, "Let the beauty of Jesus Christ be seen in you in all His glory so that your family members, friends, co-workers and the world at large may *'see your good works, and glorify your Father who is in heaven"* (Matthew 5:16).

A foundation has now been laid on which the building blocks of James' words will be placed. Let us look at the first increment of James.

## James: A Bondservant of God

*"James, a bond-servant of God and of the Lord Jesus Christ"* (James 1:1). The first thing to notice is not power or a claim to a family relationship to the God-Man, but rather an expression of *humility*. James had his entire youth to study his brother's humility. (Who can argue about our Lord's humility!) Paul, in describing Christ, said,

> *Who, though he was in the form of God [literally had all the attributes of God], did not count equality with God a thing to be grasped, but emptied himself, taking the form of a servant, being born in the likeness of men. And being found in human form he humbled himself and became obedient unto death, even [the horrible] death on a cross* (Philippians 2:6-8 RSV).

Even though James was the half-brother of Jesus, he did not emphasize the family relationship. Rather, he called himself a *doulos*, the Greek word for "slave." It means "one who is in a permanent relation of servitude to another, his will altogether consumed in the will of the other (Mt. 8:9; 20:27, 24:45-46 etc.)"[37] James recognized that Jesus Christ is both Man and God, joined in One Person forever (Hebrews

1:3, 8; cf. James 1:1). By calling himself a slave of both God the Father and the Lord, James showed Christ to be equal with the Father. He recognized that Jesus Christ was no ordinary man. He considered himself very honored to be a servant of Christ. After all, he had already learned humility by observing the Lord.

---

**Are we, like James, willing to be of service
to the Lord, no matter the cost?**

---

James' observation of his half-brother, Jesus, no doubt had an immense impact on him. Hence, by calling himself a slave, James was willing to do whatever the Lord would have him do. That's the epitome of genuine humility. The real question is, are we, like James, willing to be of service to the Lord, no matter the cost?

This connects us to the second half of the verse, "*To the twelve tribes who are dispersed abroad [diaspora]: Greetings*" (James 1:1). James' salutation underscores the idea of the "fifth Gospel" for his audience of Jewish believers in the early church, and also for you and me. We are the fifth Gospel, witnessed and "*read by all men*" (2 Corinthians 3:2).

We have already noticed the impact that Jesus (the prototype Gospel) made on James. We are acutely aware of the four written gospels, the records concerning Christ (Mark 1:1), which are rarely read by men, especially the unsaved. But the fifth one, namely us, our lives and actions, is read by everyone, every day, whether we want them to or not. Unlike the four written and sealed Gospels (Matthew, Mark, Luke and John) we remain open and are being written page by page on a daily basis. Our actions speak much louder than words.

No matter how we present Christ to the unsaved, no matter how sophisticated our message may be, no matter how much effort we make to point them to the "prototype Gospel" and the four written ones, if our lives have no reflection of Jesus Christ and the rest of the Gospels, then regrettably our efforts will be fruitless. Eric Liddell, the Scottish missionary to China (a runner and winner of the 400-meter race in the 1924 Paris Olympics), said it best: "We are all missionaries. Wherever we go we either bring people nearer to Christ or we repel them from Christ."[38]

James, with a compassionate heart and immense love, addressed his beloved brethren in Christ: *"James, a bond-servant of God and of the Lord Jesus Christ, To the twelve tribes who are dispersed abroad: Greetings."*

It is apparent that his epistle was addressed to Jewish believers, *"the twelve tribes,"* who were in enforced exile because of the persecution resulting from the Good News (Acts 1:8; cf. 8:1-4). Also, it implies that there were not yet any Gentile Christians at the time of his writing. Many scholars agree. John A. Robinson, for instance, comments, "James is addressing all who form the true, spiritual Israel, wherever they are. And he can address them in such completely Jewish terms not because he is singling them out from Gentile Christians but because, as far as his purview is concerned, there are no other Christians."[39] By saying *"greetings,"* James wishes them well.

The upcoming verses will reveal James' compassion and his heart-felt love for his beloved brethren, who were dispersed and undergoing tremendous suffering.

## FOUR

James 1:2-4

# Staying Power in Trying Times

*Consider it all joy, my brethren, when you encounter various trials, knowing that the testing of your faith produces endurance. And let endurance have its perfect result [literally work], that you may be perfect [mature] and complete, lacking in nothing* (**James 1:2-4**).

Suffering is like a bitter-coated chocolate candy; it's a blessing in disguise! But can you keep on licking this candy until the bitter coating is removed? Once the bitter outside is endured, the reward is the chocolate inside! Similarly, once suffering in our lives serves its intended purpose, God removes that suffering, and we are face-to-face with God's amazing blessing! That's the key message James conveys in James 1:2-4.

The epistle of James is entirely the work of the Holy Spirit! That includes the structure as well as the selection of words, for James' writing was *"moved by the Holy Spirit"* (2 Peter 1:21). Understanding this will spare us some intense debate over the structure of this magnificent epistle. It is a divine work!

## Encouragement in Suffering

James, with a loving heart, reaches out with words of exaltation and encouragement to his fellow believers, who were facing intense suffering. That is fascinating considering James' readers were guilty of spiritual adultery (James 4:4). They had abandoned Jesus Christ, their husband, so to say, and were engaged in an affair with the world—the cosmos (4:4). As far as God's plan is concerned, they were guilty of spiritual crimes that cannot go unpunished. (This may even explain why many of his audience were under such intense suffering.) Notice that James does not rebuke them. Why not? Grace! Rather, James begins his address with these soothing words: *"Consider it all joy, my brethren, when you encounter various trials."*

To illustrate this, let's pretend that you are a paramedic. You arrive on a scene of a massive car wreck. People are everywhere, some lying on the ground, some trapped in their cars; all are unconscious. What would be your first course of action? Would you run around and try to find out how the accident happened? Would you spend your time gathering data, to determine who the reckless driver was? No! You would check for pulses and immediately initiate cardiopulmonary resuscitation (CPR). It makes sense. You would want to stabilize the people first.

The same is true in a spiritual matter. James, in his wisdom, is doing exactly that in our passage. He knew their spiritual failures. He knew that some of their sufferings might have been related to their carnal lifestyles. Nonetheless, he writes with love and compassion, moving quickly to stabilize the minds of his readers. Later on he rebukes them, but not now.

God the Holy Spirit took a similar approach through the apostle Paul. When he received a disturbing report about the spiritual condition of the church at Corinth (1 Corinthians 1:11), Paul did not immediately rebuke all the immoral believers of that church. Instead he began by reminding them that they were *"the church of God"* (1 Corinthians 1:2) and of their position in Christ: *"to those who have been sanctified [perfect tense, meaning, once and for all—the same Greek word used in Hebrews 10:10]"* (1 Corinthians 1:2). He called them saints, which means those who have been washed and set apart unto God. He reminded them of *"the grace of God which was given"* them (1 Corinthians 1:4), of their enrichment *"in Him, in all speech and all knowledge"* (1:5), that they were *"not lacking in any [spiritual] gift"* (1 Corinthians 1:7). Moreover, he assured these believers, both carnal and spiritual, that God would *"confirm you to the end, blameless in the day of our Lord Jesus Christ"* (1 Corinthians 1:8). Paul then gave his readers the encouraging words everyone wants to hear: *"God is faithful, through whom you were called into fellowship with His Son, Jesus Christ our Lord"*

(1 Corinthians 1:9). "God is faithful!" Then, and only then, he begins, "*I exhort you, brethren*" (1 Corinthians 1:10). What genuine love!

Similarly, James moved gently to stabilize the minds of those who were weary and perhaps had lost hope. He is not writing out of compulsion but because of his compassion and love for them. Mentally, he was sharing their suffering, as is a mandate of Scripture: "*Rejoice with those who rejoice, and weep with those who weep*" (Romans 12:15).

Also, with the same care and concern, the apostle Paul wrote,

*I have been in labor and hardship, through many sleepless nights, in hunger and thirst, often without food, in cold and exposure. Apart from such external things, there is the daily pressure on me of concern for all the churches. Who is weak without my being weak? Who is led into sin without my intense concern?... The God and Father of the Lord Jesus, He who is blessed forever, knows that I am not lying* (2 Corinthians 11:27-31).

---

**We should have Christ's thinking, Christ's compassion, and His love.**

---

The height of Christian love is being able to sympathize with the sorrows of others, feeling their pressures and pains, and responding as the Holy Spirit motivates and guides us (Hebrews 2:14-17). It is sharing the burdens and agonies of those who share the same name, the same purpose and the same destiny. As Christians we should have Christ's thinking, Christ's compassion, and Christ's love flowing through our words and action.

James shows his love, and deepest concern, empathizing with his fellow Christians who were in great distress. My beloved, that's what Christianity is all about, reflecting Christ's glory that all may see Him. Seeing Christ's traits in Christ's followers is how the name "Christian" came to be. It was coined by the pagans to describe the early followers of Christ because their manner of life reflected that of Christ (Acts 11:26; 4:13). So it should be today. We should ask ourselves, "Am I such a Christian?"

To call oneself a "Christian" without applying its principles is to make a mockery of the name. (However, this does *not* mean that one is not really saved unless he manifests the life of Christ, 1 Corinthians 3:1-3, 11-15.) We unknowingly mock our Lord when the concerns of others are of no concern to us, when we fail to care and help bear the burdens of other believers. In other words, when we abandon the believer, we abandon the core of our faith (biblical truth). This is one of the main points of James' epistle.

Our Lord thought of the trials that His disciples and all the saints would face (John 16:33). The Lord soothed the panicked hearts of His disciples with words of encouragement, *"Do not let your heart be troubled"* (John 14:1).

Then Jesus followed with prayer, asking God the Father to preserve and keep us from the evil one as we endure persecution and suffering (John 17:13-21). That's what our Great High Priest did for us! We, as royal priests (1 Peter 2:9), should do the same. Other people's sorrows are not theirs alone to bear! Are you with me?

James was following our Lord's example. Because the recipients of his epistle were not local, his options were confined to prayer and words of encouragement. Scripture mandates that we encourage one another (Hebrews 10:24-25) and *"Bear one another's burdens, and thereby fulfill the law of Christ"* (Galatians 6:2).

My beloved brethren, knowing the mandates of Scripture is essential, but applying its principles in real life situations is critical for Christian living. In other words, you cannot advance an inch in your spiritual life until you begin to apply His Word to your life.

James must have been aware of false teaching with regard to suffering in his time, just as it is today. He counteracted this heresy with *"Consider it all joy, my brethren, when you encounter various trials."*

Today, many teach that suffering is a sure sign of spiritual maladjustment. But the Bible tells us suffering is inevitable (Philippians 1:29) and essential for character development (James 1:4; cf. Hebrews 5:8-9). God's ultimate plan and purpose is to conform us to the image of His Son (Romans 8:29). He wants to make us Christ-centered gold-standard believers, but this does not come without cost! The furnace of suffering is where all believers are refined, where gold is produced. "Behold, I have refined you, but not as silver; I have tested you in the furnace of affliction" (Isaiah 48:10). Hence the believer's joy should stem from God's purpose behind the testing—from His desire to strengthen and refine us.

Job was a great example of suffering induced to produce blessing!

Job compared his affliction to being cast into a "furnace." "When He has tried me, I shall come forth as gold" (Job 23:10). Note the triumphant words "I shall come forth" (through the fire). It is one thing to testify after you have passed through the fire, but Job is still in the furnace. The heat is on, his boils shoot flashes of hot pain through his body, fever parches his lips, he scraped his oozing boils with a broken piece of pottery. His head throbs with pain and his friends falsely accuse him, but he looks beyond his present fiery trial and shouts in vibrant, reassuring faith, "I shall come through."[40]

Therein is the manifestation of the glorification of God to the maximum. Job is our example of absolute confidence in Him against all odds, trusting Him even when everything, everywhere, looks so bleak.

James reassured his fellow believers that suffering is not such a bad thing (when it's not self-induced) but rather a blessing in disguise. He wanted them to rejoice in it, to *"consider it all joy"* (James 1:2). This does not mean to rejoice in the suffering itself, but rather in what suffering will produce—blessing and reward.

The Greek word *chara* rendered "joy" has a connotation of "gladness of heart."[41] It refers to a heart that is in a state of perfect tranquility, devoid of distress, anxiety and worry. It is a reference to inner feelings of gladness beyond description, even in the worst of times. This joy knows no limits! However, no human being is capable of exhibiting such joy apart from the Holy Spirit. It is the monopoly of the Holy Spirit. *"The fruit of the Spirit is...joy"* (Galatians 5:22).

The fact that James is commanding his audience to allow the Holy Spirit to produce joy in their souls is solid evidence that his epistle was addressed to believers, for an unsaved man cannot experience true joy, which is *"The fruit of the Spirit."* His mandate calls for them to rejoice in every circumstance.

Similarly the apostle Paul later exhorted, *"[In all circumstances] rejoice in the Lord always; again I will say, rejoice!"* (Philippians 4:4).

By asking them to do that which only the Holy Spirit can do, namely to exhibit joy, James is essentially calling them *"brethren,"* the special word used by our Lord to quantify those who are in union with Him (Hebrews 2:11). The New Testament writers did the same, referring to those who had trusted in Christ as *"brethren"* (Colossians 1:2; 1 Thessalonians 1:4; Hebrews 3:1; 1 Peter 5:9; 3 John 1:5). James was no exception (James 1:2). James has already begun his epistle with the word *brethren*, which signals that his epistle is for the saints (those set apart in Christ).

In essence, James is saying, "My fellow believers, consider your suffering as a God-sent, God-designed purging system for your life, designed to mature you and equip you for every good work and super-abundant blessing. Therefore do not dwell on your present predicament but look beyond your immediate suffering and see God, causing *'all things to work together for good to those who love God* [i.e., apply biblical truth], *to those who are called according to His purpose'"* (Romans 8:28).

He wanted them to have the same confidence that Job had when he was in the furnace of suffering: God knows what I am going through; when He is finished with me I shall come forth as gold (Job 23:10).

Our confidence in every circumstance of life should be that God's ultimate purpose would be manifest in our lives, once God is finished with us in the furnace of suffering!

## The Testing of Faith

We encounter James' first reference to the word *faith* in the phrase *"knowing that the testing of your faith produces endurance"* (James 1:3).

We must cultivate the habit of discerning sound biblical teaching from falsehood. We spot the first seed of falsehood. Many, by examining this phrase, *"the testing of your faith,"* erroneously introduced the idea of classifications of faith. There is no basis for such error! Douglas

J. Moo, a professor of New Testament at Wheaton Graduate School, in his work writes, "The 'testing of faith' here is not intended to determine whether a person has faith [salvation] or not; it is intended to purify faith [spiritual life] that already exists."[42] James does not doubt the salvation of the recipients of his epistle. We can dispel any thought that the testing of their faith was designed to determine whether they were truly saved or not. What's being tested is their reliance on the application of biblical knowledge to their spiritual life.

Sadly, many in the field of theology have taken the route of classification and reclassification of *faith*, which has caused much confusion in Christianity today. On the contrary, Scripture speaks nothing about "genuine" or "saving faith"; we all have a measure of faith within us, unbelievers and believers alike (Romans 12:3). It is true that a spectacular gift of faith did exist (1 Corinthians 12:9) but was the Holy Spirit's gift to a few who had already been born again (12:11). This was an apostolic gift; when the apostles died, the gift was withdrawn.

The notion that faith can be given to an unbeliever as a gift, which will compel the individual to believe in Christ, is illogical and foreign to Scripture! Faith is faith, it's on or off, there is no neutrality, either one wholeheartedly trusts in Jesus Christ and the infallible Word of God, or one doesn't. Whoever trusts is saved (eternally), and whosoever does not is forever damned (John 3:36). It's that simple!

There's a myth that has crept its way into Christianity. Because of misunderstanding of the epistle of James, Christians have invented such phrases as "intellectual faith," "heart belief vs. head belief," "saving faith," and the like. These concepts were totally foreign to the writers of Scripture and cause unwarranted confusion.

So what exactly does James mean in the phrase "*the testing of your faith*"? You may not have given this question serious thought in the past. But it's an important question! Understanding sets the tone for this section and for the entire epistle.

Let's bring the question home. Was James referring to what some refer to as of "saving faith"? Every sound Evangelical theologian knows that salvation is not based on the quality of one's faith (confidence) but rather on the *object* of faith: namely, Jesus Christ. All one needs is accurate information about the person and the work of Jesus Christ, made clear through the ministry of the Holy Spirit. Once a person believes this information, even though with *"faith the size of a mustard seed"* (Matt. 17:20), the individual is once and for all saved, according to Scripture. For instance, the Gospel of John is the only book written expressly with the unsaved in mind. *"But these [biblical doctrine proving the deity of Christ] have been written so that you may believe that Jesus is the Christ, the Son of God; and that believing [by having confidence in Him alone] you may have life in His name"* (John 20:31). *"Whoever believes that Jesus is the Christ [Messiah—God-Man] is born of God"* (1 John 5:1).

Of interest to us is the fact that the Greek word *gennao*, rendered "born" in 1 John 5:1, is in the perfect tense, indicative mood, and the passive voice. Briefly, perfect tense underscores the point that the individual who accepts these facts about Christ (John 20:31) is saved once and for all (cf. Hebrews 10:10). Indicative mood makes it a fact, and passive voice paints a vivid picture that this salvation has nothing to do with the individual's ability or work; rather, it's the work of God in its entirety, *"By His doing you are in Christ Jesus"* (1 Corinthians 1:30; see also Ephesians 2:8-9).

When we examine our passage carefully and with objectivity, we conclude that when James says *"the testing of your faith produces endurance"* he is not referring to trust with regard to salvation from the eternal penalty of sins. Would God have been testing faith that had already brought salvation to them at the point of their trust in Christ alone? Is God now testing it to see whether that faith is genuine? Or is He testing its quality to see whether it can withstand fire? James is not talking about salvation at all. It can't be "saving faith," because they were already saved. That is a fact (James 2:1)!

Rather, he is referring to the makeup of the "new species" or new man in Christ (2 Corinthians 5:17). Hence, *"the testing of your faith"* refers to their knowledge of God. Of interest to us also is the verb *knowing*, Greek *ginosko*, *"knowing that the testing of your faith produces endurance."* "Of the two Greek words for knowing, this term [here] means to know by experience."[43] Every teacher or student understands the concept of learning and testing. One's knowledge has no teeth until it's tested. The more difficult the testing, the greater the chance one has to demonstrate knowledge. When applied accurately, the knowledge increases and strengthens.

For example, a surgeon can acquire knowledge in the field of medicine, but he must have something to operate on for practice. The more complex surgeries he faces, the more his knowledge is tested and improved through experience. With time, he may come to be called "a renowned surgeon." So it is with the testing of the believer's faith in James.

*Faith* in our context, James 1:2-4, refers to the believer and the reservoir of biblical truth in his soul. Just like the surgeon, he is an ordinary man like everyone else but what differentiates him is his knowledge. When a critical health issue arises, the distinction is made between a medical resident (a new doctor) and one who is experienced. Similarly, when testing comes to believers, there will be a distinction between those who are only hearers (students) of the Word and those who both hear and apply what they know. Practice makes the difference for the believer, just like for the surgeon.

---

**The mind, heart and soul are the targets of testing and temptation in the spiritual battle.**

---

In testing, God only tests one's knowledge of His truth. Therefore *faith* here is not a reference to salvation but a reference to who we are in Christ, the makeup of the "new creature" in Him! The truth is God's testing is directed to our innermost being, our person and character as believers. The testing is geared toward our heart, soul and mind. When we are under pressure, will we apply what Bible knowledge we have learned to our lives? Will we use this knowledge to change our thoughts and actions to comply with God's plan?

In his book *Designed to Be Like Him*, Dr. D.J. Pentecost had a great deal to say about the heart, soul and mind of an individual before and after regeneration. "A NEW HEART has been given to the child of God. A new emotional capacity has been given to the believer by new creation that makes it possible for him to fulfill that for which he was created."[44]

To honor God through testing, we should respond with divine viewpoint thinking like Job did (Job 1:20-22; 6:10; 13:15; 23:10, 12; 19:25-26). Because the mind, heart and soul are the targets of testing and temptation in the spiritual battle, three writers of Scripture spoke of these.

Solomon exhorted, *"Watch over your heart with all diligence, For from it flow the springs of life"* (Proverbs 4:23).

The apostle Paul commanded, *"And do not be conformed to this world, but be transformed by the renewal of your mind, that you may prove what the will of God is, that which is good and acceptable and perfect"* (Romans 12:2).

The apostle Peter wrote, *"Beloved, I urge you as aliens and strangers to abstain from fleshly lusts which wage war [battle] against the soul"* (1 Peter 2:11).

This brings us to another element for discussion.

## Enduring Devotion

*"And let endurance have its perfect result, that you may be perfect and complete, lacking in nothing"* (James 1:4).

We begin the examination of the last portion of this section with a quotation from the editor of the *Rainbow Bible*:

> A quitter never wins…a winner never quits. What goes into our minds comes out in our actions. God never fails. Lasting joy comes through a relationship with Jesus Christ. Christians also have problems, but Christ is the power to overcome. We have no basis for pride except in our perfect example, Jesus Christ.[45]

Our spiritual life, built through faith (biblical truth), is what is being tested through the refining furnace of suffering. This testing is designed to strengthen and equip us for a greater cause! Therefore, we must not give up!

This is what James refers to as *endurance*, or staying power under adverse circumstances. No doubt, the most critical time in our testing is when the heat is on. It's the time when we pass or fail. *"If thou faint in the day of adversity, thy strength [enduring devotion] is small"* (Proverbs 24:10; cf. Hebrews 5:13-14 KJV).

The enemy will throw everything at us to compel us to fear and entice us to be bitter and complain, and whine about God's dealings in our lives. If we succumb to Satan's pressures (as did the Israelites in the wilderness), we fail (1 Corinthians 10:10; cf. Numbers 16:41). But if we hold on, expressing divine viewpoint (biblical thinking) as Job did (Job 23:10), we finish as "refined gold"! Passing "various trials" carries us to spiritual maturity. Thereby we are more equipped to represent our Savior in all His glory as well as to reap the spiritual benefits that come with faithfulness to our God. This is God's plan for you and me!

So, if we dispel the idea that this is not "saving faith" being tested but biblical truth, we can declare that the passage really makes sense! On the other hand, if we take the position that it is a "saving faith" that is being tested, then we will have a hard time interpreting the testing of Abraham when we get to James chapter 2.

---

### Endurance and patience are inseparably united.

---

*"Let endurance have its perfect result"*!

Endurance and patience are inseparably united. You cannot have one without the other. Hence, James' advice takes us back to God's ultimate objective, which is to conform us to the image of His Son Jesus Christ (Romans 8:29). To do this, God our Father must take us on a path similar to that which He took His Son on. The author of Hebrews wrote this about the path God gave Jesus: *"Although He was a Son, He learned obedience from the things which He suffered. And having been made perfect [mature], He became to all those who obey [trust] Him the source of eternal salvation"* (Hebrews 5:8-9).

Unquestionably, Jesus Christ is our role model for endurance in suffering!

Think of it! God, in His infinite wisdom and love, used unparalleled suffering to mold and equip His Incarnate Son for the ultimate sacrifice, His substitutionary death on the cross (Philippians 2:6-9). And we cannot properly identify with the trials of which James speaks without a measure of comprehension of Christ's suffering.

## Endurance of Christ

An in-depth examination of Christ's suffering is not within the scope of our study; we just want to highlight some important points. Everything that surrounds His entrance into the world points to His immense suffering. The Holy One of God was laid in a manger (feeding trough) (Luke 1:7) and wrapped with swaddling clothes. This points to a poor sanitary condition.

His parents were poor. At Christ's temple presentation, they could only afford a pair of pigeons, a poor man's offering (Luke 2:24; cf. Leviticus 5:11). Scripture concurs: *"For you know the grace of our Lord Jesus Christ, that though He was rich [before His incarnation], yet for your sake He became poor, so that you through His poverty might become [spiritually] rich"* (2 Corinthians 8:9).

During His ministry He had no place He could call home. *"The foxes have holes and the birds of the air have nests, but the Son of Man has nowhere to lay His head"* (Luke 9:58).

Think about it! In all the testing throughout His life He perfected endurance and patience. He is our example as we go through testing. His humanity passed the test which enables Him to be our sympathizer and a faithful high priest (Hebrews 2:11-17). Armed with this truth, we ought to endure every suffering in our lives with confidence. This is what the apostle Peter had in mind when he declared,

> *For you have been called for this purpose, since Christ also suffered for you, leaving you an example for you to follow in His steps, WHO COMMITTED NO SIN, NOR WAS ANY DECEIT FOUND IN HIS MOUTH; and while being reviled, He did not revile in return; while suffering, He uttered no threats, but kept entrusting Himself to Him who judges righteously* (1 Peter 2:21-23).

What was the secret to Christ's endurance? Scripture tells us it was His anticipation of future glory:

> *Therefore, since we have so great a cloud of witnesses surrounding us, let us also lay aside every encumbrance and the sin which so easily entangles us, and let us run with endurance the race that is set before us, fixing our eyes on Jesus, the author and perfecter of faith [biblical knowledge], who for the joy set before Him endured the cross, despising the shame, and has sat down at the right hand of the throne of God* (Hebrews 12:1-2).

Furthermore, He knew that one day there would be an end to all His suffering (Luke 22:37). He had confidence that His Father-God had a plan for Him. He knew there was a purpose in His suffering. He knew that, once the all-wise, all-knowing God was finished with all the suffering tailored for His life, He (Jesus Christ) would shine in glory! Assured of this infallible truth, our Lord endured every mistreatment, every injustice, and every assault from the evil one.

"*Fixing our eyes on Jesus, the author and perfecter of faith [biblical knowledge], who for the joy set before Him endured the cross*" (Hebrews 12:2). He endured because He knew that once the thick clouds cleared, **a rainbow** would surface! His eyes were on the joy set before Him!

In the same fashion, our endurance should stem from the fact that our Father, the Eternal Goldsmith, has His eyes on us. He will never take them off us, no matter what. Equally comforting is the fact that He knows the right temperature (never too high, never too low, just the right amount of heat) suitable to refine and build in us the character He **desires.**

Suffering for every believer, carnal or spiritual, is inevitable. For the carnal believer, God employs suffering to help the individual regain focus. We see this time and again. For example, in the Old Testament He inflicted His people, the Jews, with suffering: "*For God troubled them with every kind of distress*" (2 Chronicles 15:6). Subsequently, "*In their distress they turned to the LORD God*" (2 Chronicles 15:4).

"*Before I was afflicted [by means of suffering] I went astray, But now [after my suffering] I keep Your word*" (Psalm 119:67). "*For the Lord disciplines him whom he loves, and chastises every son whom he receives"* (Hebrews 12:6 RSV). That is suffering as a result of spiritual malad-justment, but there is suffering for the development of spiritual matu-rity. God exemplified this using His Son. *"Although He was a Son, He learned obedience from the things which He suffered. And having been made perfect [Greek: teleo, mature], He became to all those who obey [trust in] Him the source of eternal salvation"* (Hebrews 5:8-9). This later suf-fering is what James had in mind when he urges his brethren who were facing surmounting hardships to *"consider it all joy"* (James 1:2).

We must not forget that God in His infinite wisdom and grace uses prepared vessels for the work of His Kingdom (2 Timothy 2:20-21). In order to make us vessels of honor, He uses suffering to refine us and enable us to attain the level of spiritual maturity that James refers to as *"perfect and complete"* (James 1:4). And in reference to this phrase, Martin Dibelius (1881-1947), a professor of New Testament exegesis and criticism at the University of Heidelberg, Germany, quotes Windisch, "You are that perfect work."[46]

Equally worthy of quotation is the work of Peter H. Davis:

The battle-tested soldier, the heroic warrior for the faith [Christian cause], is highly valued. Or to change to a more accurate metaphor, the tempered metal is more precious than the raw material. So, says James, testing does a service for the Christian, for the virtue of fortitude comes out of the process, however slow and painful it may be.[47]

Obviously, suffering is unpleasant in every sense, but, if endured, the outcome is beneficial beyond measure (Hebrews 12:10-11). James and the apostle Paul agreed. Paul wrote,

*And not only this, but we also exult in our tribulations, knowing that tribulation brings about perseverance; and perseverance, proven character; and proven character, hope [absolute confi-dence]; and hope does not disappoint, because the love of God has been poured out within our hearts through the Holy Spirit who was given to us* (Romans 5:3-5).

My beloved, God is in the business of building "gold standard" believers. God wants the best for you and me! His best comes through the furnace of suffering. We don't know why God chooses that route to bring His best to us. We are not to question the all-wise God but to accept His perfect plan for our lives.

James is saying to you and me, "Learn how to remain in the furnace of suffering (endurance) until God achieves His overall objective." But how?

- By mixing the truth in our souls with absolute confidence that God will never fail or forsake us. *"Make sure that your character is free from the love of money, being content with what you have; for He Himself has said, 'I WILL NEVER DESERT YOU, NOR WILL I EVER FORSAKE YOU'"* (Hebrews 13:5).

- *"When you pass through the waters, I will be with you; And through the rivers, they will not overflow you. When you walk through the fire, you will not be scorched, Nor will the flame burn you"* (Isaiah 43:2).

- By confessing our sins to God when we fail, to ensure that we are constantly in fellowship. *"If we confess our sins, He is faithful and righteous to forgive us our sins and to cleanse us from all unrighteousness"* (1 John 1:9).

- By keeping our Lord Jesus Christ in focus at all times, thinking and meditating on the many facets of His grace toward us. *"Fixing our eyes on Jesus, the author and perfecter of faith, who for the joy set before Him endured the cross, despising the shame, and has sat down at the right hand of the throne of God"* (Hebrews 12:2).

- By taking time to analyze our trials and sufferings in light of the heroes of faith, factoring in God's promises and His faithfulness.

- By coming to an understanding that our anxieties and worrying cannot change our circumstances not even by one iota.

*"Who of you by being worried can add a single hour to his life?"* (Matthew 6:27).

• By availing ourselves to prayer on a consistent basis. *"With all prayer and petition pray at all times in the Spirit, and with this in view, be on the alert with all perseverance and petition for all the saints"* (Ephesians 6:18).

Understanding these principles, we can go about our daily lives knowing that every heartache, every disappointment, every sickness, every dilemma has been tailored to perfect us and make us "gold standard" believers! Conversely, as we remain in the furnace of suffering, we ought to make Job's words of enduring devotion ours: *"When He has tried me, I shall come forth as gold"* (Job 23:10).

May God's richest blessing in time of trials and suffering be ours in abundance.

## FIVE

James 1:5-8

# Asking for Wisdom

*But if any of you [my brethren in Christ] lacks wisdom, let him ask of God, who gives to all generously and without reproach, and it will be given to him. But he must ask in faith without any doubting, for the one who doubts is like the surf of the sea, driven and tossed by the wind. For that man ought not to expect that he will receive anything from the Lord, being a double-minded man, unstable in all his ways* (**James 1:5-8**).

God can only have one meaning in mind. In this and every section, the task is to determine *exactly* what the Bible says, for we know "*God is not a God of confusion*" (1 Corinthians 14:33). Nor is He the author of misinterpretation. Rather, **Satan, the enemy of truth, is the origin of all misinterpretations** that generate confusion. When God communicates to us, our duty is to humbly and prayerfully ask Him to help us determine its interpretation through the illuminating ministry of His Holy Spirit, to grant us wisdom. As students of His Word, if we are to "*grow in the grace and knowledge of our Lord and Savior Jesus Christ*" (2 Peter 3:18), we must develop the habit of desiring the pure spiritual milk of the infallible Word of God (1 Peter 2:2). We must earnestly ask God to guide us every step of the way so we may know how to differentiate between sound biblical teaching and falsehood.

Believing falsehood can only wreck our spiritual lives and make us unfruitful. Moreover, trusting in falsehood cannot produce the desired results and therefore leads to discouragement. Discouraged believers often abandon the Lord because their faith (confidence) in God has been shaken.

It is apparent that James' epistle was intended to exhort, rebuke and encourage his Christian audience to live like Christians. In his exhortation, he encourages them to regard their suffering as a blessing in disguise. This is true in view of the fact that a life-changing experience often comes through intense suffering. In other words, suffering uproots all human resources and causing the believer to look to God, to pray habitually, to grow in grace and to take God's Word more seriously. This is a well-documented lesson from Scripture.

> *At midnight I shall rise to give thanks to You Because of Your righteous ordinances…Before I was afflicted [by means of suffering] I went astray, But now [after my suffering] I keep Your word…It is good for me that I was afflicted, That I may learn Your statutes [literally, it has helped me take Your Word seriously]* (Psalm 119:62-71).

We have hope that once God has accomplished His desired purpose in our suffering, we *"shall come forth as gold"* (Job 23:10). In times of testing we know confusion, frustration and discouragement can become overwhelming, and so James commands us to ask for wisdom.

## Divine Wisdom, Not Human Wisdom

*"But if any of you [my brethren in Christ] lacks wisdom, let him ask of God, who gives to all men generously and without reproach, and it will be given to him"* (James 1:5). James is not mandating them to ask for human wisdom. *"But the wisdom from above is first pure, then peaceable, gentle, reasonable, full of mercy and good fruits, unwavering, without hypocrisy"* (James 3:17).

We are to ask God for a special wisdom in dealing with present suffering. A.G. Fruchtenbaum points out that "While in English this sounds like giving advice, in Greek it is imperative, making it a command."[48] He adds,

> The author [i.e., James] used the present tense: keep on asking, as in Matthew 7:7. God's response is that this is one prayer He

will answer literally and simply. That which God has not promised, He may or may not answer; but that which He has promised, He will answer. He has promised to provide wisdom, and so believers should keep on asking. The giving God will give this wisdom generously because that is a characteristic of God's nature. God will give it generously, using a word that is found only here and nowhere else in the New Testament.[49]

When we suffer, God commands us to ask for an insight to accurately apply the knowledge of His Word to our circumstances and to help us learn what we need through the suffering. "James' exhortation to his readers to ask for wisdom echoes wide spread OT and Jewish teaching. "The Lord gives wisdom,' claims Prov. 2:6, and the importance of wisdom is the central theme of this OT book. Wisdom is the means by which the godly can discern and carry out the will of God (e.g., 2:10-19; 3:13-14; 9:1-6)."[50]

In reference to the phrase "*without reproach*," M. Dibelius translated "without hesitation,"[51] meaning that God, in His infinite grace, will respond to our prayer for wisdom when we pray with a pure heart! Keep on asking God for wisdom in any and every suffering.

Have you been praying for wisdom in suffering with no answer in sight? Our next segment will give the answer.

## The Power of Faith in Prayer

"*But he must ask in faith without any doubting, for the one who doubts is like the surf of the sea, driven and tossed by the wind. For that man ought not to expect that he will receive anything from the Lord, being a double-minded man, unstable in all his ways*" (James 1:6-8). In verse 5, James commanded these believers to pray for wisdom. We know that only believers have access to the throne room of God's grace (Hebrews 4:16; 1 John 3:21-22; cf. John 9:31); hence the mandate to pray!

James used a metaphor to highlight the secret to prayer: "*But he must ask in faith without any doubting, for the one who doubts is like the surf of the sea, driven and tossed by the wind.*" He tells these believers, "Look, what you are going through is not uncommon to the saints (James 5:10-11), but to come out a winner, you must ask God for wisdom. You must do so without doubt. Whining ruptures your fellowship with God, but taking your situation as from the Lord puts you in synch with His plan for your life."

Remember this: God's objective is to mature us and make us "*vessels of...honor*" (2 Timothy 2:20) with an immense capacity to receive His overflowing blessing, both in time and in eternity. To endure the sufferings that God brings in our lives, we need the special wisdom that only comes through prayer.

But haven't we been praying for wisdom, and yet God seems to be silent? James gives us the secret to answered prayer: "*He must ask in faith [confidence] without any doubting.*" Faith in our context is **absolute confidence** that God will grant us wisdom in dealing with our present suffering. This is the key to our prayer being heard.

Make no mistake. Doubting renders our prayer powerless to ascend to the throne room of God's grace. What is doubt? It is lack of confidence in God. It is a sin. Why? Because we are not trusting God to be faithful to His promises. Doubt then describes instability of one's soul: "*The one who doubts is like the surf of the sea, driven and tossed by the wind.*"

Of course prayer must coincide with the will of God. Trusting God and His promises without wavering (Hebrews 10:23) is critical to prayer, and to the Christian experience. James commanded them to pray for wisdom with a promise that God would honor such a request. "*Let him ask of God, who gives to all generously and without reproach, and it will be given to him*" (1:5).

In other words, when you pray for wisdom, you must do so with absolute confidence that God will fulfill His promise according to Scripture. The apostle John echoed James when he affirmed, "*This is the confidence which we have before Him, that, if we ask anything according to His will, He hears us*" (1 John 5:14). Faith is the key to a favorable response from God, as long as it coincides with His will.

We, as believers, often misuse Scripture. Many today hold the erroneous idea that we can command God to do whatever we want. That's not biblical! God answers our prayers according to His will (1 John 5:14). Many people demand things from God. By a misguided faith they are "naming it and claiming it."

This can be illustrated by a story. A young Christian boy was told in his Sunday school class that with faith (trust/confidence) all things are possible. He believed this teaching with his whole heart, but the teacher didn't explain to him that "all things" must be in line with His will. One day the boy was given an outdoor school assignment, but he failed to do it before the due date. Knowing the consequences of his failure, he prayed earnestly that it would rain so that the outdoor program would be canceled. He prayed and believed with all his heart. In fact, to show that he did not doubt, he wore his raincoat to school, even though the weather was clear and sunny. But to his greatest dismay, there was not one drop of rain throughout the day! His disappointment was the result of his misconception about the principle of prevailing prayer.

This type of misapplication is addressed by Dr. D. E. Hiebert:

> The assurance of answered prayer does not mean "that God is some kind of dispensing machine into which we put a prayer and out comes whatever we select." The promise of answered prayer makes its spiritual demands upon the one asking. James points to the necessary attitude for effective prayer (v. 6a) and vividly portrays the man who does not get his prayer answered (vv. 6b-8).[52]

It is God's will to grant us wisdom in trying times in response to our prayer. But we must approach His throne in faith. *"And all things you ask [according to His will] in prayer, believing, you will receive"* (Matthew 21:22).

James says, *"But he must ask in faith without any doubting."* In other words, if your spiritual life is in order and you know that your prayer is in line with His will, you can be assured that God will answer your prayer in His due time!

## Avoid Double-Mindedness

*"For the one who doubts is like the surf of the sea, driven and tossed by the wind. For that man ought not to expect that he will receive anything from the Lord, being a double-minded man, unstable in all his ways"* (James 1:6-8).

Let us consider the word "double-minded." With a careful scrutiny of the work of Bible scholars, it becomes clear that a handful of Bible teachers erroneously attributed *"double-minded man"* in our passage to someone with a multiple personality disorder. There's no reason for such an assertion! Contextually, this is an intrusion on the text, or what theologians call an illegitimate totality transfer, which is importing some idea into a text which is not there. James is not saying that anyone who doubts when he prays has a neurological problem. If so, that would describe many of us who, an untold number of times, offer prayer with doubts. Martin Dibelius, a scholar of the past century, in his commentary on James states,

> In the interpretation of our passage [i.e., James 1:6-8] one must forgo all the examples of a metaphysical dualism…The dualism which is mentioned in our passage can in any event be only a practical dualism; what is involved is vacillation between certainty and uncertainty with regard to whether prayer will be answered…For those who have doubts towards God, these are the double-minded, and they shall not in any way obtain any of their petitions.[53]

What James is alluding to, in our passage, is typical of many believers today. I will call them "casual believers." These are not single-minded believers. No, these carnal believers have minds that are divided, part toward God, part toward the world. Instability marks their spiritual lives. They are in church today; tomorrow they skip church for a party! They are not stable enough to develop a strong and abiding relationship with God. When they pray, they are not sure whether their relationship with God is one that will produce results (1 John 3:20-22).

Believers who are not totally committed to God are like the tossing sea. They are irrational, and they waver back and forth and do not make decisions. They are often confused. They cannot trust God, let alone anyone else.

In a nutshell, that's what James is laying on the table for many of these unstable believers (James 1:13-15, 19-21; 2:1-9, 14-16; 3:14;

4:1-5, 8-11; 5:1-6). He is saying, "My brethren, such a mediocre spiritual life cannot get you anywhere, let alone get your prayer through to the throne room of God's grace." "*You ask and do not receive, because you ask with wrong motives, so that you may spend it on your pleasures*" (James 4:3).

God promises to answer our prayers when we pray in accordance with His will. "*If you abide in Me, and My words abide in you, ask whatever you wish [in line with My will], and it will be done for you*" (John 15:7; cf. 1 John 3:20-21). "*Call upon Me in the day of trouble; I shall rescue you, and you will honor Me*" (Psalm 50:15).

Beloved, these and more are the promises God made to those who are growing spiritually. We can hold Him to these wonderful promises! After all, James' exhortation is not without reason. He witnessed Jesus, the God-Man, petitioning His Father-God over and over, always with the same result. James too, according to tradition, was a prayer warrior. So, my dearly beloved, let's continue to press on! Let's stand immovable on the promises of God our Savior!

As we approach our next section, remember our twofold purpose for our in-depth study of the epistle of James:

• To dissect and accurately interpret its content
• To see ourselves as we truly are and adjust accordingly

These are the two objectives to keep in mind as we endeavor, under the mentorship of the Holy Spirit, to uncover the truth.

We have seen the stabilization of believers in suffering. In this upcoming section James underscores the believers' relationship with God and calls our attention to our spiritual lives. It is my hope that we can latch on to his admonitions and exhortations and heed his urgent call back to practical Christianity.

# Part 3

# Redefining the Relationship Between God and Man

## SIX

# The Relationship Between God and Man

Scholars, theologians and Bible teachers differ sharply on the theological content of the book of James, but they agree on one point: its message is not cohesive. James jumped from one thought to another as he was moved by the Holy Spirit (2 Peter 1:20-21). As we have seen, in James 1:2-8 he wrote about suffering, endurance, prayer for wisdom and the hindrance to such prayer. In verses 9 thru 11, his thought switched to the rich and poor believers. Then, all of a sudden, in verse 12 he returned to the unsurpassed blessing that awaits the one who passes the test of verses 2-5. This is just one of many examples of how his thoughts jumped!

Such a zigzag type of writing makes it difficult to have a cohesive outline. But the Holy Spirit did it purposely. This approach does not diminish our verse by verse exposition, though in most cases we will not examine them in sequence because the epistle, as a whole, is not sequentially written.

So in this chapter we will suspend our verse by verse study to:

- Define the effect of relationship between God and the believer, which is the underlying theme of the book of James.

- Cross-examine the spiritual status of those James was addressing.

# IRREVOCABLE RELATIONSHIP

## Relationship Defined

A good relationship requires interaction filled with love, respect, honor and enduring devotion to one another. Looking back it is evident that God, in His infinite wisdom, played His part in perpetuating His relationship between Himself and those born into His family through faith alone in Christ alone. The apostle Paul tells us, "*For you all are sons of God through faith [alone] in Christ Jesus*" (Galatians 3:26).

In unsurpassed love, God gave His Son, Jesus Christ, for the sole purpose of establishing a relationship between Himself and His fallen creatures. That's not all! In enduring devotion, He sealed our relationship with Him once and for all. "*By this will we have been sanctified through the offering of the body of Jesus Christ once for all*" (Hebrews 10:10).

That's it, once for all! Our irrevocable relationship with Him has been established once for all eternity (Romans 8:38-39).

As if eternity with God in heaven were not enough, **there is the potential to arrive in heaven with rewards of honor**. But there is a requirement: God honors only those who honor Him. "*For those who honor Me I will honor, and those who despise Me will be lightly esteemed*" (1 Samuel 2:30). God leaves the door wide open for man to reciprocate His love, which He initiated in grace.

How then should we respond to God's grace? A careful scrutiny of Scripture shows that many believers throughout the Bible, including the recipients of James' epistle, have taken their relationship with God for granted. This is still true today! How is your relationship with God?

Our relationship with God is the key to everything in this life, including marriage, parenthood and friendship (2 Chronicles 15:2; cf. Psalm 84:11)! If we take relationships for granted, as most of us do, we not only lose the glue that binds the relationship but also suffer the loss of associated blessings.

With this in mind, we now turn to discuss briefly the relationship between a son and father, which will help us lay the groundwork to explore the relationship between the believer and his Father-God.

## Son and Father Relationship

Once a son, always a son! From birth an irrevocable relationship has been established. Father and son possess the same DNA. The most a father can do to disassociate himself from his son is to deny him an inheritance. This happens in real life; fathers deny their sons access to their wealth for various reasons of relationship. In other words, children who fail the test of love, respect, honor and enduring devotion risk the loss of parental blessing, both now and long after their parents are gone. Now we can examine the relationship between the believer and His Father-God.

## Believer and Father-God Relationship

The principle of once a son, always a son is a lesson from the Bible. "*Whoever believes that Jesus is the Christ is born of God, and whoever loves the Father loves the child born of Him*" (1 John 5:1).

The truth is buried in the Greek word *gennao*, rendered "born" in the NASB, used "metaphorically of God's divine nature imparted in the believer."[54] The apostle John used *gennao* in the *perfect tense, indicative mood* and *passive voice*. Greek grammar holds the key.

Perfect tense underscores the fact that once an individual is born in God's family, he cannot be unborn! The Lord states this explicitly: "*And the slave [unbeliever] does not remain in the house forever; the son [a child of God] does remain forever*" (John 8:35; c.f. 10:27-29).

Indicative mood makes such a claim certain. Passive voice shows that the person being born into God's family does not do the work. It is entirely the work of God. Should anyone argue this point they do so based on sentimentalism, not Scripture! "*By His doing you are in Christ Jesus*" (1 Corinthians 1:30).

James also captures this truth: "*In the exercise of His will He brought us forth by the word of truth [the gospel], so that we would be a kind of first fruits among His creatures*" (James 1:18).

Being born into God's Family accords the privilege and opportunity to take our relationship with God to the next level if we so desire. There is no limit to which we can take our relationship with Him!

As we know, a relationship demands unlimited sacrifices: time, resources and enduring devotion. We cannot get around this! Sadly, many believers are not willing to meet the rigorous demands of the Christian life and fall along the wayside. But for those who remain steadfast, their "new names" will be inscribed "*on the stone which no one knows but he who receives it*" (Revelation 2:17). These will be recognized in a special way with exclusive honors and rewards. This our Lord makes certain:

> "*He who overcomes will thus be clothed in white garments;…I will confess his name before My Father and before His angels…He who overcomes, I will make him a pillar in the temple of My God, and he will not go out from it anymore; and I will write on him the name of My God, and the name of the city of My God, the new Jerusalem, which comes down out of heaven from My God, and My new name…I will grant to him to sit down with Me on My throne, as I also overcame and sat down with My Father on His throne*" (Revelation 3:5-21).

## Pursue a Strong Relationship With God

So the blessing of living eternally in heaven is based on our irrevocable relationship with our heavenly Father, because of Christ. However, super-abundant blessings (rewards for both time and eternity) are based on our fulfillment of His plan for our lives. There are no shortcuts! If we develop undiminished love and respect for Him and practice obedience to His Word, He will shower us with blessings beyond description! This extraordinary truth is captured beautifully in Psalms: "*For the Lord God is a sun and shield; The LORD gives grace and glory; No good thing does He withhold from those who walk uprightly*" (Psalm 84:11; cf. 34:10).

God will go an extra mile, so to say, for any believer, male or female, who develops a strong relationship with Him! A solid relationship with God is the key that unlocks our rapport with others, in marriage and friendship and with fellow believers. In fact, no believer can have a strong relationship with anyone apart from a strong and deepened relationship with God (Luke 2:52). A mediocre relationship with God spells out mediocre relationships with our fellow believers, friends and spouse, making us poor witnesses to the world. This was the condition of the believers whom James addressed.

> What is the source of quarrels and conflicts among you [believers in Christ]? Is not the source your pleasures that wage war in your members? You [believers] lust and do not have; so you [believers] commit murder. You are envious and cannot obtain; so you fight and quarrel. You do not have because you do not ask. You ask and do not receive, because you ask with wrong motives, so that you may spend it on your pleasures. **You adulteresses, do you not know that friendship with the world is hostility toward God? Therefore whoever wishes to be a friend of the world makes himself an enemy of God.** Or do you think that the Scripture speaks to no purpose: "He jealously desires the Spirit which He has made to dwell in **us** [James plus his audience]" (James 4:1-5, emphasis added).

---

**The question is not if they were believers, but what kind of believers were they?**

---

Who can examine this passage and question whether the recipients of James' epistle were believers? James put to rest any doubt by pointing out that they have the indwelling Holy Spirit (James 4:5)! The question is not if they were believers, but what kind of believers were they? Were they spiritual or carnal? This question takes us to the spiritual condition of James' audience.

## JAMES' AUDIENCE'S RELATIONSHIP WITH GOD

To better appreciate James' train of thought, we need to look at the spiritual status of the recipients of his epistle.

### Spiritual Condition of Jewish Believers

We know that these were undoubtedly believers. This is clear from his writing: "In the exercise of His will He brought **us** forth by the word of truth, so that **we** would be a kind of first fruits among His creatures" (James 1:18, emphasis added). "He jealously desires the Spirit which He has made to dwell in **us** [James plus his audience]" (James 4:5, emphasis added).

The "we" and "us" of James 1:18 and 4:5 respectively are more evidence that James' audience was believers. If they were his brethren by virtue of regeneration, then the "we" and "us" of the quoted passages refer to James and his audience, those who were brought forth (born) in God's family (James 1:18) and sealed by the indwelling presence of His Holy Spirit (James 4:5; cf. 2 Corinthians 1:22; Ephesians 4:30). We cannot get around this simple fact. Let us stand on the side of truth!

Now that we have settled, once and for all, that James' audience was composed of believers, let's see why James addressed them with such a derogatory word in James 4:4. Why the shift from *"my brethren"* (James 1:2) and *"my beloved brethren"* (James 2:5) to *"adulteresses"* (James 4:4)? This is inspired wisdom! Spiritual wisdom teaches us not to meet confrontation head-on, for *"A gentle answer turns away wrath, But a harsh word stirs up anger"* (Proverbs 15:1).

Paul, much later, used the same approach. Despite the fact that he had received a bad report on the spiritual status of the Corinthian Church (1 Corinthians 1:11), he did not chastise them right away. He used wisdom.

First, he called their attention to the fact that they were saints in Christ, sanctified once and for all (1 Corinthians 1:2).

Second, he wished God's grace upon every one of them (1 Corinthians 1:3).

Third, he then let them know that he had not ceased to offer thanksgiving to God for His grace upon their lives (1 Corinthians 1:4-5).

Fourth, he assured them that their salvation was secured according to God's faithfulness (1 Corinthians 1:7-9).

Then Paul helped defuse their spiritual tension: *"Now I exhort you, brethren, by the name of our Lord Jesus Christ, that you all agree and that there be no divisions among you, but that you be made complete in the same mind and in the same judgment"* (1 Corinthians 1:10).

What a message of maturity! In his first approach, Paul did not blast them with a more serious sinful indictment, like incest

THE RELATIONSHIP BETWEEN GOD AND MAN

(1 Corinthians 5:1-5), prostitution (1 Corinthians 6:15-18) or even being disrespectful to the Lord's Table (1 Corinthians 11:18-30). He carefully worked his way from the least offense to the worst. That's the wisdom mentioned in Galatians 6:1. He applied grace, knowing that he too was immensely graced-out by God (1 Timothy 1:15). Of course, there is a time for castigation, but it must be done discretely and with great wisdom. After all, the Lord did not call us to help tear the Church down but to build it up by encouraging one another (Hebrews 10:25). Undoubtedly, James, Paul, Peter and a few others copied the Lord's unmatched problem-defusing technique that He applied in the case of a woman caught in adultery: "*He who is without sin among you, let him be the first to throw a stone at her*" (John 8:7).

James used the same approach! Perhaps he had received feedback about the condition of the churches from those coming from or going to Jerusalem. James knew that all was not well with them spiritually, so he began on common ground, their suffering. That's the height of sensitivity! That's the hallmark of grace-orientation! He withheld his real blow until chapter 4, and there he released it with full force—"*You adulteresses*"!

This is a lesson for us all! Now we can discuss the spiritual infidelity of James' audience.

## Marked by Infidelity

You see how we are building a superstructure of part III. It's all about relationship! James selected the most deplorable concept in a relationship—adultery. But why not use the masculine word, since it is the custom of the Bible to address the human race in the masculine? For example, in Galatians, both male and female believers are addressed as "sons." "*For you are all [male and female] sons [masculine] of God through faith in Christ Jesus*" (Galatians 3:26). This perplexing question had some translators adding the word *adulterer* to the text: "*Ye adulterers and adulteresses*" (James 4:4, KJV).

There's no room for such an addition! In fact, doing so allows for misinterpretation of the passage. "The best MSS, however, have only the single word [i.e., adulteress].[55]

We ask again, why the feminine word? The answer is found in the word *relationship*! Keep in mind that James was writing to Jewish believers who knew that in the Old Testament the believers' relationship to God is often described in terms of marriage (Deuteronomy 31:16; Isaiah 54:5). Therefore any disloyalty can be described metaphorically as adultery. Dr. D.J. Moo tells us:

> As this text [Isaiah 54:5-6] suggests, the Lord is consistently portrayed as the husband and Israel as the wife in this imagery. Accordingly, therefore, when Israel's relationship with the Lord is threatened by her idolatry, she can be accused of committing adultery; see Jer. 3:20: "But like a woman unfaithful to her husband, so you have been unfaithful to me, O house of Israel, declares the Lord."[56]

Dr. D. J. Moo brings this to focus:

> James, following this tradition, uses "adulteresses" to label his readers as unfaithful people of God…As [L.T.] Johnson points out, the ancient view of friendship sheds light on the seriousness of the charge James is making here. We speak rather casually of "friends" in our day, but in Hellenistic world friendship "involved 'sharing all things' in a unity both spiritual and physical."[57]

The picture James is painting becomes clear when we read his next words: "*Do you not know that friendship with the world is hostility toward God? Therefore whoever wishes to be a friend of the world makes himself an enemy of God*" ( James 4:4).

Both the apostles John and Paul agree with James on this point (1 John 2:15; Romans 8:5, 8; James 4:4). This sobering indictment tells us that those James wrote to were in a state of spiritual anarchy. Their relationship with God was not in question; otherwise, calling them "adulteresses" would have been baseless. James knew that you cannot commit adultery unless you are married. The twelve tribes (Christian believers) scattered to the nations were "married" to the Lord, who is portrayed as the bridegroom of the church (John 3:29; Ephesians 5:22-32; Revelation 18:23).

Instead, what was in question was their faithfulness to the One to whom they were joined. What effect does this infidelity have on James' readers? The answer is chilling, and we can't wait to flip to the next chapter. Until then, my beloved, keep meditating on this: No believer can have a strong relationship with anyone apart from a strong and deepened relationship with God.

Dear Heavenly Father, it is my fervent prayer that we as believers take our relationship with You seriously today, tomorrow and until we are face to face with the King of kings, Lord of lords, our Great Savior, Jesus Christ, in whose name I pray. Amen!

## SEVEN

# Consequences of Spiritual Unfaithfulness

We are still laying the background for an in-depth scrutiny of the book of James. In this chapter we again postpone our verse-by-verse study in order to examine the consequences of spiritual infidelity. Since the epistle of James was to encourage his audience back from spiritual unfaithfulness, we must thoroughly understand the grave dangers James knew them to be facing, and not only them but all who lapse in their spiritual lives.

We ought not deceive ourselves. A mediocre relationship with God sooner or later will lead to spiritual infidelity and ultimately will manifest itself in tragedy in all areas of life. This is true of James' readers, whom he labeled "adulteresses" because of their spiritual infidelity (James 4:4). It sounds extreme; but it got their attention! We shall discuss the effect of spiritual infidelity toward both God and man and then look at the consequences of such a lifestyle. Our study here is crucial to determining why James rebuked his readers with such a harsh word—*adulteresses*.

## Effect of Spiritual Infidelity Toward God

Adultery is a threat to any marriage! It's the only grounds in Scripture for a divorce (Matthew 19:9). But wait! What about the indictment of unfaithfulness of James' audience, "*You adulteresses*"? Could that be grounds for the Lord to "divorce" them? No! Not at all! Here we can appreciate the apostle Paul's dogmatic assertion in a later epistle:

*It is a trustworthy statement: For if [since] we died with Him, we will also live with Him [both in time and eternal state guaranteed]; If we endure [hardships and trials], we will also reign with Him; If we deny Him [if we fail in our spiritual lives], He will also deny us [reward according to context 2:5-6]; If we are faithless [unfaithful], He remains faithful, for He cannot deny Himself [He cannot alter His character and His promises to us]* (2 Timothy 2:11-13).

Drs. John Walvoord and Roy B. Zuck agree: "True children of God cannot become something other than children, even when disobedient and weak. Christ's faithfulness to Christians is not contingent on their faithfulness."[58] Thank God for that!

Isaiah underscores God's covenant relationship with His people:

*Lift up your eyes to the sky...the sky will vanish like smoke...But My salvation will be forever, And My [imputed] righteousness will not wane...My righteousness will be forever, And My salvation to all generations... "For the mountains may be removed and the hills may shake, But My lovingkindness will not be removed from you, And My covenant of peace will not be shaken," Says the LORD who has compassion on you* (Isaiah 51:6-8; 54:10; cf. Jeremiah 31:3).

As we saw in chapter 1, there's nothing a believer can do, no degree of infidelity on our part, that can undo our salvation wrought in grace (Ephesians 2:8-9) and signed off with the unblemished blood of the Lamb of God (1 Peter 1:18-19; cf. Romans 8:38-39)!

Those who are on fire for the Lord and are fed up with the spiritual infidelity infesting Christianity today may find this hard to accept. Many of them undoubtedly love the Lord passionately. Some believe that if an individual does not bear fruit he is probably not really saved in the first place. This is an honest attempt to stir up believers to get on with their spiritual lives, but that's going too far. We cannot help God! Our job is to declare the whole realm of God's truth and leave the results to the One who controls history.

There are scores of passages of Scripture that show that one can be truly saved with no sign of spiritual production (Romans 13:11-14; 1

Corinthians 3:1-3; 5:1-5; Ephesians 5:14; 2 Thessalonians 2:6; James 4:1-5). Furthermore, there is not one shred of evidence in the entirety of James' epistle that shows that James' audience were unsaved, God seekers or those who had not really believed. We know that many of these were saved on the Day of Pentecost by an act of a simple faith in Christ alone (Acts 2:41, 47). What concerns James is not their salvation but rather the effect of their lack of spiritual productivity.

Four things to note in the epistle of James:

1. God's glory is His ultimate purpose in both creation and regeneration of man. *"Everyone who is called by My name, And whom I have created for My glory, Whom I have formed, even whom I have made [for My glory]"* (Isaiah 43:7).

2. God is glorified through the life of a believer who pledges fidelity to Him, who daily allows the indwelling Holy Spirit to enable him to manifest the character of Christ in all His glory. *"I am the vine, you are the branches; he who abides in Me and I in him, he bears much fruit, for apart from Me you can do nothing"* (John 15:5, cf. Philippians 2:13).

3. Spiritual infidelity incites spiritual anarchy and indifference toward God. *"Do you not know that friendship with the world is hostility toward God? Therefore whoever wishes to be a friend of the world makes himself an enemy of God"* (James 4:5).

4. Therefore, a believer in a state of spiritual anarchy cannot honor God, let alone enjoy fellowship with Him. *"Because the mind set on the flesh is hostile toward God; for it does not subject itself to the law of God [His Word], for it is not even able to do so, and those who are in the flesh cannot please God"* (Romans 8:7-8).

James knew that with such an impoverished spiritual life, these believers' conduct would be a poor testimony to the cause of Christ, our Savior. He knew that such a life would violate our Lord's command to *"Let your light shine before men in such a way that they may see your good works, and glorify your Father who is in heaven"* (Matthew 5:16).

More than that, James knew that those who are hostile toward God will also be hostile toward others. Consequently, relationships with them are difficult. He knew that they would make a mockery of the Lord's mandate for believers to love one another as He loved them (John 13:34-35).

## Effect of Spiritual Infidelity Toward Man

By nature, human beings are prone to evil. *"For I know that nothing good dwells in me"* (Romans 7:18).

Even after regeneration, evil still wants to control believers (Romans 7:14-21). We are in a tug of war constantly, *"For the flesh sets its desire against the Spirit, and the Spirit against the flesh; for these are in opposition to one another, so that you may not do the things that you please"* (Galatians 5:17).

People, by nature, are neither humble nor grace-oriented. Grace-orientation is the monopoly of maturing believers—those who are consistently under the influence of the Holy Spirit. A believer without the power of God cannot relate to others in a harmonious or gracious manner. Remember, a mediocre relationship with God guarantees a flawed relationship with others. This was the condition of the churches James addressed. Let us examine how this affected all areas of their spiritual lives.

Once a believer is in carnality, he is powerless against the sin nature. In other words, the moment the sin nature takes control of our lives, it empowers and moves us in the direction where we are most vulnerable. This was true of the recipients of James' epistle. Their spiritual infidelity affected them all, from elders to lay people. The indictments begin from the top and work their way down. He addressed the elders.

*My brethren, do not hold your faith in our glorious Lord Jesus Christ with an attitude of personal favoritism. For if a man comes into your assembly with a gold ring and dressed in fine clothes, and there also comes in a poor man in dirty clothes, and you pay special attention to the one who is wearing fine clothes, and say, 'You sit here in a good place," [because he will enrich your church] and you say to the poor man, "You stand over there, or sit down by my footstool," [because he is too poor to contribute to the church] have you not made distinctions among yourselves, and become judges with evil motives?* (James 2:1-4).

James indicates that, though their spiritual infidelity had driven them to practice evil, they were still among those born in the "*exercise of His will*" (James 1:18) and indwelt by His Spirit (James 4:5). Interestingly, he uses "Present active imperative of echo with negative me, exhortation to stop holding or not to have the habit of holding in the fashion condemned."[59] In other words, he was telling them as believers in Christ to stop the evil they were already involved in. This is a sharp rebuke to the elders of the church! Now, he turns to the congregation.

*What use is it, my brethren, if someone says he has faith [i.e., if a man says he has an arsenal of biblical truth] but he has no works [application]? Can that faith [biblical knowledge] save him [from discipline and even premature physical death]? If a brother or sister is without clothing and in need of daily food, and one of you says to them, "Go in peace, be warmed and be filled," and yet you do not give them what is necessary for their body, what use is that?* (James 2:14-16).

These believers were indifferent to the needs of their fellow believers (2:15-16). Is that surprising? Not really. If you are indifferent to God, you will be indifferent to those around you. It's that simple! The apostle John later asked a similar question: "*But whoever has the world's goods, and sees his brother in need and closes his heart against him, how does the love of God abide in him? Little children, let us not love with word or with tongue, but in deed and truth*" (1 John 3:17-18).

The backdrop of James 2:14-16 is the Old Testament teaching on caring for the poor or needy (Leviticus 25:35; Deuteronomy 15:4-11; Proverbs 14:21; 19:7). These sound teachings of the Bible are collectively called *biblical truth*, or what Dr. James Orr refers to as, "the truth, or body of truth, which is trusted, or which justifies trust."[60] It's this body of truth that James refers to as "faith" in James 2:14. We recognize that others hold different views, but context and logic will prevail as our study shifts gear.

The believers of James' day had failed miserably in their response to this biblical teaching about helping their needy brethren, a failure repugnant to Almighty God. So James asked, "Can your orthodoxy— your doctrine or biblical truth—save you from discipline, if your lifestyle is not in agreement with what you know?"

---

**Can your knowledge of biblical truth save you from discipline, if your lifestyle is not in agreement with what you know?**

---

In James 3 and 4, he chastised them for the misuse of their tongues in vituperation, gossip, maligning, backbiting, slander, covetousness and judging of others. It is striking how James reprimanded these adulterous believers. On the one hand, he held them with a grip of love and grace-orientation; and on the other he lambasted them: *"My brethren, do not hold your faith in our glorious Lord Jesus Christ with an attitude of personal favoritism"* (James 2:1).

This gesture shows us that they were unquestionably believers in Christ! It's obvious that his audience were those saved by grace. But the danger, as the apostle Peter pointed out, was that they were *"blind…[and] short-sighted, having forgotten [their] purification from [their] former sins"* (2 Peter 1:9).

But is that all? Will God continue to look the other way? He cannot, for His justice will not allow it. Even Thomas Jefferson (principal author of the U.S. Declaration of Independence and third president of the United States of America, 1743-1826) commented on God's justice: "I tremble for my country when I reflect that God is just; that His justice cannot sleep forever."[61]

James certainly knew that God's judgment was on the horizon, and that explains his remarks. *"Therefore, putting aside all filthiness and all that remains of wickedness, in humility receive the word implanted, which is able to save your souls [physical life]"* (James 1:21).

## Consequences of Spiritual Infidelity

*"MY SON, DO NOT REGARD LIGHTLY THE DISCIPLINE OF THE LORD, NOR FAINT WHEN YOU ARE REPROVED*

*BY HIM; FOR THOSE WHOM THE LORD LOVES HE DIS-CIPLINES, AND HE SCOURGES EVERY SON WHOM HE RECEIVES"* [God deals with us as sons] (Hebrews 12:5-7).

We have viewed briefly the effect of spiritual infidelity, both toward God and toward man. We noted that apart from a deepened relationship with God, we will be unhappy and miserable. Those around us will share in our misery! More than that; spiritual unfaithfulness sidelines our spiritual life temporarily.

Let us recall the overriding principle of James' epistle, namely that prolonged carnality will ultimately result in premature physical death. James' concern was the deteriorated spiritual condition of his Jewish audience.

James was esteemed by Paul as one of the pillars of the church (Galatians 2:9) As a shepherd, James was acutely aware of his duty, both to the Lord and to the recipients of his epistle. He knew, as the spiritual leader of his Christian audience, that he was responsible to warn them of God's impending judgment because of their infidelity (James 4:4; cf. Hebrews 13:17). Undoubtedly, he was familiar with, and took seriously, the words of the prophet Ezekiel:

*"Son of man, I have appointed you a watchman to the house of Israel; whenever you hear a word from My mouth, warn them from Me. When I say to the wicked, 'You will surely die,' and you do not warn him or speak out to warn the wicked from his wicked way that he may live, that wicked man shall die in his iniquity, but his blood I will require at your hand.* **Yet if you have warned the wicked and he does not turn from his wickedness or from his wicked way, he shall die in his iniquity;** *but you have delivered yourself. Again, when a righteous man turns away from his righteousness and commits iniquity, and I place an obstacle before him, he will die; since you have not warned him, he shall die in his sin, and his righteous deeds which he has done [while in fellowship] shall not be remembered [will not save him from premature death]; but his blood I will require at your hand. However,* **if you have warned the righteous man that the righteous should**

*not sin and he does not sin, he shall surely live because he took warning; and you have delivered yourself"* (Ezekiel 3:17-21, emphasis added; cf. James 5:19-20).

The issue is not if a believer is capable of entering into carnality, for the potential abounds. *"Indeed, there is not a righteous man on earth who continually does good and who never sins"* (Ecclesiastes 7:20; cf. Ezekiel 3:21; 1 John 1:8-10).

The issue is whether the individual will recover when he finds himself in sin (1 John 1:9; cf. Ezekiel 3:21). Many scholars agree that James was well acquainted with the writings of the prophets of the Old. *"However, if you have warned the righteous man that the righteous should not sin and he does not sin, he shall surely live because he took warning; and you have delivered yourself"* (Ezekiel 3:21). These words may have been on his mind in his exhortation: *"Therefore, putting aside all filthiness and all that remains of wickedness, in humility receive the word implanted, which is able to save your souls* [physical life]*"* (James 1:21).

And then he outlined for them the path to premature physical death:

*Let no one say when he is tempted, "I am being tempted by God"; for God cannot be tempted by evil, and He Himself does not tempt anyone. But each one is tempted when he is carried away and enticed by his own lust. Then when lust has conceived, it gives birth to sin; and when sin is accomplished, it brings forth death. Do not be deceived, my beloved brethren* (James 1:13-16).

Apparently, some false teachers were distorting biblical truth regarding God's sovereignty, as is true today. They may have been teaching that man has no free will, that whatever happens is the way God designed it. In other words, God's sovereignty is behind everything good or bad—man is just a robot without the ability to make choices.

James steps forward to refute such a notion in James 1:13-16 and rests his case with words of caution: *"Do not be deceived, my beloved brethren"* (James 1:16).

You see, premature physical death was clear to him as he wrote the epistle. Therefore he sought to inspire these adulterous believers to turn back to God and thus avoid God's temporal (not eternal) judgment.

If a man knows the whole realm of God's Word and does not put it into practice but continually engages in an adulterous behavior (James 4:4), can such knowledge of God's Word save him from premature death? (James 2:14).

Premature physical death was on James' mind. He was no doubt thinking back to Ezekiel 3:21 when he urged, "*My brethren, if any among you strays from the truth [spiritual life] and one turns him back, let him know that he who turns a sinner [believer] from the error of his way will save his soul [physical life] from [premature physical] death and will cover a multitude of sins*" (James 5:19-20).

In other words, God can forgive the sinning believer and wipe his slate clean. "*Blessed are those whose iniquities are forgiven, and whose sins are covered; blessed is the man against whom the Lord will not reckon his sin*" (Romans 4:7-8 RSV).

On the other hand, the Bible is not silent regarding God's judgment of believers in time. So let's look into the biblical teaching on temporal judgment and premature physical death of believers, or what some refer to as "sin unto death," a consequence of spiritual infidelity.

## Sin Unto Death

In eternity past, God in His infinite grace, wisdom and fairness allocated the number of years every believer would spend on earth (Psalm 139:16). The good news is no one but God can shorten these years. However, the believer can contribute to God's decision, as we shall see. Saul, in the Old Testament, is a perfect example. Of his case we read,

> So Saul died for his trespass which he committed against the LORD, **because of** the word of the LORD which he did not keep; and also **because** he asked counsel of a medium, making inquiry of it, and did not inquire of the LORD. Therefore He killed him and turned the kingdom to David the son of Jesse (1 Chronicles 10:13-14, emphasis added.).

119

Is it not obvious that Saul contributed to his own premature death?

Now we turn to the apostle Paul's epistle to the carnal Corinthians: *"For, in the first place, when you come together as a church [to partake of Communion], I hear that divisions exist among you; and in part I believe it [knowing what you are capable of doing]"* (1 Corinthians 11:18).

Paul continues to charge them with failures, one after another, ranging from fighting for communion bread (1 Corinthians 11:20-22) to partaking of the Eucharist while intoxicated with communion wine (1 Corinthians 11:21). Then he explains the consequences: ***"For this reason many among you are weak and sick, and a number sleep [die early]"*** (1 Corinthians 11:30). It is obvious from this passage that carnality is the only reason why many of these believers were suffering and a good number were dead already! Other passages abound:

> *"If anyone does not abide in Me, he is thrown away as a branch [being plucked out of the Vine, John 15:5] and dries up [intensive discipline]; and they gather them, and cast them into fire and they are burned [a metaphor for premature death and a loss of reward, 1 Corinthians 3:15]"* (John 15:6).

> *The fear of the LORD is a fountain of life, That one may avoid the snares of death* (Proverbs 14:27).

> *The fear of [respect and application of the Word of] the LORD prolongs life, But the years of the wicked will be shortened [premature death]* (Proverbs 10:27).

> *A man who wanders from the way of understanding Will rest in the assembly of the dead [before his appointed time]* (Proverbs 21:16).

As demonstrated, discipline is the result of spiritual infidelity, and great blessing is the result of a life marked with love, respect, honor and enduring devotion to God.

## Review of Foundational Material Studied in Chapters 6 and 7

1. James' epistle was addressed to born-again believers. Otherwise he would not have called them "my brethren" or "my beloved brethren" so often.

2. James labeled them "adulteresses" because they, as the Lord's "wife," had deserted Him and turned back to the world (i.e., another man) (James 4:5).

3. James' epistle was to show them the two sides of Christianity,

- Discipline and possible premature physical death if one remains in carnality

- Abundant blessing if one applies the truth in their souls to the maximum!

With this solid foundation laid in the last two chapters we are now ready to return to our verse-by-verse exposition.

## EIGHT

## James 1:9-11

# Pursue Eternal Glory

> *But the brother of humble circumstances is to glory in his high position; and the rich man is to glory in his humiliation, because like flowering grass he will pass away. For the sun rises with a scorching wind and withers the grass; and its flower falls off and the beauty of its appearance is destroyed; so too the rich man in the midst of his pursuits will fade away* (**James 1:9-11**).

*Sic transic gloria mundi* is a Latin phrase that means "thus fades worldly glory" or simply "the glory of this world passes away." In the time of the Roman Empire, this famous inscription could be read on their banners. It was a reminder of the transience of life, riches and earthly honor.

James shifts from his exhortation to "*Consider it all joy*" and moves on to wealth, riches, earthly nobility and the alarming rate in which these fade away.

We cannot say it often enough: James is an exceptional Bible teacher. Under the principle that Scripture must harmonize with Scripture, his epistle harmonizes with the book of Hebrews. We see the parallel of James' message in Hebrews 10:24. "*Let us consider how to stimulate one another to love and good deeds.*"

James has done this in his epistle in a stunning manner. In a grand display of wisdom, grace-orientation and love, he strongly reproved his Christian audience as "*adulteresses.*" He knew that spiritual infidelity would not only tear the church apart but also nullify the effect of the gospel. James also knew that premature physical death was looming for many of these who were in spiritual degeneracy. *"Then when lust has conceived, it gives birth to sin; and when sin is accomplished, it brings forth [premature physical] death"* (James 1:15).

He did what every Bible teacher should do; he exhorted them to regain their spiritual momentum through confessing their sins. *"Therefore, putting aside all filthiness and all that remains of wickedness [through confession], in humility receive the word implanted, which is able to save your souls [life from premature physical death]"* (James 1:21; cf. 1 John 1:9).

He stirred his readers to "good deeds" using Abraham as a perfect example (James 2:21-22). By doing so, in essence he was saying, "Listen, there's more to the Christian life after faith [confidence] alone in Christ alone for salvation. God has more in mind, and it is beyond description!" He wanted them to know that in God's household, there is going to be a distinction. Some will be justified temporally and eternally for greater blessing, beyond their wildest imagination, because they have applied God's Word to the maximum. God honored Abraham with the title *"the friend of God"* (James 2:23; cf. Malachi 3:13-18; cf. 1 Corinthians 3:11-15; James 2:24). God wants to honor you in the same manner that He honored Abraham. James was saying, "Let's stop messing around and get with God's program so we can develop the capacity for super-abundant blessings."

Now we come to our passage. *"But the brother of humble circumstances is to glory in his high position; and the rich man is to glory in his humiliation, because like flowering grass he will pass away"* (James 1:9-10). As you can see, this passage, James 1:9-11, is not in continuity with James 1:2-8 but rather contains a new thought.

Martin Dibelius agrees: "The saying about the downfall of the rich man introduces a new antithesis which is not combined by the author in any way with the preceding antithesis [faith and doubt of the previous passage]."[62]

The other issue is whether *the rich man* mentioned is a believer or an unbeliever. We stand on the side that the rich man is a believer. This conviction is based on three reasons.

First, all New Testament epistles (letters to churches and pastors) were written for the edification of believers. *"For whatever was written in earlier times was written for our instruction"* (Romans 15:4).

Second, we have no credible scriptural evidence that any epistolary author addressed any portion of his letter to the unsaved. This is because a local church serves as a meeting place for the saints. Occasional visitation of unbelievers in such an assembly is too insignificant to require an epistle.

Third, James is judging those in the church and not unbelievers, as noted in Scripture: *"For what have I to do with judging outsiders? Do you not judge those who are within the church? But those who are outside, God judges"* (1 Corinthians 5:12-13).

With these two issues settled—the manner in which James wrote and the recipients being believers—we begin the scrutiny of our passage by examining a quote by Douglas J. Moo:

> James in these verses addresses two believers, a poor one and a rich one. He exhorts each of them to look toward their spiritual identity as their measure of their ultimate significance. To the poor believer, tempted to feel insignificant and powerless because the world judges a person on the basis of money and status, James says: take pride in your exalted status in the spiritual realm as one seated with Christ in the heavenlies with Jesus Christ himself. To the rich believer, tempted to think too much of himself because the world holds him in high esteem, James says: take pride not in your money or in your social position— things that are doomed all too soon to fade away forever—but, paradoxically, in your humble status as a person who identifies with one who was "despised and dejected" by the world.[63]

---

**"Spiritual identity...[our] measure of...
ultimate significance."**

---

Character is revealed under pressure. Maintaining a biblical viewpoint while under pressure is a hallmark of maturity. We all have pressures. No one is immune. Prosperity can exert as much pressure on the rich as poverty does on the poor. How we handle adversity or prosperity reveals our level of growth in the Lord. Being poor is not a sin! On the contrary, *"The poor will never cease to be in the land; therefore I command you, saying, 'You shall freely open your hand to your brother, to your needy and poor in your land"* (Deuteronomy 15:11). Our Lord at the end of His earthly ministry stated, *"For you always have the poor with you"* (Matthew 26:11).

The idea that every believer should be wealthy is a demonic teaching. It contradicts Scripture! Dr. Fruchtenbaum agrees: "It is not true that He wants every believer to be wealthy; He does not want believers to 'name it, claim it, and frame it.'"[64]

Rather, James wants every believer of humble means to have the right attitude toward his lowly estate. Glory in it! Let there be no misunderstanding; poverty in itself does not translate one to a high position in the Lord. It is always the inner quality of a believer's soul that spirals him to God's bosom. But often it's the believer in a lowly state who is freed from the worries that prosperity brings. Solomon captured this beautifully: *"The sleep of the working [poor] man is pleasant [he's not worried about protecting his investments], whether he eats little or much; but the full stomach of the rich man [because of worries about maintaining his wealth] does not allow him to sleep"* (Ecclesiastes 5:12).

Often it's the poor who spend more time in prayer. It's the poor who attend church, or Bible study, on a regular basis. It's the poor who, because of consistency in their spiritual life, develop harmony and closeness with God more easily than the rich, who may be distracted in finding ways to expand or protect their wealth. Pause and consider this profound prayer: *"Keep deception and lies far from me, Give me neither poverty nor riches; Feed me with the food that is my portion, That I not be full and deny You"* (Proverbs 30:8-9). The author in Proverbs prayed for just enough to not forget the Giver!

James is saying, "Those of you who are of humble means but spiritually rich in the Lord, rejoice! Your reward is accumulating for you in heaven, where spiritual wealth counts and lasts for all eternity!"

To the rich, his message is only slightly different. He's not rebuking riches. On the contrary, there's nothing sinful about prosperity; after all, riches are of the Lord (1 Chronicles 29:12). It is the attitude one has toward prosperity that counts. James is not saying that rich believers will never make it. Zaccheus, a rich man, hit the jackpot with the Lord (Luke 19:2-9). Abraham, Job, and David, just to name a few rich men of the Old Testament, came out on top spiritually, having one thing in common—the Lord was their portion. So to the rich James is saying, "Consider your wealth as a blessing from the Lord, and yourself as a steward who is to manage God's assets wisely. View all this as temporary because, like a fading flower or withering grass, you will pass away, leaving wealth, power and possessions behind." He agrees with Jeremiah, who said, "*Let not a wise man boast of his wisdom, and let not the mighty man boast of his might, let not a rich man boast of his riches; but let him [wise, mighty, or rich] who boasts boast of this, that he understands and knows Me*" (Jeremiah 9:23-24).

So my beloved, let your boasting be in the Lord. Value your spiritual identity as your true identity. Eventually a rich person will be brought low, because in death "he can't take it with him." Let it be that you have come to know our Lord as your Savior and that you have seen Him working in your life! In all you do, remember this: the glory of this world passes away—*sic transit Gloria mundi.*

In the next chapter we shall examine "the crown of life," James 1:12. Until then, may the Lord continue to enrich our souls through His Word.

## NINE

James 1:12

# The Crown of Life

*Blessed is a man who perseveres under trial; for once he has been approved, he will receive the crown of life which the Lord has promised to those who love Him* (**James 1:12**).

In ancient Greece and Rome, the winners of an athletic competition received a crown of laurel leaves. In today's Olympic games the prize is a gold medal. Every culture has its athletic games, and every athlete has his eye on the prize.

This may explain why the apostle Paul and the writer of Hebrews both described our spiritual journey as a race.

## Run with Endurance

*"Do you not know that those who run in a race all run, but only one receives the prize [or crown]?"* (1 Corinthians 9:24). *"Let us run with endurance the race that is set before us"* (Hebrews 12:1).

Jesus Christ, our role model, persevered through many trials but kept His focus on *"the joy set before Him"* (Hebrews 12:2). He looked forward to the day when His suffering would be over, when He would once again sit down at the right hand of the Father, the place of victory and honor. The Lord exhorts us, saying,

*"I am coming quickly; hold fast what you have, so that no one will take your crown. He who overcomes, I will make him a pillar in the temple of My God, and he will not go out from it anymore; and I will write on him the name of My God, and the name of the*

129

*city of My God, the new Jerusalem, which comes down out of
heaven from My God, and My new name"* (Revelation 3:11-12).

Since the crown was the highest award for a runner of his day, it's
fitting that James would also call attention to a "crown," for both time
and eternity.

When we consider our passage (James 1:12) carefully, it seems to
fit right after James 1:2-3:

*Consider it all joy, my brethren, when you encounter various tri-
als, knowing that the testing of your faith produces endurance..."*
(James 1:2-3).

*"Blessed is a man who perseveres under trial; for once he has been
approved [literally passed the test], he will receive the crown of life
which the Lord has promised to those who love Him* (James 1:12)

You can see why a sequential outline for James' epistle is difficult to
come by. Keep in mind, though, that James' epistle is not a "three-point
sermon," with introduction, body of the message and conclusion.

We have used the three most important fundamentals undergird-
ing serious students of the Word of God to reveal the text:

1. We check sentimentalism and emotion at the door of our soul.
2. We approach God's Word with humility, objectivity, reverence and awe under the influence of the Holy Spirit.
3. We follow the rules of interpretation, allowing Scripture to
interpret Scripture.

---

**When one sticks to his premise at the expense of truth,
the potential to corrupt the Word of God abounds.**

---

The basic principles of hermeneutics (biblical interpretation)
require that we compare one verse with another verse, one context with
another context, and a verse with the context of the whole Bible. We
debase God's Word when we start from our own premise and work our
way into Scripture. The right approach is to analyze Scripture first and
let it reveal the premise, never the other way around! If we begin with

our own premise we bring along our bias and tradition and therefore may reject an interpretation that cannot be made to fit our view. Clearly, when one sticks to his premise at the expense of truth, the potential to corrupt the Word of God abounds! We must use great caution to come to the text free from bias.

We say this because some hold a position that the "crown of life" means eternal life which would be awarded to those who persevere to the end. So, if one begins with the premise that "saving faith" must persevere to the end, it makes sense that he would conclude that eternal life is in view.

Does "*the crown of life*" in our passage reference eternal life? No, because James said eternal life is a gift (James 1:17-18 c.f. Romans 6:23b). Therefore it cannot be earned or worked for (Romans 4:4; Ephesians 2:8-9; 2 Timothy 1:9). Do we agree on this?

If we insist that the crown of life is eternal life, then the phrase "*those who love Him*" becomes a condition for eternal life. But such an assertion does not concur with the rest of Scripture, where perseverance precedes the crown. If the crown (eternal life) is gained through perseverance, that means the one who is persevering is an unbeliever. But Scripture tells us one cannot persevere unless he has been born anew and given the power to do so (John 1:12).

Also consider "*Apart from Me [apart from My life and continued fellowship] you can do nothing*" (John 15:5; cf. 1:12). "*These things I have written to you who believe in the name of the Son of God, so that you may know that you have eternal life*" (1 John 5:13). Consider the meaning of *eternal life*. If eternal life is everlasting, when does it begin and end? Simply, it begins at the point one "*believes in the Son*" (John 3:36) and continues throughout eternity. It never ends (John 10:28-29)!

---

**Nothing in Scripture teaches that failure in one's spiritual life is a sign that one is not saved.**

---

My beloved, we should not twist a verse around to fit it into the mold of a false premise. As tempting as it may be, that's a misrepresentation of God's Word, and it carries a warning label (a subject of James 3:1)!

A serious student of God's Word may ask, "What about Galatians 5:21?" *"Envying, drunkenness, carousing, and things like these, of which I forewarn you, just as I have forewarned you, that those who practice such things will not inherit the kingdom of God"* (Galatians 5:21).

Good question. In Galatians *"inherit the kingdom of God"* is not eternal life but rewards! Eternal life is a gift. There's only one condition for receiving it: that one trusts in Christ alone (John 3:36). One is saved not according to one's works (2 Timothy 1:9). Conversely, lack of works cannot cause God to retract His *"irrevocable"* gift (Romans 11:29). But when it comes to possessing God's kingdom, as an inheritance, it comes with a price, namely, fulfillment of God's plan for one's life. In Colossians 3:23-24, the apostle Paul underscores, *"Whatever you do, do your work heartily, as for the Lord rather than for men, knowing that from the Lord **you will receive the reward of the inheritance**. It is the Lord Christ whom you serve."* Here, and in other passages, one takes an inheritance to mean a reward (Galatians 5:5; Hebrews 10:36; Luke 6:20; Revelation 22:12). The truth is that God tests His own for character development. Often we falter; then we pass the test! Nothing in Scripture teaches that failure in one's spiritual life is a sign that one is not saved. For example, Abraham (after he received God's imputed righteousness) had three obvious tests. He failed two as a baby in the Lord and passed the third as a mature believer. Of course, passing the test came with much learning and growing in the grace of Yahweh!

Test one: After the Lord made a promise to Abraham (Genesis 12:1-7), He then tested him by taking him to Egypt for food. But en route, Abraham failed the test. He feared that the Egyptians would kill him and take his beautiful wife. Fear gripped him. So he told his wife to lie because of fear of death (Genesis 12:10-13) But wait a minute. Hadn't God just made a promise to him that had not yet been fulfilled? What made him think that someone could terminate his life before God's plan was completed? Fear! But in maturity fear gave way to confidence that whatever God has promised, He is able to fulfill (Romans 4:18-21; cf. 1 John 4:18).

Test two: This was a test of patience. God promised him a son (Genesis 12:2; 15:1-5). Abraham waited for years and later succumbed to the temptation of impatience. Abraham tried to help God fulfill His promise by impregnating Sarah's housemaid, Hagar (Genesis 16:1-3). Can we say that Abraham's faith (confidence) was not genuine when he failed these two tests as a believer in Yahweh? No. Abraham was eternally saved (his confidence for salvation was genuine). What was weak was his patience because of immaturity.

Test three: On the third test God asked Abraham to offer his only son as a sacrifice. He not only passed (Genesis 22:1-10) but was justified for the title "*the friend of God*" (James 2:23). We shall cover this in greater detail in a later chapter.

Like Abraham, the apostle Peter had two notable tests; he failed miserably on one (Matthew 26:69-75) and shone in the other (Acts 2:14, 22-24, 36-38). Neither Abraham nor the apostle Peter lost his salvation when they failed spiritually!

"*Blessed is a man who perseveres under trial*" (James 1:12). Blessing and rewards should not be at the forefront of our minds when we are fulfilling God's purpose for our lives. Rather, our love for Him! As D.J. Moo points out, "Far too many Christians bring a selfish and calculating 'bottom line' mentality into their service of the Lord, asking, 'what's in it for me?' at every step."[65]

Believers should not have this mentality, especially when we consider that was Satan's claim against Job: "*Does Job fear God for nothing?*" (Job 1:9). **We should serve, not because of what God will do for us but because of what He has already done for us.** God gave of Himself for us, in the Person of His Son, Jesus Christ, who suffered immensely to redeem us from the eternal consequences of sin. Therefore we should all be offended by this "what's in it for me?" attitude.

However, some brethren have overreacted and therefore reject the idea of reward. That too is going to an extreme, because scriptural references abound with regard to rewards. "Jesus certainly did not shrink from speaking of rewards. 'Great is your reward in heaven,' He said (Matt. 5:46; 6:1, 2, 4, 6, 17, Luke 6:35)."[66]

The apostle Paul, too, followed the Lord's footsteps in spotlighting reward (1 Corinthians 3:11-15; 9:24-27; 2 Corinthians 5:10; 2 Timothy 2:3-6; 4:6-8). Regardless of other people's opinions, we should declare the whole realm of God's Word without compromise! God will reward those *"who love Him"* (James 1:12; I Corinthians 2:9; 8:3).

This phenomenal concept is also mentioned in the Old Testament: *"Because he [mature believer] has loved Me, therefore I will deliver [protect] him; I will set him securely on high [esteem], because he has known My name"* (Psalm 91:14).

Grammatically, the word *because* highlights the rest of the sentence. *"Because he has loved Me...I will set him securely on high."*

*"No good thing does He withhold from those who walk uprightly"* (Psalm 84:11). The phrases *"who love Him," "has loved Me,"* and *"walk uprightly"* describe believers with spiritual integrity. God promises to honor these believers in a special way.

*"For those who honor Me I will honor"* (1 Samuel 2:30). That reward is for a special group. That reward is for gold-standard believers! The idea that every believer will be rewarded alike, or that there will be no rewards at all, does not agree with Scripture. The Bible teaches there will be distinction in the eternal state: *"So you will again distinguish between the righteous [believer of spiritual integrity] and the wicked [carnal believer], between one who serves [honors] God and one who does not serve [honor] Him"* (Malachi 3:18; cf. 1 Corinthians 3:11-15).

We now proceed to examine the phrase *"love for God."*

## Love for God

The phrase *"who love Him"* in James 1:12 must be clarified before we can understand the rest of the passage.

We know that love in any relationship is not automatic. It takes time to flourish through knowledge and experience. The idea that someone can trust in Christ today and be full of love for God the next is unrealistic. A normal excitement about our new life within should not be misconstrued as a love for God. The truth is, we cannot love God without getting to know Him; and we cannot know Him apart from a serious study of His Word. The more we know about Him through His Word, the greater the potential is to love Him. As we fill ourselves with the understanding of His Word, applying it through the trials of life's experiences, we behold His faithfulness in our every circumstance. Love and appreciation for who and what He is soars to new heights! Simply "love for God" is a mark of spiritual maturity.

The apostle John gave us a vivid picture of mature love:

*We have come to know and have believed the love which God has for us God is love, and the one who abides in love abides in God, and God abides in him. By this, love is perfected with us, so that we may have confidence in the day of judgment; because as He is [matured in His incarnation, Hebrews 5:8-9], so also are we [when we follow in His footsteps] in this world. There is no fear in love; but perfect [mature] love casts out fear [a symptom of babyhood], because fear involves punishment [divine discipline], and the one who fears is not perfected [mature]* 67 *in love* (1 John 4:16-18).

Note, the apostle John did not say, "The one who fears is still unsaved." Rather, *"and the one who fears is not perfected in love"* (a spiritual baby).

Immature believers are more prone to mishandling the ball of suffering, through whining and complaining, before they can even get to the goal line, let alone score! The author of Hebrews captured this concept:

*For everyone who partakes only of milk is not accustomed to the word of righteousness [he has no capacity for advanced truth; is not proficient in handling life's many problems], for he is an infant. But solid food [advanced truth] is for the mature [teleios, same Greek word for "perfect love"], who because of practice [applying God's Word to life] have their senses trained [maturity] to discern good and evil* (Hebrews 5:13-14).

The author of Hebrews never questioned the salvation of these babies. He simply underscored what characterized them, namely silliness.

Often spiritual babies retrogress and never grow up, as seen in the apostle Paul's frustration with the Corinthians. About two years after their conversion, many Corinthian believers were still babies, creating problems and messes of all kinds in their local church (1 Corinthians 3:1-3). In spite of this, Paul assured them that God would *"confirm...[them]*

to the end, blameless in the day of our Lord Jesus Christ" (1 Corinthians 1:8), highlighting God's faithfulness. "God is faithful" (1 Corinthians 1:9; cf. 2:7-9; 2 Timothy 2:13). That's grace!

"Love for God" is an expression of a deeper relationship with Him, characterized by love, respect for His Word, honor and enduring devotion. Love for God is a phrase we hear all the time, but what is it? Love for God is the same as spiritual maturity, righteousness, or spiritual integrity. At this stage of growth the thinking and character of Christ dominate the thinking of the believer and are consistently displayed in his life. A baby believer may indeed have a heart for God but development of love for God takes time, effort, patience and, above all, discipline.

God introduces trials to turn our focus to Him. As we mix life's experiences with His Word in our souls, as we strengthen our confidence in His providential care and faithfulness, capacity to love God becomes inevitable!

Now we can go back and tie this section to James' earlier thought: "Consider it all joy, my brethren, when you encounter various trials, knowing that the testing of your faith produces endurance. And let endurance have its perfect result, that you may be perfect [mature, with love for God] and complete, lacking in nothing (James 1:2-4). Love for God which is synonymous with maturity (or capacity), attracts God's ultimate blessing. God has accorded us everything in grace, including the availability of His Word, the power of His Spirit, and the capacity for, and execution of, His plan. The "crown of life" is a reward for those who have developed the capacity for such an honor! We must point out that even blessing above and beyond is based completely on God's grace (Romans 8:32).

## Receiving the Crown of Life

So what is "the crown of life?" According to Leslie Milton,

It is called a "CROWN" because it is a source of joy, a high privilege, a wonderful honour. It is the mark of God's approval, the symbol of His "Well done"...In modern times a crown is usually made of very precious materials and is intrinsically valuable. In ancient times, however, it was usually of little value in itself, its value lying entirely in the honour it represented…Crown combined with life speaks of its quality and duration. "Every good thing bestowed and every perfect gift is from above, coming down from the Father of lights" (James 1:17). The word "life" points to the duration of God's honor— eternal! We might as well refer to it as a **"crown of a lifetime."** In the ancient time, crowns are made of perishable wreaths (1 Corinthians 9:25); but in our case, we will "Obtain an inheritance which is imperishable and undefiled and will not fade away, reserved in heaven for you" (1 Peter 1:4; cf. 5:4).[68]

This honor awaits mature believers both for now and forever. Zane Hodges underscores this concept, saying, "Indeed, every time we successfully endure a period of trouble, the crown of life will be awarded to us anew."[69] This means that the believer can acquire many crowns if he stays focused in his Christian life.

God blesses us in time as our capacity grows. James points to Job as an example: *"We count those blessed who endured. You have heard of the endurance of Job and have seen the outcome of the Lord's dealings, that the Lord is full of compassion and is merciful"* (James 5:11). Job didn't have to wait until the eternity to have a taste of what the eternal state would look like. God gave him a double portion in time! *"The LORD restored the fortunes of Job…and the LORD increased all that Job had twofold"* (Job 42:10).

This brings up another issue, the eternal state.

## The Eternal State

As for the eternal state, it's indescribable. Paul expresses it thus: *"THINGS WHICH EYE HAS NOT SEEN AND EAR HAS NOT HEARD, AND which HAVE NOT ENTERED THE HEART OF MAN, ALL THAT GOD HAS PREPARED FOR THOSE WHO LOVE HIM"* (1 Corinthians 2:9). So whatever blessing we enjoy in time is just the tip of the iceberg in view of the many crowns and blessings in the future. Paul was looking forward to his rewards when he said,

*I have fought the good fight, I have finished the course, I have kept the faith [church age biblical truth]; in the future [eternal state] there is laid up for me the crown of righteousness [crown of spiritual integrity], which the Lord, the righteous Judge, will award to me on that day; and not only to me, but also to all who have loved His appearing [matured—winner believers]* (2 Timothy 4:7-8).

What a future to look forward to! What a hope! So, in essence, James is saying, "My beloved brethren, look! God has something special that will make whatever suffering you are facing right now appear insignificant. God wants to bless you. He wants to honor you in a way that will make the angels' jaws drop in great amazement!" To look forward to such a state is motive enough to strive for maturity.

My beloved, can it be said of you right now that your love for God is immeasurable? Remember,

*Run in such a way that you may win. Everyone who competes in the games exercises self-control in all things. They then do it to receive a perishable wreath, but we an imperishable. Therefore I run in such a way, as not without aim; I box in such a way, as not beating the air; but I discipline my body and make it my slave, so that, after I have preached to others, I myself will not be disqualified [for a crown]* (1 Corinthians 9:24-27).

It's my heartfelt prayer that our love for the One who first loved us may abound, that we may grow in knowledge and obedience, that we might receive the crown of life!

This closes chapter 9 and opens up another more in-depth study of James' epistle.

---

## TEN

James 1:13-16

# Path to Premature Death

*Let no one say when he is tempted, "I am being tempted by God";*
*for God cannot be tempted by evil, and He Himself does not tempt*
*anyone. But each one is tempted when he is carried away and*
*enticed by his own lust. Then when lust has conceived, it gives*
*birth to sin; and when sin is accomplished, it brings forth death.*
*Do not be deceived, my beloved brethren* (**James 1:13-16**).

James, and later Paul, dealt with the issues of spiritual degeneracy with divine insight. When Paul received a report that the church at Corinth was in spiritual disarray, his letter did not begin with a rebuke but rather by gently reminding them that they were the "*church of God*" (1 Corinthians 1:2), set apart unto God, namely "*saints*" (1 Corinthians 1:2). He reserved his rebuke of this carnal church until he had awakened them to the reality of who they were in Christ and God's immeasurable grace upon their lives (1 Corinthians 1:2-8).

Then he started with a mild rebuke, citing "*divisions among you*" (1 Corinthians 1:10). In chapter 3 he called these believers "*men of flesh...infants in Christ*" (1 Corinthians 3:1). In chapter 5, he handled the problem of incest; there he exhorted, "*You have become arrogant and have not mourned instead*" (1 Corinthians 5:2). The apostle Paul's castigation got more and more severe as the chapters progressed.

Likewise, James knew that his readers had deserted the Lord and were immersed in carnality. But he did not call them adulteresses in James 1:1, even though he knew that's what they were. He reserved such a reprimand for chapter 4. James' rebukes of his audience get harsher and harsher as his epistle progresses. That's discernment! He first stabilized them with words of encouragement about suffering when he told them to "*consider it all joy…when you encounter various trials*" (James 1:2).

Then James warned his readers that the last stop on their path was premature physical death. "*When lust has conceived, it gives birth to sin; and when sin is accomplished, it brings forth* [premature physical] *death*" (James 1:15). Make no mistake, the death James has in mind here is physical. However, James did not say that anytime one sins he will die. Far from it! He employed the example of conception and childbearing. Birth does not follow immediately after pregnancy; it takes time. Likewise, one who habitually lives in sin will finally, after time, arrive at the day of labor where premature death will be born.

It appears that James' audience had some kind of misconception with regard to God's sovereignty. They are not alone. Many of us, centuries later, are still lacking knowledge on this topic. We shall briefly examine God's sovereignty in order to help us more fully comprehend our passage.

## SOVEREIGNTY OF GOD

Basically, there are three major theological schools on this subject, Calvinist, Armenian and Biblicist. We are Biblicists (meaning we stand on what Scripture says). This does not imply that our beloved brethren (Calvinist and Armenian) do not consult Scripture. They do. We whole heartedly embrace their teachings were they line up with Scripture. But were they come short, we go with what we believe to be a more accurate interpretation of the Bible. We appreciate the great work, done in all honesty, by our beloved brothers (Calvin and Arminius). That not with-standing, we take into account the danger of group divisionism, "*I am of Paul,*" and "*I am of Apollos,*" and "*I am of Cephas*" (I Corinthians 1:12), which the apostle Paul himself sought to correct, "*Has Christ been divided?*" (v. 13). My beloved, hear me: The danger is that if one attaches oneself wholly to any particular theological group, the temptation of becoming a *defender* of its doctrine at all cost abounds. With this in mind, we approach the subject of *sovereignty*, with brand new eyes under the lens of the Holy Spirit. The Calvinists believe that God has already predetermined everything, including man's salvation. Many passionate children of God claim that in salvation God gives "a saving faith" to those He has chosen and thus makes them willing to believe. The rest [reprobates] He condemns to eternal damnation according to His will and purpose. John Calvin, a proponent of this theology, called it "a horrible decree"[70] but nevertheless remained resolute on his position.

---

**God is sovereign.**
**This is an undeniable truth.**

---

In the other camp, the Armenians say that man has free will to do whatever he pleases. Some who share this view go a step further in saying that the free will of man and the sovereignty of God coexist. Both camps use a mountain of Scriptures to support their position. But opposing views cannot be right at the same time. Since Scripture cannot contradict itself and each group uses it to their advantage, it means one camp (or both) must have misinterpreted Scripture. Both can be wrong, but both cannot be right.

God is sovereign! This is an undeniable truth.

In eternity past, the all-wise, all-knowing God, without any outside counsel, decided how He would direct the course of human history. As sovereign God, He made a decision to allow man to operate within a marked boundary: "*And his [man's] limits You have set [put in place] so that he cannot pass*" (Job 14:5). This includes free will, which we define as man's ability to make limited decisions on his own— including salvation. But our Calvinist brethren claim that man is incapable of making a decision on his own accord, citing the "depravity of man." This too is extreme.

To challenge their claim, we turn to the apostle Paul. It's clear from Paul's writing under the influence of the Holy Spirit, which declared that even a depraved man is capable of sound judgment (or decision) for or against God. Paul explains,

*For I am not ashamed of the gospel, for it is the power of God for salvation to everyone who believes, to the Jew first and also*

*to the Greek. For [in] it [the gospel] the righteousness of God is revealed from faith to faith; as it is written, "BUT THE RIGHT-EOUS man SHALL LIVE BY FAITH." For the wrath of God is revealed from heaven against all ungodliness and unrighteousness of men who suppress the truth in unrighteousness* (Romans 1:16-18, emphasis added).

Read the passage again. Now, stop and answer two questions.

1. What is the subject of the above passage? That's right; the gospel!
2. Who in this passage "*suppress the truth in unrighteousness*"? The unbelievers!

Therefore, those who suppress the truth of the gospel must have come to a full comprehension of it before they can suppress it! Right? One cannot suppress the truth unless one knows it.

Paul goes on to say they have no excuse not to turn to God:

*Because that which is known about God is evident within them; for God made it evident to them. For since the creation of the world His invisible attributes, His eternal power and divine nature, have been clearly seen, being understood through what has been made, so that they are without excuse. For even though they knew God, they did not honor Him as God or give thanks, but they became futile in their speculations, and their foolish heart was darkened* (Romans 1:19-21).

---

**Accountability requires free will.**

---

The apostle is saying that they understood the gospel as spiritually dead people, but they suppressed it. Above all, they had a God-given ability to choose for or against God, and so he concludes, "*They are without excuse*" (v. 20). Accountability requires free will.

Let us take the apostle's charge and ask, "*They are without excuse*" for what? For their unbelief! In other words God's sovereignty did not play a role in their negative volition; nor did total depravity. That man is totally depraved explains why the work of the Holy Spirit is needed. He must make the issue of a relationship with God, through the Person and the work of Jesus Christ, completely clear. This provides man with the understanding needed to choose for or against God (John 16:8-9; 2 Corinthians 4:6; John 3:18).

Total depravity therefore means man in his status quo, spiritual death, can think and make rational decisions for or against God with regard to salvation but cannot do anything to provide salvation for himself. However the illuminating ministry of the Holy Spirit, impartially works in every heart that hears the good news concerning the work of Jesus Christ on the cross and thereby affects the faith of whosoever believes in the finished work of Christ unto salvation.

Let's underscore the definition. There are two parts to God's response to man's condition of total depravity. First, God in His fairness instills in man the ability to examine or observe facts and come to an intelligent conclusion based on those facts. This the apostle Paul capitalized on when he wrote,

> *Because that which is known about God is evident within them [all totally depraved individuals]; for God made it evident to them. For since the creation of the world His invisible attributes, His eternal power and divine nature, have been clearly seen, being understood through what has been made, so that they are without excuse* (Romans 1:19-20; cf. Romans 2:14-15).

What God does in the second part is critical. Once a man comes to the conclusion that this magnificent orderliness in creation demands a Supreme Being and wants to know Him personally, God responds to that signal in a marvelous way. We see this in the case of the Ethiopian eunuch who had a desire to know this Being. God sent him the evangelist Philip, who, through the illuminating ministry of the Holy Spirit, opened his eyes to the work of Christ on the cross (Acts 8:26-37).

This was true also of Cornelius and his household. Cornelius, in his total depravity, was quite aware of the existence of a Supreme Being. He too wanted to know Him personally. Of course, his desire in itself was not a result of receiving a special favor from God. His desire did not amount to instant salvation. Faith in Christ, which comes not as a gift but by hearing the word of God (Romans 10:17), is essential for salvation. To this, God responded by sending the apostle Peter, a two-day journey away.

Arriving, the apostle began speaking to them, saying,

> *"Of Him all the prophets bear witness that through His name everyone who believes in Him receives forgiveness of sins." While Peter was still speaking these words, the Holy Spirit fell upon all those who were listening to the message [because faith in Christ had come through the gospel information]* (Acts 10:43-44).

We consult another passage of Scripture to underscore God's fairness to all. When speaking to a religious crowd (legalistic unbelievers), our Lord called out, *"Come to Me, all who are weary and heavy-laden, and I will give you rest"* (Matthew 11:28).

My beloved, it is inconsistent with Scripture to say that our Lord's reference to *"all"* applies only to the elect, as some maintain. If so, that would make the elect the only ones who are *"weary and heavy-laden."* But the Scripture says we all bear the burden of sin.

*"For all have sinned and fall short of the glory of God"* (Romans 3:23). That means *all* are weary! There is a *big* hole in our brother's doctrine of depravity. This biblical truth stands the test of time. However, it can be taken to the extreme if one is not careful. Those who are true to the cause of our Lord's Kingdom, they will concede that Matthew 11:28 and Romans 3:23 plus Romans 1:16-21 are roadblocks to our brother John's position on the doctrines of election and predestination.

This leads us to look at the relationship between evil, temptation and the Sovereignty of God.

## God Does Not Tempt

Someone may ask, "What connection does sovereignty have with our passage in James?" Read James' words again: *"Let no one say when he is tempted, 'I am being tempted by God'; for God cannot be tempted by evil, and He Himself does not tempt anyone"* (James 1:13).

Perhaps some of his readers were having a hard time understanding their spiritual failures in light of the sovereignty of God and the role of their personal responsibilities. Maybe some false teachers had been teaching these born-again believers not to worry about their sins, perhaps encouraging them to relax and live it up. Maybe they said, "After all, God's sovereignty rules and determines everything, including our conduct."

James responded in 1:13. In essence he is saying, "Don't even think about blaming God!" Straight away, James dispels this falsehood and points toward man's free will. "*But each one is tempted when he is carried away and enticed by his own lust*" (James 1:14). **James is saying that man is accountable for his own actions.**

Often, when we hear the word *lust*, our mind runs to sexual covetousness. Sure, that's one aspect, but many others abound. Consider power lust, approbation lust, and materialism lust, just to name a few. James warns that any one of these lusts contains enough pathogen to slowly kill its object. My beloved, lust can draw us in any direction. For James' readers, it has pulled them into spiritual adultery: "*You adulteresses, do you not know that friendship with the world is hostility toward God? Therefore whoever wishes to be a friend of the world makes himself an enemy of God*" (James 4:4).

---

**Lust can draw us in any direction.**

---

Adultery in James 4:4 is not sexual, but rather mental unfaithfulness to God. It is abandoning the love one has for God in pursuit of various lusts. It is forming an alliance with the world in all its ungodly ways. It is bringing turmoil to one's soul (1 Peter 2:11). James' message is crystal clear for anyone pulled by the power of lust—the individual makes himself "*an enemy of God.* " What James is saying is this: "Whatever brand your lust may be, its source is the devil, not God."

The truth of the matter is that the moment we lust for something, God credits that desire to our account as a sin. Our Lord says, "*You have heard that it was said, 'YOU SHALL NOT COMMIT ADULTERY'; but I say to you that everyone who looks at a woman with lust for her has already committed adultery with her in his heart*" (Matthew 5:27-28).

The only thing holding us back from carrying out our desire is an opportunity. But in the eyes of God, we have already sinned! James goes a step further: "*When sin is accomplished, it brings forth death.*" The question is, what kind of death? The answer is simple: physical death.

The Greek construction in James 1:14 is of great interest in our discussion. Both "*carried away*" and "*enticed*" are in the present, passive participle. It is significant because the present tense highlights a continuous action. James wrote to believers on the path of perpetual carnality racing toward physical death, "*When sin is accomplished, it brings forth death*" (James 1:15).

Zane Hodges states,

> Death, then, is the grandchild of sinful lust or desire! Death is the cul-de-sac into which our lust can lead us. This point is reaffirmed by James in 5:20: He who turns a sinner from the error of his way will save a soul from death. The truth that physical death is the ultimate end of sinful conducts is stated repeatedly in the Book of Proverbs (e.g., 10:27; 11:19, 12:28; 13:14; 19:16). Since James is writing to his Christian brothers [1:2], it is plain that even a born-again Christian can flirt with premature [physical] death by indulging his sinful lusts.[71]

The apostle Paul, later, touched on this issue: If you are living according to the flesh, you must die (literally in Greek: "You are about to die"[72]).

The issue of premature physical death, as Hodges mentions, is taught throughout Scripture. James, because of his compassion and immense love for his brethren, is seeking to perhaps inspire them to turn their focus toward God so as to avoid going home to heaven early, leaving God's perfect plan for their lives unfinished. Just in case any of his readers doubts the possibility of a premature death, James concludes, "*Do not be deceived, my beloved brethren*" (James 1:16).

Paul took this a step further: "*Do not be deceived, God is not mocked; for whatever a man sows, this he will also reap. For the one who sows to his own flesh will from the flesh reap corruption, but the one who sows to the Spirit will from the Spirit reap eternal life*" (Galatians 6:7-8).

## God Is Not the Source of Evil

In James 1:13-16, James presents a biblical truth, that God's sovereignty cannot be involved in luring a believer to drift off course. Scholars have earnestly debated the subject of God's sovereignty. Although James clearly spells out that God is not involved in one's temptation to sin, regrettably some still take the position that God is the source of evil. To support their position, they often refer to God's incitement of David to commit sin by taking a census of Israel (2 Samuel 24:1). Of this sin he confessed, "*I have sinned greatly, in that I have done this thing [i.e., taken a census]. But now, please take away the iniquity of Your servant, for I have done very foolishly*" (1 Chronicles 21:8).

Biblicists, Calvinists and Armenians can all agree on one point: Scripture cannot contradict itself. We need to clear up what seems to be a gray area to many scholars. Some see 2 Samuel 24:1 to be in contradiction of 1 Chronicles 21:1. "*Now again the anger of the LORD burned against Israel, and it incited David against them to say, 'Go, number Israel and Judah*" (2 Samuel 24:1). "*Then Satan stood up against Israel and moved David to number Israel*" (1 Chronicles 21:1).

On the surface, these passages may appear to be contradictory, but when Scripture is compared with Scripture, the question of contradiction is resolved. Dr. Ronald F. Youngblood, one of the contributors to the *Expositor's Bible Commentary*, states, "The older record [2 Sam. 24 v. 1] speaks only of God's permissive action: the later [1 Chronicles 21:1] tells us of the malicious instrumentality of Satan. The case is like that of Job."[73]

Dr. J.F. Walvoord and others agree: "This is no contradiction for the Lord had simply allowed Satan to prompt David to an improper course of action...In any case, the Lord Himself did not incite David to do evil for 'God cannot be tempted by evil, nor does He tempt anyone' (James 1:13)."[74]

Here the truth is magnified. God simply permitted Satan to incite David to fulfill the lust of his heart, namely taking a census. God knew that David had already lusted in his heart and had equally given in to temptation (cf. James 1:13-15).

David had regressed to the point where pride had overtaken his thinking. Pride had partially, or totally, obliterated from his frame of reference his earlier confidence when he was face-to-face with Goliath. "*The LORD does not deliver by sword or by spear; for the battle is the LORD'S and He will give you into our hands*" (1 Samuel 17:47). That trust and humility was then replaced by pride, which caused him to assume that his military might depended on a large army or in his military skills. So he desired a census so that its result might boost his ego. But not without a price! For David would be severely disciplined for this sin.

One may ask, "How did you arrive at this conclusion?" We know that Joab, his chief army commander, was unhappy about the idea of taking a census. So he asked, "*But why does my lord the king [David] delight in this thing [census]?*" (2 Samuel 24:3). In other words: "David, what are you doing? Don't you still believe that the number of soldiers is inconsequential to God in granting us victory?" Obviously, Joab was reluctant to comply with David's order. "*Nevertheless, the king's word prevailed against Joab and against the commanders of the army*" (2 Samuel 24:4).

But God would punish David for that and, of course, all the Israelites for their spiritual failure as well (2 Samuel 24:1).

Here's the scenario: David had a desire in his heart to take a census (to increase his army); God credited his desire as a sin. In other words David had already sinned in God's sight. This is the truth of Scripture, "*for God [judges or] sees not as man sees, for man looks at the outward appearance, but the LORD looks at the heart*" (I Samuel 16:7; cf. Matthew 5:27-28).

Consequently, in order for his mental sin of lust to be manifested so we can see it and link his punishment to it, God granted Satan the permission to move David. "*Then Satan stood up against Israel and moved David to number Israel*" (1 Chronicles 21:1).

Therein is the truth of a seemingly apparent contradiction of Scripture! This is similar to the apostle Peter's temptation: "*Simon, Simon, behold, Satan has demanded permission to sift you like wheat*" (Luke 22:31).

Both the temptations of David and Peter produced the same results—failure—but with different outcomes. David was punished, and he later confessed (1 Chronicles 21:8). Both the books of Samuel and Chronicles reveal David's arrogant heart and his mental attitude of humility.

Peter failed miserably during our Lord's trial. He denied knowing Him three times. Later our Lord, after His resurrection, met up with him. Peter was restored to fellowship and moved on in his spiritual life (Matthew 26:69-74).

James goes beyond 1:13-16 to contrast the idea that God could be involved with evil. "*Every good thing given and every perfect gift is from above, coming down from the Father of lights, with whom there is no variation or shifting shadow*" (James 1:17).

James points out that everything God does is *always* in agreement with God's character of holiness. We know that God's character is unchanging (Malachi 3:6) and so are His actions. In other words, God is consistent; He cannot will good for us today and tomorrow will evil. "'*For I know the plans that I have for you,' declares the LORD, 'plans for welfare and not for calamity to give you a future and a hope*'" (Jeremiah 29:11).

---

**Temptation is not of God;
testing is of Him.**

---

James wants to underline this point. Essentially, he is saying, "God cannot will that you honor Him and reap His blessing as a result and at the same time tempt you to sin so that He will punish you for your failure and thereby forfeit His blessing." That would be the work of a mad man. The truth is our lusts are the source of our sinful acts! Of course, temptation is not a sin; it is the desire behind it. We must keep the record straight; temptation is not of God; testing is of Him (Matthew 4:1-10).

This prepares us for the next chapter, where we will further explore God's greatest gift, eternal life, to those who put their confidence alone in His Son, Jesus Christ.

## ELEVEN

## James 1:17-18

# The Gift of Eternal Life

*Every good thing given and every perfect gift is from above, coming down from the Father of lights, with whom there is no variation or shifting shadow. In the exercise of His will He brought us forth by the word of truth, so that we would be a kind of first fruits among His creatures* (**James 1:17-18**).

Every perfect gift is from above! This is a fact of Scripture. James now takes up another subject, namely salvation. Remember, our objective is to observe and accurately interpret James' epistle, to polish the mirror of God's Word observed so we can see ourselves reflected as we truly are and adjust accordingly to the glory of our heavenly Father.

James links our salvation to one of God's many "perfect gift[s]" from above: "*In the exercise of His will He brought us forth by the word of truth, so that we would be a kind of first fruits among His creatures*" (James 1:18).

Salvation is a gift; that is the teaching of the Bible! We have seen that James and the apostle Paul agreed that salvation is a gift (James 1:18; cf. Ephesians 2:8, 9; Titus 3:5; 2 Timothy 1:9). Many also hold the position that, in salvation, faith is a gift. They often use the misinterpretation of Ephesians 2:8-9 to support their stance. But this is totally inconsistent with the rest of Scripture. In Romans 6:23, for instance, the gift is not "faith" but "eternal life." The apostle Paul further underscores this: "*And how shall they believe [have confidence] in*

*Him Whom they have not heard? So faith comes [is activated or switched on] by hearing, and hearing by the Word of Christ"* (Romans 10:14b,17).

We know that our salvation is not based on the quality of our faith (confidence) but on the object of that faith, Jesus Christ. Many scholars agree that salvation is a gift. But some believe faith is a gift, and that is where the camps split. *"Faith comes by hearing"* does not mean faith is delivered as a gift. Rather, faith (confidence) in Christ is arrived at by means of hearing a gospel message illuminated by the Holy Spirit. Everyone has a measure of faith which is in on or off mode at any given time. Information given is processed and acted upon. You either agree—faith on, or disagree—faith off. For example, John the apostle systematically presented his gospel to demonstrate that Jesus is Christ. If one examines all these facts, he is forced to one of two conclusions: The info is true therefore I believe (faith/trust) is turned on. Or I do not believe this information (faith remains in off position).

There is a difference of opinion about man's responsibility in salvation between the Biblicists, the Armenians and Calvinists. These groups share history and many doctrines, but one of the places they part ways is over the doctrine of salvation.

Some maintain that the will of man is not involved in salvation. They quote the passage *"In the exercise of His will He brought us forth"* as support for their position.

Others maintain that free will is involved in salvation, that man is free to choose because the sins of the entire human race have been paid for through the cross. Therefore, we may use our free will to accept Christ by faith and be saved. Some who believe man's free will plays a part in salvation also believe the gift of salvation cannot be lost, since man did nothing to earn it.

My beloved, you may never fully realize the impact of this split on the church at large. At best, it has weakened our cause! Let us reason together to see if we can bring these groups to unity with the Scripture, and thereby strengthen the church. We need to lift up the phrase *"In the exercise of His will"* and behold it by itself.

# GOD'S WILL

No doubt about it, James 1:18 is a passage we all need to approach with objectivity and reverence, knowing that its misinterpretation has divided the church. Sadly, our Calvanistic brethren have misused the preceding passage to defend their position against man's free will. This in turn is used to support their version of the doctrine of the total depravity of man. Let me be absolutely clear: the depravity of man is a biblical doctrine, but our definitions differ. A careful examination of Scripture reveals that this group went too far with their teaching on the total depravity of man, which serves as a bedrock for their other teachings, which together are referred to by the acronym TULIP: Total depravity of man, Unconditional election, Limited atonement, Irresistible grace, and Perseverance of the saints. Join me as we reexamine this crucial truth, the total depravity of man.

We have already briefly looked at it, but let's go a step further. We agree about the depravity of man, but what does the Bible teach on this subject? It clearly teaches that man is sinful and spiritually dead (Romans 3:23; Ephesians 2:1; Colossians 2:13). It teaches that no one seeks for God (Romans 3:11); *"THERE IS NONE WHO DOES GOOD, THERE IS NOT EVEN ONE"* (Romans 3:12). Obviously, no serious student of God's Word would argue about the inerrancy of Scripture—one can only argue about its interpretation. So what does it mean that man is depraved? Does depravity affect man's will? Answering these questions is critical to our study.

First let us begin by examining this passage: *"In the exercise of His will He brought us forth by the word of truth, so that we would be a kind of first fruits among His creatures"* (James 1:18). Here James speaks of God's will alone. He assumes man's will to be active in responding to God's grace. The apostle Paul also speaks of God calling us *"according to His own purpose and grace"* (2 Timothy 1:9). Paul charges that *"they are without excuse"* (Romans 1:20) for not answering.

Scripture magnifies God's will. The truth is that without God making a decision to initiate salvation for mankind, we would be forever separated from Him. God did all this *"according to His purpose who works all things after the counsel of His will"* (Ephesians 1:11). Thank God for that!

Consequently, whatever "*the counsel of His will*" entails, one thing is clear. Scripture tells us time and again that Christ died for all because He wishes all to come to repentance:

- *The Lord is not slow about His promise, as some count slowness, but is patient toward you, not wishing for any to perish but for all to come to repentance* (2 Peter 3:9).

- *This is good and acceptable in the sight of God our Savior, who desires all men to be saved and to come to the knowledge of the truth* (1 Timothy 2:3-4).

- *My little children, I am writing these things to you so that you may not sin And if anyone sins, we have an Advocate with the Father, Jesus Christ the righteous; and He Himself is the propitiation for our sins; and not for ours only, but also for those of the whole world* (1 John 2:1-2; cf. John 4:42).

- *For the grace of God has appeared, bringing salvation to all men* (Titus 2:11).

Mark these words: *wishing* (2 Peter 3:9) and *desires* (1 Timothy 2:3). These are words of what one would like, but not necessarily words of certainty. They are simply wishes. God wishes that all *would* come to repentance and be saved, but He does not will that all *should* come to repentance. He does not will that all *must* be saved.

## MAN'S WILL

But let's begin with this question: what does the Scripture mean when it says, "*THERE IS NONE WHO SEEKS FOR GOD*" (Romans 3:11)? Does it mean that man in his depraved state is not able to seek God? The apostle Paul answered this question with a strong *No!* In the following passage Paul makes the case that a depraved man can seek God:

*Brethren, my heart's desire and my prayer to God for them [the Jews] is for their salvation. For I testify about them that they [depraved Jews] have a zeal for God, but not in accordance with knowledge [truth]. For not knowing about God's righteousness and seeking to establish their own, they did not subject themselves to the righteousness of God* (Romans 10:1-3).

Who is the apostle referring to in this passage? That's right, the depraved and unbelieving Jews. You see, they are capable of seeking God!

*"For I testify about them that they have a zeal for God, but not in accordance with knowledge"* (Romans 10:2). These lack not the will, but the true knowledge of the simple grace gospel, faith alone in Christ alone (Romans 9:30-32).

The Bible tells us that man is aware of the existence of a Supreme Being (Romans 1:18-21). Because of this, there's an appetite for worship within man. This explains why there are thousands, even millions, of temples across the globe. Hinduism alone has over 330 million gods and goddesses!

The apostle Paul's encounter in Athens is a perfect example. The Athenians were god seekers, and for this reason they built a temple for every god they knew of. Just to be sure they didn't leave any god out, they built one with an inscription *"TO An UNKNOWN GOD"* (Acts 17:23). This was the apostle's point of contact.

*So Paul stood in the midst of the Areopagus and said, "Men of Athens, I observe that you are very religious in all respects. For while I was passing through and examining the objects of your worship, I also found an altar with this inscription, 'TO AN UNKNOWN GOD' Therefore what you worship in ignorance, this I proclaim to you...He Himself gives to all people life and breath and all things; and He made from one man every nation of mankind to live on all the face of the earth, having determined their appointed times and the boundaries of their habitation, **that they would seek God, if perhaps they might grope for Him and find Him, though He is not far from each one of us;** for in Him we live and move and exist, as even some of your own poets have said, 'For we also are His children.' Being then the children of God, we ought not to think that the Divine Nature is like gold or silver or stone, an image formed by the art and thought of man. Therefore having overlooked*

*the times of ignorance,* **God is now declaring to men that all peo-**
**ple everywhere should repent**" (Acts 17:22-30, emphasis added).

Beloved, it is true, man on his own is incapable of seeking God.
But it's clear from this passage that God implanted in man the ability
to seek Him, if man so desires (Acts 10:1-5), "*Having determined their*
*appointed times and the boundaries of their habitation, that they [all crea-*
*tures] would seek God, if perhaps they might grope for Him and find Him*"
(Acts 17:26-27). You see, the apostle's indictment here is not total
depravity but ignorance: "*I also found an altar with this inscription, 'TO*
*AN UNKNOWN GOD' **Therefore what you worship in ignorance, this***
***I proclaim to you***" (Acts 17:23, emphasis added).

These Greeks, like many Jews, were zealous but lacked accurate
information. The Bible says they were "*not in accordance with knowl-*
*edge*" (Romans 10:1). These passages are clear. They were depraved. But
still they were capable of worshiping, even if in ignorance. Remember,
a rule of interpretation is to go from a clear passage to an obscure one.

Repeat, man is capable of seeking God; therefore Paul's assertion
"*God is now declaring to men that all people everywhere should repent*
*[change their minds about Christ]*" (Acts 17:30)!

Depravity then, means that a spiritually dead man is incapable of
providing a solution for his own sinful condition. In other words,
there's nothing a man can do or contribute to untangle the condition
of his spiritual death. Apart from God's intervention, man would be
*forever lost!* That's where grace comes in: "*But God demonstrates His own*
*love toward us, in that while we were yet sinners [depraved], Christ died*
*[as a substitute] for us*" (Romans 5:8).

The issue of man's free will is clearly taught in Scripture. In our
introduction we noted that James' epistle was written to Jewish
Christians because at the time of James' writing, there were not yet any
Gentile Christians. James includes himself among this group of Jewish
believers who had been born anew into God's family and indwelt by
His Holy Spirit (James 4:5): "*In the exercise of His will [apart from man's*
*effort] He brought **us** forth [gave new birth to us] by[means of] the word of*
*truth, so that **we** would be a kind of first fruits among His creatures*"
(James 1:18, emphasis added).

He called them "*first fruits*," a term they were familiar with (Jeremiah 2:3), because they were the first harvest of the Church Age. Others would follow—namely the Gentile believers. James highlighted "*the word of truth*," namely the gospel (Ephesians 1:13), as the means by which they were brought into God's family.

Of course, all this is possible because of "His will," as he indicates. That's to say, without the sovereign will of God, our will would be totally fruitless. Simply stated, had God not taken the steps necessary to bring into His family "whosoever" will accept His grace gift (John 3:16), we would still be in darkness, forever separated from "*the Father of lights, with whom there is no variation or shifting shadow*" (James 1:17). Thank God for "*the exercise of His will*"! No doubt, it was God's decision, His plan, His purpose, and His will that triggered the work of our so great salvation.

As you can see, James did not go beyond this point, and we shouldn't either. We should resist outright the temptation of reading or forcing our theologies into Scripture!

\* \* \*

The truth is that we cannot properly discuss man's will without talking about the mind. Interestingly, Paul used the word *mind* more extensively than any other New Testament writer. The reference in his epistle to Titus is pertinent to our study: "*To the pure, all things are pure; but to those who are defiled and unbelieving, nothing is pure, but both their mind and their conscience are defiled*" (Titus 1:15).

Elsewhere, Paul talks about the darkening of understanding and man's hardness of heart (Ephesians 4:18). On the surface, no one can read such verses and not subscribe to Calvinism's definition of total depravity. But we must ask, does spiritual death affect one's ability to make rational decisions?

This is where we need to dig deeper. We have already proven from Scripture that man is quite capable of perceiving and making rational decisions for or against God.

Bear with me as we reason this out from four vantage points:

1) Justice of God

2) Christ's grace offer rejected

3) Paul's view of free will

4) Christ's atonement

## The Justice of God

"*For there is no partiality [favoritism] with God*" (Romans 2:11). God is fair. His fairness calls for Him to ensure that each of us has the ability to know and make a rational decision for or against his Creator-God. Beloved, repetition is the key to inculcation, retention and recall, so we are compelled to revisit a passage that the apostle Paul used to make his case: "*For the wrath of God is revealed from heaven against all ungodliness and unrighteousness of men who suppress the truth in unrighteousness [all depraved people], because that which is known about God is evident within them; for God made it evident to them*" (Romans 1:18-19, emphasis added).

Again, what is "*evident within them*"? That God exists! In some mysterious way, God made it evident in all of us. Why? So that when those who reject Christ stand before the Great White Throne Judgment (Revelation 20:11-15), they will have no excuse for that decision. Therefore God will be justified to sentence them to the Lake of Fire. "*For since the creation of the world His invisible attributes, His eternal power and divine nature, have been clearly seen, being understood through what has been made, so that they are without excuse*" (Romans 1:20).

## Christ's Grace Offer Rejected

"*Jerusalem, Jerusalem, who kills the prophets and stones those who are sent to her! How often I wanted to gather your children together [Lord's effort emphasized], the way a hen gathers her chicks under her wings, and you were unwilling [free will highlighted]*" (Matthew 23:37).

Clearly, *man's will* is the issue in "*you were unwilling.*" One may ask, "Why didn't the Lord use His sovereignty and thus accomplish His purpose?" Because forcing a decision would not establish a relationship (which we earlier defined as a two-way street)! Moreover, that would be inconsistent with justice, for justice demands that the Lord do the same for every person (Romans 2:11)! That means, if He forced one, He would have to force all to accept His grace offer, and that does not agree with Scripture.

"*He came to His own, and those who were His own did not receive Him [negative decision]. But as many as received Him [positive decision], to them He gave the right to become children of God, even to those who believe in His name*" (John 1:11-12).

Again, *man's free will* is in focus. They "*did not receive Him,*" even though they had the God-given ability to do so!

## Paul's View of Free Will

"*They are without excuse*" (Rom. 1:20). This is Paul's reaction to the pagan world. He never gave any hint that man is not capable of responding to God's initiation of grace.

> *When they had set a day for Paul, they came to him at his lodging in large numbers; and he was explaining to them by solemnly testifying about the kingdom of God and trying to persuade them concerning Jesus, from both the Law of Moses and from the Prophets, from morning until evening. Some were being persuaded by the things spoken, but others would not believe* (Acts 28:23-24).

How can we read this passage and conclude that the apostle thought those whom he was persuading might not be capable of understanding and responding to his persuasion? The answer is obvious. There is no evidence from the passage that he ever thought in terms of man's lacking free will (predestination, election). No! On the contrary, He knew they could, for some of them did: "*Some were being persuaded by the things spoken, but others would not believe*" (Acts 28:24).

These Jews clearly understood his gospel presentation about Christ and all used their free will. Some used it to accept Him and some used it to reject Him. Those who "*would not believe*" (Acts 28:24) are "*without excuse*" (Romans 1:20). That is the fact of Scripture.

In conclusion, it takes two wills to give birth to a relationship. There is no relationship if one party is willing and the other is not. In salvation, God is the initiator. He makes all the sacrifices necessary to start a relationship with the depraved human race. He sent His Son to the cross to pay the penalty for our sins (Romans 5:8). He sent His Holy Spirit, whose work is to wake us up and cause us to see our hopelessness, to see our need for a Savior. In other words, the job of the Holy Spirit is to make the issue clear, to challenge our volition so we can make a clear choice for or against Christ.

> "And He [the Holy Spirit], when He comes, will convict the world concerning sin and righteousness and judgment; concerning sin, because they do not believe in Me" (John 16:8-9).

God did all this! That's grace! Now He patiently awaits us at the meeting point of the crossroads of wills, His and ours. Scripture is not silent on this. In case anyone misses this clear teaching of the Bible, we revisit the apostle Paul's position on this issue.

> For I am not ashamed of the gospel, for it is the power of God for salvation to everyone who believes, to the Jew first and also to the Greek. For in [through] it [the gospel] the righteousness of God is revealed from faith to faith; as it is written, "BUT THE RIGHTEOUS man SHALL LIVE BY FAITH." For the wrath of God is revealed from heaven against all ungodliness and unrighteousness [depravity] of men who suppress the truth in unrighteousness (Romans 1:16-18).

Remember, a depraved person is under indictment for suppressing the truth!

God reveals the work of Christ to man so that man may respond. Those who fail to respond, "They are without excuse" (Romans 1:20). In essence Paul was saying, "You have no excuse not to turn to God!" (cf. Numbers 21:8-9; John 3:14-15). Free will equals accountability!

As Dr. M. F. Unger tells us, "The lost are without excuse because they deliberately and knowingly choose the course of lawlessness and rejection of God...the lost are without excuse because they stifle the voice of conscience...[for] God implanted [an] inner monitor that tells a man right from wrong [Romans 2:14-15]."[75]

## Christ's Atonement

*"For God so loved the world, that He gave His only begotten Son, that whoever believes in Him shall not perish, but have eternal life"* (John 3:16). It is sad to note that for centuries a good number of our brethren have wrestled and twisted the words of the following passages, particularly the words *all* and *world*. They say *all* and *world* refer only to the elect. They also say that the word *whoever* of John 3:16 refers only to the elect.

If so, that would mean Jesus Christ died only for some, the "elect," a position known as limited atonement. This is contrary to our position, unlimited atonement, that Christ died for *all*—those who would believe as well as those who would not. Justice demands it!

Beloved of God, the only reason to twist the words *all* and *whosoever* and *world* is to ensure that the Calvinistic definition of total depravity stands. In His omniscience, God knew ahead of time that some would quarrel over the use and meaning of these words and concepts. His Holy Spirit inspired the apostle Paul to settle any ambiguity when he wrote, *"It is a trustworthy statement deserving full acceptance. For it is for this we labor and strive, because we have fixed our hope on the living God, who is the Savior of all men [the whole world], **especially** of believers"* (1 Timothy 4:9-10, emphasis added).

So then, if His death on the cross is for the whole world, as the apostle Paul indicates, by separating "believers" from the rest of "all men" (the whole world), then holding onto the teaching of limited atonement, and other similar teachings built around it, must give way to the truth of the infallible Word of God. This is because the five points of Calvinism are woven together, as a renowned Calvinist scholar, Lorraine Boettner affirmed:

> The Calvinistic system emphasizes five distinct doctrines. These are technically known as "The Five Points of Calvinism" and they are the main points upon which the superstructure rests. These are not isolated and independent doctrines but are so inter-related...Prove any one of them false and the whole system must be abandoned.[76]

Based on the clarity of the Scriptures mentioned, is it fair to say that the doctrine of total depravity as taught by our beloved brother John Calvin is not biblical? Let Scripture be the judge and jury!

What about "limited atonement"? I suggest that you carefully, under the mentorship of the Holy Spirit, reexamine this section of our study and then decide for yourself. As for me, Scripture is my guide. "*It is a trustworthy statement deserving full acceptance. For it is for this we labor and strive, because we have fixed our hope on the living God, who is the Savior of all men [the whole world], **especially** of believers*" (1 Timothy 4:9-10, emphasis added). We cannot get around or twist this distinction, "***Savior of all men [the whole world], especially of believers.***" Therein is the truth italicized and highlighted for our edification.

It is my fervent prayer that this truth alone will be our yardstick for "*rightly dividing the word of truth*" (2 Timothy 2:15 KJV). With this said we turn to the next chapter.

## TWELVE

## James 1:19-21

# Exhortation for Restoration to Fellowship

*But everyone must be quick to hear, slow to speak and slow to anger; for the anger of man does not achieve the righteousness of God. Therefore, putting aside all filthiness and all that remains of wickedness, in humility receive the word implanted, which is able to save your souls [lives]* (**James 1:19-21**).

James' ultimate purpose in his epistle is to steer his readers away from the road of premature death and consequently guide them back to spirituality. In this passage he made an appeal to his brethren to return to the path of life.

Now we are ready to tap into James' new thought, which is crucial if we are to grasp the meaning of James 2:14, coming up in our study.

James 1:19-21 would be better exegetical if it were linked sequentially right after 1:13-15 (as we covered in chapter 10). This is because James 1:13-15 deals with temptation, spiritual failure and its consequences, and James 1:19-21 focuses on the means of restoration to fellowship. Hence, the question that faced James is how to reach out to people who perhaps had grown complacent and were in perpetual carnality.

The same challenge confronts us today! How can we reach out to those who have grown cold toward the Lord? How can we reach out to believers who have fallen by the wayside and are totally indifferent to

God? How can we stir up our complacent brethren, whether they be pastors or laymen?

With these questions in mind, James, in his spiritual wisdom, dealt with their past and present failures head-on.

First, he clears any ambiguity by affirming that God is not responsible for our spiritual failures (1:13-14).

Second, he shifts his attention to exhortation in two areas: restoration and implantation of God's Word (1:21).

Third, he highlights the ramifications of "*the word implanted*," namely, saving one from physical death (1:21; cf. 1:15).

This is the epitome of exhortation from a brother who was esteemed by the apostles as the leader of the Jerusalem church. On the other hand, the idea that most of his audience are not genuinely saved is an idea that some simply read into the text. James wrote with love, passion, and concern to those he knew were saved. You can't read his epistle objectively and not sense his inner pain for his brethren whom he describes as "*adulteresses*" (James 4:4). Adultery is a sin that only a spouse can commit. Because these were married to the Lord Jesus Christ (Ephesians 5:22-27, 32), James could indict them for spiritual adultery with no trouble at all (James 4:4-5; cf. Ezekiel 16:32). That's the Word of God! That's the only explanation that makes sense!

Spiritual life functions under the mentorship of the Holy Spirit. It never functions with a divided lifestyle, (99 percent directed to God and 1 percent to sin). In other words, a lifestyle of spiritual adultery, for instance, disables one's spiritual life completely **until that sin is dealt with through confession** (1 John 1:9). Sin must be dealt with right away, for when the sin of unfaithfulness or any other sin remains unconfessed, the believer can slide down the slippery slope into the mire of carnality.

David is a perfect example. His first sin was arrogance. He was supposed to be at war, leading his men, but he stayed home (2 Samuel 11:1). His next sin was lust, which led to adultery (11:2-4). His spiritual life was in total disarray. He sunk to the depths of hypocrisy and eventually murder (11:6-17). David had lost fellowship with God and was miserable (Psalm 31:9-10). But God did not retract David's title "*a man after [God's] own heart*" (1 Samuel 13:14) even during his chain of sins.

Why? Because God's love for him did not change. God's love had not diminished since David first trusted in Yahweh (Jeremiah 31:3). However, he lost every spiritual vitality, and God made his life miserable (Psalm 38:10) until he confessed his sin (Psalm 32:5). The same is true of every believer. We remain in carnality and are miserable until we confess our personal sins (1 John 1:9) and subsequently change our direction (Proverbs 28:13). This is what James is trying to get these adulterous believers to do (James 1:21)!

---

*The Lord knows those who are His*
**(2 Timothy 2:19).**

---

Let us be clear: we cannot dogmatically say that one who is out of touch with the life of Christ is not truly saved. We confuse people when we make such a dogmatic statement. On the contrary, spiritual failure is possible after regeneration. That is why the Holy Spirit laced the Word of God with a great number of imperative mood commands, exhortations and warnings, such as *"Do not be conformed to this world"* (Romans 12:2), *"Do not give the devil an opportunity"* (Ephesians 4:27), and *"Your adversary, the devil, prowls around like a roaring lion, seeking someone [a believer] to devour [disable]"* (1 Peter 5:8).

Those who live in carnality will die prematurely (Romans 8:13). When a believer is in the flesh, his lifestyle will be the same as that of an unbeliever (1 Corinthians 3:3)! Consequently, there is no way one can look at such a person and catch even a glimpse of the life of Christ. Is that not true?

We have said this before; it's a difficult task, if not an impossible one, for anyone to examine someone else's lifestyle and label the person "saved" or "unsaved." Obviously, the apostle Paul came across many people in his ministry, some were wonderful and some were anything but wonderful. Most likely at one point or another, he may have even questioned himself whether certain men like *"Hymenaeus, and Alexander"* whom he *"delivered over to Satan, so that they may be taught not to blaspheme"* (1 Timothy 1:20) and *"Demas...[who] loved the present world"* (2 Timothy 2:10), were wolfs in sheep's clothing (Matthew 7:15). The apostle couldn't, by observation, be absolutely certain regarding who was truly saved or not! He just took everyone, who professed faith in Christ to be a Christian. He loved these with the same intensity of love as he had experienced from the Lord. He never doubted the genuineness of anyone's profession in Christ. We ought to do likewise; love everyone unconditionally, as Christ loved us. What's more, it's on this platform of uncertainty that he summed up his admonition, *"Nevertheless, the firm foundation of God stands, having this seal, 'The Lord knows those who are His,' and, 'Everyone who names the name of the Lord is to abstain from wickedness'"* (2 Timothy 2:19).

We mentioned briefly in our introduction, that one can be saved without any spiritual production. The truth of the matter is that we all start as spiritual babies. Some grow up (2 Peter 3:18), leave childish behavior behind and bear fruit to the glory of God. However, many never advance and thus remain wrapped up in carnality. These become like one who is *"blind or short-sighted, having forgotten purification from his former sins"* (2 Peter 1:9).

There are many examples in both in the Old and New Testament. Saul was truly saved, but he never grew up spiritually. After he disobeyed God, he lived a life that never revealed that he was once empowered by the Holy Spirit. He continued on such a deadly course that he *"died [prematurely] for his trespass which he committed against the LORD"* (1 Chronicles 10:13). You see; he did not persevere to the end, and yet he was eternally saved.[77]

Make no mistake; Scripture never teaches anywhere that "perseverance," as taught by brother Calvin or anyone else, is a condition, or even an indication, of eternal life.

Eternal life is

- A gift (Romans 6:23)
- Issued on the basis of grace (Ephesians 2:8, 9)
- Guaranteed not to be revoked (Romans 11:29)
- Based on the character of the Giver (1 Corinthians 2:9; Romans 8:38-39; John 10:28)

It is that simple!

The books of Hebrews and James share much in common. Both books were addressed to believers who were in suffering, not growing up, and in danger of severe punishment. In Hebrews, the author voiced his frustration: *"For though by this time [perhaps many years after regeneration] you have need again for someone to teach you the elementary principles [basics] of the oracles of God, and you have come to need milk and not solid food"* (Hebrews 5:12).

But what are the fruits of babyhood? The apostle Paul wrote,

> *And I, brethren, could not speak to you as to spiritual men, but as to men of flesh, as to infants in Christ. I gave you milk to drink, not solid food; for you were not yet able to receive it. Indeed, even now you are not yet able, for you are still fleshly. For since there is jealousy and strife among you, are you not fleshly, and are you not walking like mere men?* (1 Corinthians 3:1-3).

In the same manner, James described his readers as carnal believers marked with *"quarrels and conflicts"* (James 4:1). It's the same manifestation of babyhood that James entreated his audience to put away. *"Therefore, putting aside all filthiness and all that remains of wickedness, in humility receive the word implanted, which is able to save your souls"* (James 1:21)!

Let's pause here and make some connections.

## Connecting the Dots

You may wonder why we are taking all this trouble to connect the dots of Scripture. This is because James' epistle is not an ordinary epistle. It is the most hotly contested, and its misinterpretation is a source of many false teachings. Consequently we must consult other passages of Scripture to help shed light.

In view of "perseverance of the saints," for instance, we consult 1 Corinthians 3:3. Surely you will agree that the Corinthian church was the worst in the apostolic era. Paul's epistle to the Corinthians, particularly the first letter, was used to correct and urge them on to fruit-bearing. As we have already delineated, Paul handled the report about their spiritual carnality with love, compassion, poise and grace (1 Corinthians 1:2-10).

167

"*The church...those who have been sanctified in Christ*" (1 Corinthians 1:2). "*I thank my God always concerning you*" (1 Corinthians 1:4). What is Paul thanking God for in 1 Corinthians 1:4? Is he thanking God for division among the Corinthian believers (1:10; cf. 3:1-3)? Or for the incestuous lifestyle in the church (5:1-5)? No! He's thankful to God for His grace upon their lives! Yes, *grace!*

Verses 8 and 9 say that Jesus puts a seal on the eternal security of these believers.

> **Our Lord Jesus Christ, who will also confirm [Greek: bebaioo, "to make true," "warrant security" to] you [i.e., the carnal Corinthian believers 3:3] to the end, blameless in the day of our Lord Jesus Christ. God is faithful, through whom you [carnal, 3:3] were called into fellowship with His Son, Jesus Christ our Lord** (1 Corinthians 1:7-9).

God's faithfulness is not dependant on our faithfulness. Thank God for that! The passive voice indicates that salvation is the work of God in its entirety (1 Corinthians 1:30). God alone will finish what He has begun! Of that "*I am confident*" (Philippians 1:6; cf. Romans 8:38-39).

Having reminded them of their position in Christ, Paul draws attention to their spiritual status: "*men of flesh...infants in Christ*" (1 Corinthians 3:1). Notice: even though they were fleshly, behaving like unbelievers, they were still "*in Christ*" and equally "*God's building*" (v. 9). In verse 23, the apostle signs off with these words: "*And you belong to Christ; and Christ belongs to God.*"

Who belongs to Christ? The carnal believers of 3:1-3!

Can you read Paul's treatment of this subject with objectivity and still claim that, unless a believer is "persevering" or producing fruit, more than likely he is not truly saved? I know what some of us may be saying: "Well, if a person is truly saved, he will not remain in carnality for too long." I ask, how long is too long? More than two years for the Corinthians? Perhaps fifteen to thirty years for the audience of the book of Hebrews?

These died the sin unto death. "*Saul died [suddenly] for his trespass which he committed against the LORD*" (1 Chronicles 10:13). The apostle Paul reminded his Christian audience at Corinth that carnality was one major reason why many of their church members had died (1 Corinthians 11:30). The point we wish to make here is that born again believers can remain in perpetual carnality until God finally removes the believer prematurely (Proverbs 10:27). Sin unto death does not terminate one's salvation (Romans 8:37-38), *"absent from the body"* face-to-face with the Lord" (2 Corinthians 5:8). This position stands in opposition to our brother John Calvin. He maintained that true believers would persevere to the end. But Saul was a true believer; he didn't persevere spiritually to the end. King Solomon was a believer, no record that he remained in constant touch with the life of God to the end. Rather, *"his wives turned his heart away after other gods"* (1 Kings 11:4). The same record was true of so many carnal believers at Corinth, who died and did not persevere to the end (1 Corinthians 11:30). This is the teaching of the Bible!

These died without recovery. You ask, "How is one certain?" Scripture answers: *"But if we judged ourselves rightly, we should not be judged"* (1 Corinthians 11:31). In other words, had these believers taken the steps for spiritual recovery, this may have cancelled the *"sin leading to death"* (1 John 5:16; cf. James 5:19-20)

Beloved, again, there is no reason to read into Scripture that which the inspired authors did not intend. In fact, it is a misconception—that every believer must produce fruit—that led to misinterpretation of James 2:14. *"What use is it, my brethren, if someone says he has faith but he has no works? Can that [literally, the]* [78] *faith save him?"* (James 2:14). Lack of spiritual production led to the coinage of the phrase "saving faith," which the Bible never mentions.

We have said before that the fruit of infidelity is a sure sign of anarchy. It destroys relationships in the human and spiritual realm. Many of the recipients of James' epistle were no longer living the spiritual life. Many had abandoned it altogether, in exchange for what the world offered. We ask, "Can one look at a believer who has *'forgotten his purification from his former sins'* (2 Peter 1:9), who now *'participate[s] in the unfruitful deeds of darkness'* (Ephesians 5:11), and conclude that such a one is a fruit bearer of our Lord?" No way! Are they not like the *"DOG [THAT] RETURNS TO ITS OWN VOMIT"* and the *"sow, [that] after washing, returns to wallowing in the mire*" (2 Peter 2:22)? Paul is telling us that these believers could not be recognized as believers by their actions. He said they "*walk…as the Gentiles [pagans]*" (Ephesians 4:17). They were not lacking a "saving faith" but were believers who, due to perpetual carnality, looked like unbelievers. My heartfelt prayer is that God the Holy Spirit, who inspired the words of Scripture, would impress this truth into our hearts!

Now let us examine our passage more closely.

## Putting Aside All Filthiness

*This you know, my beloved brethren. But everyone must be quick to hear, slow to speak and slow to anger; for the anger of man does not achieve the righteousness of God. Therefore, putting aside all filthiness and all that remains of wickedness, in humility receive the word implanted, which is able to save your souls [lives]* (James 1:19-21).

According to Professor Tasker, the most ancient manuscripts of James 1:19 begin with "Ye know this" or "Know this," as in RV and RSV. "Translating it this way," he says "gives a more forceful meaning: 'You are aware of (or "rest assured of") the heavenly origin of your new birth, but you must see to it that it reflects in your personal conduct.'"[79]

In other words, James does not doubt their new birth. On the contrary, he calls their attention to it: "*This you know, my beloved brethren*" is like saying "You are aware of your new birth, my beloved brethren." He wants their manner of life to match their new birth, to be in tune with the life of Christ: "*But everyone must be quick to hear, slow to speak and slow to anger*" (James 1:19b).

What James was saying to his audience, and is telling us today, is simply this: "Be a good listener; avoid a quick reply. Take your time to hear, dissect, and digest the information!" It appears that the recipients of James' epistle were fond of emotional and irrational responses to a message without giving it much thought. This conclusion is based on comparing James 1:19-21 with 2:18: "*But someone may well say, 'You have faith and I have works; show me your faith without the works, and I will show you my faith by my works*" (James 2:18).

This is an example of someone who heard something and immediately fired back an answer without thinking about what he heard. This is often done! It is not a trait of a good listener. A Spirit-filled believer, under the guidance of the Holy Spirit, would, like the Bereans, receive the message wholeheartedly and then prayerfully analyze it to see whether the message is in accordance with Scripture (Acts 17:11). This is the type of attitude James was hoping the recipients of his epistle would cultivate.

We too should be people who welcome a message with an open heart, people who don't thoughtlessly respond, or rush to teach others, until we have mastered the message ourselves. Tasker admonishes, "Christians must be swift to hear. Conversely they must be slow to speak, not rushing hastily to proclaim God's Word to others before they have really paid attention to it themselves."[80]

You may ask, "Why should one not rush to teach others God's Word?" James gave the answer: "*Let not many of you become teachers, my brethren, knowing that as such we will incur a stricter judgment*" (James 3:1).

James was a compassionate leader, very concerned with the well-being of his Christian audience. He knew too well that the ultimate consequence of taking one's spiritual life carelessly was premature death. His words of warning to them are still applicable to us today, to avoid descending into the valley of death prematurely (James 1:13-15; 5:19, 20; cf. 2:14). James adds, "*Be...slow to anger*." This brings us to a short discussion on the subject of anger.

### • *Anger*

Anger is an emotional reaction that can split into one of two directions—unrighteous or righteous anger. The former is characterized by a high-powered and uncontrollable rage. It is an emotional reaction that carries with it the venom of bitterness and the poison of wrath. James warned all believers to avoid this. As was said earlier, Christians should always keep in mind that they represent Christ and are under the world's scrutiny 24/7. People watch our every move, every action, to see if they line up with what we profess (Philippians 1:27; cf. 2 Corinthians 2:15; 3:2-3).

On the other hand, there's another kind of anger, righteous anger, which in itself is not a sin but can lead to sin if not checked: "*BE ANGRY, AND yet DO NOT SIN; do not let the sun go down on your anger*" (Ephesians 4:26).

One can be angry at sin (John 2:13-16), but what Scripture warns about is nurturing that anger. If that anger lingers on, it can give "the devil a foothold (lit., 'a place'), an opportunity for leading that Christian into…sin."[81] Let us illustrate this with the sin of murder. We need not be deceived; believers are capable of committing any sin, even murder (James 4:2). David is a perfect example. He committed murder as a believer in Yahweh (2 Samuel 12:9).

Our ministry often receives letters from believers who are in prison, many on charges of murder. They are believers who strayed from their spiritual life. Their unchecked carnality manifested itself in anger and hatred. This animosity incubated until it turned into rage, resulting in the crime of murder. They destroyed not only their own lives but also the lives of others and in the process delivered a barbaric testimony!

So, my beloved, we should always consider our words and actions in view of our witness to those who are lost. "*Let your light shine before men in such a way that they may see your good works, and glorify your Father who is in heaven*" (Matthew 5:16).

So let's consider two keys that will help unlock this mighty epistle.

## Keys to James

Restoration to fellowship and perception and application of God's Word are crucial keys to understanding James. These two keys will unlock some of its mystery. Without fellowship with God, our spiritual life comes to a halt (Psalm 32:2-5). Without His infallible Word, direction for life's journey is reduced to a blind path (Psalm 119:105). Here we shall examine the first key. The second key will be introduced here and is the subject of our in-depth study in part IV.

## • *Restoration to Fellowship*

Any sin ruptures our fellowship with God. No ifs or buts about it. With a careful scrutiny of our text, one concludes that the believers to whom James wrote had been in carnality for a long time.

We have already noted some of the sins that caused the derailment of their spiritual life, such as the sin of partiality (James 2:1-5), sin of indifference to the needs of others (2:15-16), sin of the tongue (3:1-12) and sin of judging (4:11) just to name a few. James simply summed up their spiritual maladjustment with one word, "*adulteresses*" (4:4)!

As a result of all this, James realized their spiritual life was at a halt. With knowledge of the Old Testament regarding restoration to fellowship, he directed, "*Therefore, putting aside all filthiness and all that remains of wickedness*" (James 1:21). Beloved of God, take notice. James did not issue a call for salvation.

James knew that no unbeliever is capable of putting away sins by his own effort; nor is one saved because one confesses one's sins to God. Salvation is based on faith alone in Christ alone!

Dr. Robinson Haddon once said in a sermon that one rule of Bible study is when one sees the word *therefore* in a passage, one ought to find out what the word is *there for*. This we intend to do, as our next sentence starts with the word *therefore*, or as A. T. Robertson put it, *therefore* should be translated "Because of this."[82]

The word *therefore* is like glue. It connects James' previous thought to this new one. In other words, James was saying, "Because of the consequences of broken fellowship and the risk of premature death (James 1:13-15), because of your new birth and new nature (1:18), because of all this, 'Therefore [put] aside all filthiness and all that remains of wickedness.'"

---

**We all fail regardless of our
level of spiritual growth.**

---

Where does the filthiness and wickedness come from, since all believers are cleansed at the point of regeneration?

Tasker answers this question succinctly: "Every converted Christian brings with him into his new life much that is inconsistent with it. This has to be laid aside, that he may give himself more completely to the positive work of receiving with meekness the engrafted (RV rightly 'implanted') word."[83]

We are trapped in the coat of our sin nature. We must face this truth head-on with honesty, if we have any aspiration of coming clean before a Holy God. We all fail, regardless of the level of our spiritual growth. Some recover; others do not.

David, a mature believer, failed spiritually and bounced back (Psalm 32:1-5). Scripture is not silent about Saul's and Solomon's failures; it is silent about their recovery. We know that both were believers in Yahweh. Saul disobeyed God and continued on the road of carnality until premature death caught up with him (1 Chronicles 10:13). Solomon began well but ended up in idolatry. *"For when Solomon was old, his wives turned his heart away after other gods"* (1 Kings 11:4).

There is no scriptural evidence that Solomon recovered. But where is Solomon today? I hope you would enthusiastically say, "In heaven!" If we can grasp this truth, if we can come to terms with what the Bible reveals about the believer's potential to fail and never recover, it will motivate us to do everything within our means to help fallen Christian soldiers (Galatians 6:1; cf. James 5:19-20) instead of lifting Scriptures out of context to label them "unsaved."

James resisted this route. Instead, he moved with love and compassion to help them jump start their spiritual lives, as seen in our verse. *"Therefore, putting aside all filthiness and all that remains of wickedness"* (James 1:21).

Of interest is the fact that the Holy Spirit guided James to choose the right tenses in his admonitions! We ought not to overlook this. The phrase *"Putting aside,"* for example, is in the aorist participle.[84] This is very significant. What James was saying is this: "Stop and take an inventory of your spiritual failures and take time to acknowledge them to God." In other words, deal with these sins, and any others, whenever they rear their ugly heads in your soul (1 John 1:9).

Take, for instance, a believer who fails in the area of theft. If he confesses that sin, God forgives him with a promise to remember it no more (Isaiah 43:25). If the individual never commits that sin again, he remains cleansed of that sin forever! He does not need to confess it over and over, out of guilt, like many of us do. This illustrates the emphasis of the aorist tense in Greek. In other words, deal with that particular sin at that moment and cast it behind you. God knew that we would fail even after salvation; hence His grace provision: *"If we confess our sins, He is faithful and righteous to forgive us our [known] sins and to cleanse us from all unrighteousness [evil or forgotten sins]"* (1 John 1:9).

This passage is only meant for the believers' restoration to fellowship when they fail. Make no mistake, believers can go into spiritual coldness. Our Lord, in His last message to the churches in Asia Minor, spoke about this (Revelation 3:1-2, 14-16). The question is, how can one whose spiritual life has been quenched because of prolonged carnality get back on track spiritually?

James offers the solution:

1. They are to approach the throne of His grace with a confession, *"Therefore, putting aside"* (James 1:21; cf. 1 John 1:9).
2. They must make it a priority to draw near to God through learning and converting Bible knowledge into thinking and action (James 1:21-22).
3. They are to be consistent in resisting Satan and his bag of temptations (James 4:7).
4. If, for any reason, they are defeated and lured to sin, they are to return to the first solution as soon as they become aware of their failure.
5. They are to remain in constant touch with God through study, application of His Word and prayer (James 4:8).

James knew that the way back from spiritual failure is through spiritual cleansing, and hence the mandate *"Cleanse your hands"* (4:8; cf. Exodus 40:30-32; 1 John 1:9). He knew about the greatness of God's love and the depth of His compassion (Isaiah 55:7). He knew that God forgives and restores everyone to fellowship who takes the necessary steps. James was convinced that they could avoid the judgment of premature death and loss of reward. *"But if we judged ourselves rightly, we would not be judged"* (1 Corinthians 11:31, cf. 3:15). Armed with this knowledge, he therefore sternly admonished, *"Therefore, putting aside all filthiness and all that remains of wickedness, in humility receive the word implanted, which is able to save your souls [lives, from premature physical death]"* (James 1:20-21).

It's clear then, from our investigation, that James was concerned about their physical life, not their salvation. For these believers had been born anew once for all (James 1:18; cf. 1 John 5:1; Hebrews 10:10). If this is not clear, please take time to review before proceeding to the next topic.

## Application of God's Word

God's Word accomplishes four basic things in every generation:

1. The Bible offers spiritual nourishment for our souls and the fountain of life (Matthew 4:4; cf. Psalm 36:9; Deuteronomy 32:47).

2. The Bible gives us insight in decision-making. *"Your word is a lamp to my feet And a light to my path"* (Psalm 119:105; cf. vv. 98-100; 37:31).

3. The Bible serves as a restrainer against spiritual failure. *"Your word I have treasured in my heart, That I may not sin against You"* (Psalm 119:11; cf. 40:8).

4. The Bible provides the only means of advancement to spiritual maturity, maximum glorification of God and super-abundance of blessings now and forever more. *"And now I commend you to God and to the word of His grace, which is able to build you up and to give you the inheritance among all those who are sanctified"* (Acts 20:32; cf. 2 Timothy 3:16-17; 2 Peter 3:18).

When a believer ignores God's Word, what happens? He injures himself in two areas:

- He blocks his access to God through prayer. *"He who turns away his ear from listening to the law [God's Word], Even his prayer is an abomination [to God]"* (Proverbs 28:9).

- He begs for an early death. *"For he who finds me [God's Word] finds life And obtains favor from the LORD. But he who sins against me [the Word] injures himself; All those who hate me [indifferent to the Word] love death"* (Proverbs 8:35-36; cf. 21:16).

So James stressed that proper application of God's Word can save a believer from an untimely death: "*Therefore, putting aside all filthiness and all that remains of wickedness, in humility receive the word implanted, which is able to save your souls [lives]*" (James 1:21).

Let us concentrate and study our next section together, for it holds the key to understanding the whole of the epistle of James. Oh, how I pray and hope that the message of this book would awaken sleeping believers everywhere to God's amazing gift to us—His written Word.

# Part 4

# Perception and Application of God's Word

## THIRTEEN

James 1:21b-25

# Being a Hearer and a Doer of God's Word

*In humility receive the word implanted, which is able [has potential] to save your souls [lives, from physical premature death]. But prove yourselves doers of the word, and not merely hearers who delude themselves. For if anyone is a hearer of the word and not a doer, he is like a man who looks at his natural face in a mirror; for once he has looked at himself and gone away, he has immediately forgotten what kind of person he was. But one who looks intently at the perfect law [mirror of God's Word], the law of liberty, and abides by it [application], not having become a forgetful hearer but an effectual doer, this man will be blessed in what he does* (**James 1:21b-25**).

Before we look at our verses, we first need to review and pull in additional background information in preparation for our study. We concluded section III with James' exhortation to put "*aside all filthiness and all that remains of wickedness*" (1:21a). His aspiration was to save his fellow brethren from becoming losers in the spiritual race—going to heaven empty-handed with no reward for all eternity. This was not a reference to making it to heaven but rather the loss of reward, which should be a horrible thought for anyone (1 Corinthians 3:15).

This thought consumed even the great apostle Paul. We know this from his epistle to the Corinthians. "*Therefore I run in such a way, as not without aim; I box in such a way, as not beating the air; but I discipline my body and make it my slave, so that, after I have preached to oth-*

*ers, I myself will not be disqualified [from the prize, v. 24]"* (1 Corinthians 9:26-27).

James, therefore, passionately urged his readers, with the hope of steering their course toward God in order to *avoid* the judgment that would ultimately bring about a premature physical death and strip them of any tangible reward in the eternal state (Revelation 3:11; cf. 1 Corinthians 3:14-15). *"Therefore, putting aside all filthiness and all that remains of wickedness, in humility receive the word implanted, which is able to save your souls [lives from premature death]"* (James 1:21).

It has been said that "where there's smoke, there's fire." Conversely, James' exhortation was based on his fiery indictment *"You adulteresses, do you not know that friendship with the world is hostility toward God? Therefore whoever wishes to be a friend of the world makes himself an enemy of God"* (James 4:4).

James was writing to believers who were totally complacent spiritually. Earlier he had warned them that a habitual lifestyle of carnality would surely give birth to a premature death: *"When lust has conceived, it gives birth to sin; and when sin is accomplished, it brings forth [physical] death"* (James 1:15). Make no mistake; James is not talking about spiritual death. Rather, the death in question is physical! This we know based on his last words: *"My brethren, if any among you strays from the truth [or falls away] and one turns him back, let him know that he who turns a sinner from the error of his way will save his soul [physical life] from death and will cover a multitude of sins"* (James 5:19-20).

If we understand that James was referring to physical death, the answer to the question *"Can that [the] faith [biblical truth] save him?"* (James 2:14) is clearly understood as "save him" from physical death (more on this as our study progresses).

There is hope for the fallen Christian soldier (James 5:19-20)! How can anyone miss this? My beloved, listen: it is this imminent judgment that prompted him to ask, *"What use is it, my brethren, if someone says he has faith but he has no works? Can that faith [literally the faith,*[85] *i.e., biblical truth] save him?"* (James 2:14).

We know that James was not talking about salvation; that's not his subject! Rather, he asked, could knowledge of God's Word without application save the individual from the judgment of premature death (1:15, 21, 5: 20; cf. 1 Corinthians 11:30)? Scriptural references abound in regard to God calling His children home earlier than their scheduled time due to lack of spiritual production. Solomon warned, "*The fear of the LORD prolongs life, But the years of the wicked will be shortened*" (Proverbs 10:27; cf. 14:27; 21:16).

Elsewhere we are told, "*So Saul died for his trespass which he committed against the LORD, because of the word of the LORD which he did not keep... Therefore He [God] killed him and turned the kingdom to David the son of Jesse*" (1 Chronicles 10:13-14).

\* \* \*

---

**To put the message into practice is the real challenge in Christian living.**

---

The question is, how can any serious student of the infallible Word of God miss the crucial point of James' message, that the believer who is not a doer of the Word risks judgment and severe punishment, which may include untimely death? Everyone can hear the Word, but not everyone does what it says. To hear the Truth, all one needs is to listen to the teaching of God's Word, through face-to-face teaching or recorded messages. Literature is another good source for receiving Bible teaching. But to put the message into practice is the real challenge in Christian living.

On the one hand, the good news is that acting upon God's Word is blessing immeasurable (Psalm 84:11). It is life (Deuteronomy 32:47). On the other hand, the bad news is that failure to act on its instruction is a recipe for divine discipline and possibly death.

Our Lord graphically drove the point home. In Luke's account we read, "*But the one [believer in Christ] who has heard [His Word] and has not acted accordingly, is like a man who built a house on the ground without any foundation; and the torrent burst against it and immediately it collapsed, and the ruin of that house was great*" (Luke 6:49; cf. 11:28).

Can you see? This is similar to James' message, namely, being a hearer and not equally a doer cannot save anyone from severe discipline

(James 2:14). Believers who only accumulate God's Word in their minds, without incorporating it into action, will one day come to the end of grace and experience untimely death. This is the Word of God. "*The fear of the LORD [learning and applying biblical truth] prolongs life, But the years of the wicked [carnal believer, apathy to application of biblical truth] will be shortened*" (Proverbs 10:27).

God has spoken! If we keep in mind that knowledge alone can never save us from total collapse and ruination, that knowledge without application can never save us from divine discipline and premature death, then we shall have no trouble at all in understanding James 2:14.

Repeat, impending premature physical death is the cause of James' alarm: "*When sin is accomplished [full grown], it brings forth [premature] death*" (James 1:15; cf. 21; 5:19, 20).

We continue with James' appeal for his readers to be doers of the Word of God.

## Restoration Precedes Being a Doer of the Word

James drew a distinction between those who apply what they hear to life and those who only hear the Word but don't apply it. Before we can be doers, we must first be cleansed, or restored to fellowship, for we cannot move forward in the spiritual race until the sin issue in our lives is dealt with through acknowledgment of sin (Psalm 66:18; cf. 1 John 1:9) and a subsequent change in our direction (Proverbs 28:13).

Since James' audience were Jewish believers, they were familiar with the Mosaic Law. They were aware of the Old Testament provisions regarding restoration to fellowship. They knew the protocol and the sacrificial elements required for the sin offering, such as doves, pigeons, bulls, goats and lambs (Leviticus 6:4-13). All these rituals were a shadow of Christ, the true Lamb of God (Hebrews 10:1-10; cf. 1 Corinthians 5:7). Because they knew all this so well, it explains why James did not dwell much on the subject of restoration. He simply admonishes, "*Therefore, putting aside all filthiness*" (James 1:21).

Of course, after the cross we are no longer required to bring sacrificial elements for our sin offering. This is what the author of the book of Hebrews had in mind:

> *Therefore leaving the elementary teaching about the Christ, let us press on to maturity, not laying again a foundation of repentance from dead works and of faith toward God [the Son]…For in the case of those who have once been enlightened…and then have fallen away, it is impossible to renew them again to repentance [toward God the Son]* (Hebrews 6:1-6).

When a believer falls away and then desires to come back to fellowship, the believer does not need to go back to the cross to be saved anew; it's impossible! Rather, the believer is to recall the finished work of Christ on the Cross and confess his sins to God alone (1 John 1:9). In light of this, James admonishes his audience, "*Therefore, putting aside all filthiness [same as confession, 1 John 1:9] and all that remains of wickedness*" (James 1:21a).

## Receive the Word Implanted

"*In humility receive the word implanted, which is able to save your souls* " (James 1:21). The proper rendering would be save your "lives" and not "souls," for souls are immortal (1 Samuel 19:11; Jeremiah 48:6), and their souls had already been saved from the eternal damnation (John 5:24; cf. James 1:18). Consequently, with a cleansed, fertile heart through confession of one's sins, God's Word can then be implanted. The implanted Word, when applied, accomplishes many things. Although we mentioned this in our introduction to part IV, it's worthy of a revisit from another perspective.

First, the implanted word will serve as healing balm to our souls (Psalm 119:154, 50). In other words, it will help in the reconstruction and healing of a sin-broken life. "*Before I was afflicted I went astray, But now I keep Your Word…It is good for me that I was afflicted, That I may learn Your statutes*" (Psalm 119:67-71).

Second, "*the word implanted*" when applied will serve as building blocks in building the believer up again (Acts 20:32). That's not all; it will be a guiding light (Psalm 119:105) and a shield against premature death to all who love to learn and use it (Proverbs 8:36). Being armed with the most practical biblical truth but not putting it into practice will not save anyone from premature death, let alone divine discipline.

185

This, in light of our context, is what James had in mind when he uttered these words: *"What use is it, my brethren, if someone says he has faith [biblical truth or creed] but he has no works [application of that Bible knowledge]? Can that [literally, 'the' acquired knowledge of God's Word] faith save him?"* (James 2:14).

James is saying, "We cannot escape divine discipline simply because we have stored in our minds volumes of academic knowledge of God's Word!" We must remember, mastering the entire Scripture is not enough; putting it into practice is the fountain of life! We are reminded of this in the book of Ezra. *"For Ezra had set his heart to study the law of the LORD and to practice it, and to teach His statutes and ordinances in Israel"* (Ezra 7:10).

This brings us to James' next topic of discussion.

## Delusion

*"But prove yourselves doers of the word, and not merely hearers who delude themselves"* (James 1:22).

---

**God's Word is designed to shape our wills and actions**
*"to the praise of His glory."*

---

*Delusion* is a perfect word to describe believers who think God owes them a blessing simply because they have a massive accumulation of God's Word in their souls. Application is necessary! God's Word is designed to shape our wills and actions *"to the praise of His glory"* (Ephesians 1:12, 14). But it must be applied consistently in order to achieve this goal.

James makes his point by using a mirror analogy to contrast the two: *"For if anyone is a hearer of the word and not a doer, he is like a man who looks at his natural face in a mirror; for once he has looked at himself and gone away, he has immediately forgotten what kind of person he was"* (James 1:23-24).

This is like a believer who goes to Bible study and takes good notes but goes home and puts them away without review or reflection. Such a lifestyle is not what God had in mind when He gave us His very own life. He desires that we bear fruit (Ephesians 2:8-10; Titus 2:11)! So, what James' epistle seeks to correct is apathy to the application of the Word of God.

When we stand in front of a mirror and see dirt on our faces but walk away without washing it off, then the information in the mirror is of no use—it does not bring change. Similarly, the information in God's Word is of no use (technically, rendered dead or useless), if we walk away and don't take action or adjust our behaviors.

Conversely, there is great blessing for those who are consistent doers of the Word. *"But one who looks intently at the perfect law [mirror of God's Word], the law of liberty, and abides by it, not having become a forgetful hearer but an effectual doer [application], this man will be blessed in what he does"* (James 1:25).

James contrasts the believer without application in verses 23-24 with another whose delight is in the fulfillment of His Word in verse 25. In doing so he alludes to Psalm 1.

> *How blessed is the man who does not walk in the counsel of the wicked, Nor stand in the path of sinners, Nor sit at the seat of scoffers! But his delight is in the law of the LORD, And in His law he meditates day and night [i.e., reflects on God's Word day and night until it becomes part of his thinking and action, 2 Timothy 2:7]. And he will be like a tree firmly planted by streams of water, Which yields its fruit in its season And its leaf does not wither; And in whatever he does, he prospers* (Psalm 1:1-3).

Success, in every sense of the word then, is a reward (or crown as we saw in chapter 9) for those who love God, who love learning and who love applying His Word on a consistent basis!

With the ground tilled and thoroughly watered, we now implant the main seed. You ask, "What seed?" Keep reading; the answer is coming in the next chapter.

## FOURTEEN

# James 1:26-2:9

# Faith Without Works Is Dead

Beloved of God, we are set to tackle one of the most pivotal passages in all of Scripture, namely James 1:26-2:26. It has become a stumbling block to a proper understanding of the book of James. Its difficulty has been the source of misinterpretation by such passionate and honest servants of God as Martin Luther and John Calvin. As a result, many have been led astray. The passage we are about to study is the central passage of the entire epistle. Hence, to understand it is to grasp the heart of James' entire work.

Scholars point to 2:14-26 as the most difficult passage of all. And the backdrop for that passage is 1:26-2:13. We cannot separate them and expect an accurate interpretation of the whole passage. So, we must treat James 1:26 through 2:26 as one complete thought, like a tapestry that is woven together with the thread of rebuke, admonition and exhortation, embellished with examples of hero believers of the past.

Considering the difficulties that many great scholars have had for centuries in deciphering what James was trying to communicate to his readers, let us adjust our approach. Simply, let us set aside our scholastic and linguistic knowledge and approach the throne room of His grace. Let us humbly ask God afresh for His illumination through His Spirit, so at the end of this passage we can with great joy shout, "Thank God; at last, we fully understand James' message!"

Father-God, admittedly, this passage has caused men immeasurable agony for centuries. Scholars have tirelessly wrestled with its content, producing little or no clarity. We know that You authored this passage and that You are not a God of confusion. Father, we look to You alone to illuminate our passage so that the message might be crystal clear to us all. This and more we ask in the name of Your Son, Jesus. Amen.

> *If anyone thinks himself to be religious, and yet does not bridle his tongue but deceives his own heart, this man's religion is worthless. Pure and undefiled religion in the sight of our God and Father is this: to visit orphans and widows in their distress, and to keep oneself unstained by the world* (**James 1:26-27**).

For a maximum benefit of the study of this section, you may wish to pause and read the entire twenty-eight verses from your Bible (1:26-2:26).

This passage flows like a mountain stream. Therefore, if we are to appreciate James' work, it is imperative that we flow along with his thoughts to the end. But first we need to survey our stream's source. Using our analogy, we know the water that flows to the end is the same water that flows from where the stream begins. In other words, James' thought or premise from the onset of this passage is no different from his conclusion. His conclusion supports his premise.

We have already demonstrated that James' message is not about salvation. His audience was believers. We have seen that his emphasis is on "*the word implanted*" and "*doers of the word*." If we look at James' ending thought in verse 2:26, it will help us understand his flow of thought from the beginning of the passage. So let us examine the last verse of this entire section. "*For just as the body without the spirit is dead, so also faith [biblical truth] without works [application] is dead*" (James 2:26).

Any interpretation must match the premise. We must not overlook or deviate from his thinking. Remember, James has just been discussing "*the word implanted*" and "*doers of the word*." Therefore, the second part of James 2:26 would be better rendered "The implanted word without application is useless [dead]."

## Dead Faith

Having translated it this way, we begin with a question: What is dead faith?

The answer to this question has been elusive. Book after book has been published in an attempt to answer the question "Is 'dead faith' a reference to a faith that cannot bring about salvation from the lake of fire?" That cannot be, since James is not talking about salvation.

James' premise is "*the word implanted*" and the application thereof. Logically, his conclusion must agree with his premise: "*the word implanted*." This would lead us to translate "the word implanted that is not used and applied is utterly useless." It does not make sense for him to conclude his sentence by switching topics from "*the word implanted*" to "salvation."

We can explain it this way: Assume you own the best and most sophisticated gun, and it is fully loaded. An armed robber breaks into your house and robs you, but you never use the gun to fire a single bullet. Your gun is useless (or dead), not in the sense that it doesn't work but in the sense that you did not use it to defend yourself when you could have.

We consult two passages to further explain the meaning of dead faith. The first passage is in Revelation, where our Lord used the same Greek word, *nekros,* for "dead." There, the apostle John records Him saying,

> "*To the angel [pastor] of the church in Sardis write: He who has the seven Spirits of God and the seven stars, says this: 'I know your deeds, that you have a name that you are alive, but you are dead. Wake up, and strengthen the things that remain, which were about to die; for I have not found your deeds completed in the sight of My God. So remember what you have received and heard; and keep it, and repent [change your mind]. Therefore if you do not wake up, I will come like a thief, and you will not know at what hour I will come to you [contextually, a metaphor for an imminent temporary judgment]*" (Revelation 3:1-3).

Apparently, the name of their church was Christ's Living Church. "*You have a name that you are alive.*" But the Lord rebuffed them: "It is not the name that defines who you are but the temperament of the people in that church. As for you, your carnal lifestyle makes you a dead church." There's no indication that the Lord ever doubted their salvation. You see, *dead* here does not mean that they cannot hear or function again; otherwise, what is the need for the admonition "*Wake up*" (3:2)? It simply means that their spiritual life has been stalled; hence the metaphor "you are dead." Furthermore, it doesn't mean that they have dead faith either! The apostle Paul uses the same metaphor in writing to the Ephesians: "*For this reason it says, 'Awake, sleeper, And arise from the dead, And Christ will shine on you*" (Ephesians 5:14).

Paul issued an order. You may ask, "Can someone command a dead man to wake up if he cannot hear?" My beloved, we must not be too hasty, lest we fall short of "*rightly dividing the word of truth*" (2 Timothy 2:15 KJV). James is not talking about dead faith (biblical truth) in the sense of a corpse but rather in the sense of uselessness or ineffective or, as Frank Gaebelein suggests, "barren."[86] This does not imply that their theology, which James refers to as faith, is dead per se, but stagnant in the sense that it is not beneficial. James is not talking about salvation.

## EXAMINING CONDUCT

Now, we go to the beginning of this passage. In James 1:25, he indicated the recipients of his epistle as hearers of the Word only. Then, in 1:26 he made his case that they stand guilty as indicted.

### Misuse of the Tongue

"*If anyone thinks himself to be religious [spiritual], and yet does not bridle his tongue but deceives his own heart, this man's religion [spiritual life] is worthless*" (James 1:26). If we believe that James used the word "religion" to mean salvation, then none of us is truly saved because we all struggle with keeping our tongues under control. Often we fail to bridle them! Does that make our religion (salvation) worthless or dead? That would be absurd. James is not talking about salvation but of the spiritual life. So in verse 1:26 our religion [spiritual life] is stagnant or not operational—therefore rendered useless. Basically, James is saying, "If a believer thinks he is living the spiritual life and yet does not bridle his tongue, he is deceiving himself."

Next, James contrasts this with an example of application.

## Orphans and Widows

"*Pure and undefiled religion [spiritual life] in the sight of our God and Father is this: to visit orphans and widows in their distress, and to keep oneself unstained by the world*" (James 1:27). His selection of orphans and widows is noteworthy. It does not mean that, if we should decide today to start helping orphans and widows, our action would make us pure in the sight of God. Rather, the underlying element in James' message is *tenderness of heart*. We are acutely aware that in biblical times orphans and widows were generally helpless when it came to caring for themselves. It takes a compassionate heart to understand their situation! In other words, once a believer is preoccupied with Christ, the individual will imitate and follow Christ's footsteps in his daily living. He will be sensitive to the needs of others, orphans and widows included. He would never look the other way when confronted with the needs of others (Philippians 2:4) but would take action according to his means, ability and God's leading. On the other hand, he would resist outright friendship with the world where materialism abounds (James 4:4).

James is not finished. He presented more examples to prove that these stand guilty as indicted.

## Sin of Partiality

*My brethren, do not hold your faith [trust] in our glorious Lord Jesus Christ with an attitude of personal favoritism. For if a man comes into your assembly with a gold ring and dressed in fine clothes, and there also comes in a poor man in dirty clothes, and you pay special attention to the one who is wearing the fine clothes, and say, "You sit here in a good place," and you say to the poor man, "You stand over there, or sit down by my footstool," have you not made distinctions among yourselves, and become judges with evil motives? Listen, my beloved brethren: did not God choose the poor of this world to be rich in faith and heirs of the kingdom which He promised to those who love Him? But you have dishonored the poor man. Is it not the rich who oppress you and personally drag you into court? Do they not blaspheme the fair name by which you have been called?* (**James 2:1-7**).

Note the words *"you have been called."* Paul used the same words *"For those whom He foreknew, He also predestined…He also called…He also justified; and…glorified"* (Romans 8:29-31) to show his audience was truly saved. Since James is using *"you have been called"* in the same way as the apostle Paul did, this dispels any thought that James' audience was not truly saved. The phrase *"you have been called"* is also critical in settling the ambiguity of James 2:14. In other words, James was not talking about salvation.

Read the following slowly: *"My brethren, do not hold your faith [confidence] in our glorious Lord Jesus Christ with an attitude of personal favoritism."* Here James uses faith in the sense of trust, and the object is "Jesus Christ." However, this verse is not as praise, but as rebuke.

Let us consider the above passage. On the one hand, James confirms their salvation: *"your faith in our glorious Lord Jesus Christ."* On the other hand he calls their lifestyle of favoritism *"evil"* (James 2:4). In fact, the Greek construction of the above passage is sobering. This mandate "do not hold" is the "present active imperative of echo with negative *me*, exhortation to stop holding or not to have the habit of holding in the fashioned condemned."[87] In other words, as children of God, "Stop (cease) holding onto the practice of favoritism!"

It fascinates me when I reflect on the many facets of God's grace toward us especially when we are in a state of spiritual maladjustment. This is what God does: He holds the carnal believer in the grip of His love and simultaneously disciplines him with the iron hand of justice. God's love for the believer is not changed by one iota! Why? Because God is love (John 14:3). He is immutable and does not change (Malachai 3:6).

---

**God's love for all believers never
changes, no matter what!**

---

Perhaps you have read Hebrews 12:6, *"FOR THOSE WHOM THE LORD LOVES HE DISCIPLINES"* many times and overlooked this concept. Though the believer has failed miserably, the Lord still loves him with an everlasting and undiminished love (Jeremiah 31:3). It's clear: God's love cannot change! No matter what!

Often we erroneously think that God loves us because of what we do or think. The truth is that He loves us because we possess the object of His love—His very righteousness (Romans 3:22; cf. Psalm 33:5). That's grace! It has nothing to do with our attitude or who we are. That explains why James still called those who had failed wretchedly in their spiritual life "My brethren." Circumstances change, people change, times change, but God's love for all believers never changes. It's that simple. That's grace!

James urges believers in Christ to stop misusing their faith in our glorious Lord Jesus Christ by showing an of attitude personal favoritism. Like many in church today, they granted seats of honor to those who gave generously to their church and wished the shameful poor would leave or stay home. To them, poor people in the church were not profitable. To such a mental attitude, James thunders, "This is evil to the core!"

Dr. Fruchtenbaum noted, "Admiring a person because of his position in life was expressly forbidden by the Mosaic Law in Leviticus 19:15."[88] The motive behind their favoritism was purely financial. They had elevated their love for money above Christ, and that's what James calls evil, as did the apostle Paul (James 2:4; cf. 1 Timothy 6:10).

After James addressed the evil behavior of most of his audience, he also addressed those who might have been acting properly. In the process he gave the "Royal Law," which is a guideline for all time—not only for James' audience, but also for us now—as to how we should treat others.

> "*If, however, you are fulfilling the royal law according to the Scripture, 'YOU SHALL LOVE YOUR NEIGHBOR AS YOURSELF,' you are doing well*" (**James 2:8**).

This verse quotes directly from the Old Testament, with which they would be familiar: "*You shall not take vengeance, nor bear any grudge against the sons of your people, but you shall love your neighbor as yourself; I am the LORD*" (Leviticus 19:18).

James went on again to address partiality and let them know that such a lifestyle disgraced the One in whom they had placed their trust as their Savior. They were mocking God by mistreating the poor

(Proverbs 17:5). This action begs for divine judgment, which James wants his beloved to avoid. Hence the exhortation: *"My brethren, do not hold your faith in our glorious Lord Jesus Christ with an attitude of personal favoritism"* (James 2:1).

> *"But if you show partiality, you are committing sin and are convicted by the law as transgressors"* (**James 2:9**).

This passage tells us we all sin in many ways (James 4:17)!

May the God of truth impress upon our hearts His Word communicated so that, without fail, we may continue on the path of truth!

The foundation has been laid; now we are ready to begin laying the rest of the bricks. This we shall do beginning with the next chapter.

## FIFTEEN

James 2:10-14

# Understanding the Faith of James 2:14

*For whoever keeps the whole law and yet stumbles in one point, he has become guilty of all. For He who said, "DO NOT COMMIT ADULTERY," also said, "DO NOT COMMIT MURDER." Now if you do not commit adultery, but do commit murder, you have become a transgressor of the law. So speak and so act as those who are to be judged by the law of liberty. For judgment will be merciless to one who has shown no mercy; mercy triumphs over judgment* (James 2:10-13).

We will examine this passage on two fronts: first, as a warning; second, as instruction for correcting those who think acceptance before God is based on observation of the Mosaic Law. Though salvation was not what James was referencing, this truth can still be applied to believers and unbelievers.

The apostle Paul also warned about the consequences of seeking to establish a relationship with God through the observations of the Mosaic law:

*What shall we say then? That Gentiles, who did not pursue righteousness, attained righteousness, even the righteousness which is by faith [trust]; but Israel, pursuing a law of righteousness, did not arrive at that law. Why? Because they did not pursue it by faith [trust], but as though it were by works [of the Law]. They stumbled over the stumbling stone* (Romans 9:30-32).

In addition to the Decalogue (10 commandments), there are over 600 laws in the Bible. Anyone who wishes to have a relationship with God based on the Law must be diligent to keep the entire Law, all 613 commandments! "*For whoever keeps the whole law and yet stumbles in one point, he has become guilty of all*" (James 2:10). That's a demand of perfection! That's bad news for the entire human race, for no one can keep the whole Law without stumbling.

---

**A believer in Christ no longer stands before God in his own righteousness, but in Christ's righteousness.**

---

The good news is that "*Christ is the end of the law for righteousness to everyone who believes*" (Romans 10:4; cf. Matthew 5:17). In other words, faith alone in Christ alone cancels all the requirement of holiness based on the Law for acceptance before God. A believer in Christ no longer stands before God in his own righteousness, but in Christ's righteousness. That is the epitome of God's grace! This is what the apostle Paul had in mind when he recorded these words: "*And may be found in Him, not having a righteousness of my own derived from the Law, but that which is through faith in Christ, the righteousness which comes from God on the basis of faith*" (Philippians 3:9; cf. Romans 3:22; Galatians 3:10-13; 5:4-5).

James' message to his readers is that the spiritual life is all or nothing. One cannot claim spirituality and simultaneously show favoritism or partake in any other unrighteousness (1 John 5:17).

Sin, no matter how small, ruptures our fellowship with God. Fellowship is only restored through acknowledgment of that very sin. "*If we confess our [known] sins, He is faithful and righteous to forgive us our sins and to cleanse us from all unrighteousness [unknown sins]*" (1 John 1:9).

This too is grace!

## Showing Mercy to the Destitute

James warns against an uncompassionate heart: "*So speak and so act as those who are to be judged by the law of liberty. For judgment will be merciless to one who has shown no mercy; mercy triumphs over judgment*" (James 2:12-13).

A child of God who is on track spiritually will have a heart of compassion. His heart will immitate Christ's heart of love, compassion and mercy. There is no room for ego or self-centeredness, no room to look down on those less fortunate. When pride causes us to look down on another, arrogance takes over, and mercy flies out the window.

James reminded his Jewish Christian audience that their lack of mercy and compassion toward others would adversely affect how God would treat them. He knew the Old Testament Scriptures and was familiar with our Lord's teachings. His epistle, being the earliest, had scripture references from the Old Testament as in James 2:13. What's more, our Lord Himself said, "*In everything, therefore, treat [present imperative: keep on treating] people the same way you want them to treat you, for this is the Law and the Prophets*" (Matthew 7:12; cf. 5:7).

This is what is referred to as the "golden rule." In essence James was saying, "You risk the mercy of your heavenly Father when you treat the rich with an attitude of favoritism because of their economic status." King Solomon captures it beautifully: "*He who oppresses the poor taunts his Maker [God], But he who is gracious to the needy honors Him*" (Proverbs 14:31).

Our attitude toward everyone, rich or poor, is measured by our spiritual life. If our spiritual life is poor, it will manifest itself on many levels, including looking down on the poor while esteeming the rich for what we might get from them. James called this evil (James 2:4)!

Finally, we are ready to examine the pivotal verse in James' epistle. This is the heart of our entire work.

## THE FAITH OF JAMES 2:14

"*What use is it, my brethren, if someone says he has faith [biblical truth, beliefs] but he has no works [application]? Can that faith [literally 'the faith,' i.e., accumulated biblical truth] save him [from premature physical death]?*" (**James 2:14**).

As we said earlier, many great and honest communicators of God's

Word have fumbled the ball of biblical interpretation of this passage. Consequently, many souls have been taken captive by falsehood. One sheds tears when he considers the effect of the misinterpretation of this verse on the Church. It has brought more confusion and division among the body of Christ than most any other passage of Scripture.

Knowing that God's wrath is poured out in full measure on anyone who misinterprets His Word (James 3:1), let's pause in awe for a quick prayer.

> Father-God, we humbly ask that You would cast a beam of light on James 2:14 and all other passages. Guide us along the way through the mentorship of Your Holy Spirit to uncover the truth of Your Word, which for centuries has eluded many great scholars. May You open the eyes of Your children to grasp the depth, the width, and the height of Your truth communicated herein. In Christ's name. Amen.

We need to take into account James' train of thought. This takes us back to James 1:15, "*when sin is accomplished, it brings forth [physical] death.*" He developed this idea in 1:21 to 2:13. "*Therefore, putting aside all filthiness and all that remains of wickedness, in humility receive the word implanted, which is able to save your souls [lives]*" (James 1:21). All this was preparation for his main point: "*What use is it, my brethren, if someone says he has faith [biblical truth, beliefs] but he has no works [application]? Can that faith [literally 'the faith,' i.e., accumulated biblical truth] save him [from premature physical death]?*" (James 2:14).

Let us proceed with objectivity, humility and concentration.

## Defining Faith

Keep in mind that the word *faith* is the main point of contention in James 2:14. It would benefit us tremendously to reconsider this word as James used it. We mentioned earlier that *pistis*, the Greek word for **"faith," does not always mean "trust" or "confidence."**

First, let us consider the whole Bible. From Genesis to Revelation, it's apparent that none of the writers of Scripture ever doubt, or question, the salvation of those whom they knew were already saved. For example, Moses never doubted Israel's salvation despite their colossal spiritual failures. The same is true of the prophets Isaiah, Ezekiel and Jeremiah. Similarly, the apostles John and Paul never question the salvation of their audience in their epistles. The apostle Paul would have questioned if the Corinthians had only "intellectual assent" instead of the so-called "saving faith," but he **did not**! Rather, he called them "*the church of God*" (1 Corinthians 1:2).

Second, every author of Scripture seemed to be consumed with the ramifications of spiritual failure. Knowing this helps us understand James' epistle! The thought of severe punishment and loss of rewards for all eternity prompted James to ask, "How can your knowledge of God's Word shelter you from discipline if what you know is not applied? For example, how can your knowledge of Scripture: "*not be partial to the poor nor defer to the great*" (Leviticus 19:15), shield you from discipline if you know this truth, but in disobedience you still favor the rich over the poor (James 2:1-4)?

This is like a pilot who knows every technique to control an airplane in turbulence but merely folds his hands when his aircraft is severely hit. Can his knowledge save him from crashing? Only if he applies it.

Beloved of God, let us consider our ways. We superimpose sentimentalism over the principle of hermeneutics (comparing Scripture with Scripture) when we maintain that a "'genuine believer" must show an evidence of his salvation by his deeds! If we hold to this dogma we must then reject outright many passages of Scripture, particularly the first book of Corinthians, which reveals that believers can live from day to day, month to month and even year to year without any manifestation of the life of Christ (1 Corinthians 3:1-3).

Furthermore, this position is saying, in essence, that believers can never fall away. But we know they can (James 5:19-20; cf. Galatians 6:2; Hebrews 6:4). Scripture must harmonize with Scripture! We cannot take just one portion and leave the rest hanging.

Upon a thorough examination of the entire text, under the illuminating ministry of the Holy Spirit, one understands the effort of some scholars to try to redefine the word *faith* in James 2:14. They use phrases such as "saving faith," "head believism," "intellectual assent" and the like. We shall demonstrate that James is not talking about salvation from hell, but before we do, let us trace James' train of thought in 1:13-22.

There James warned his readers with a sobering message, that knowing the right thing to do and doing the opposite would bring divine punishment: "*when lust has conceived, it gives birth to sin; and when sin is accomplished, it brings forth death*" (1:15). In light of this concern, James exhorted, "*Therefore, putting aside all filthiness*" (James 1:21; cf. 1 John 1:9), "*receive the word implanted, which is able to save your souls [lives]* " (James 1:22). You see, James' train of thought on one hand is laced with "the word implanted" and its application and on the other the consequences of lack of application thereof. This is where the question of James 2:14 fits in.

"*What use is it, my brethren, if someone says he has faith [biblical truth] but he has no works [application]? Can that faith [literally 'the faith,' i.e., accumulated biblical truth] save him [from premature physical death]?*" (James 2:14). James asked, "*Can that faith [literally 'the faith']*[89] *save him?*" Regrettably, here is where many teachers of the Word drop the ball of accurately interpreting James' thought. As a result of an oversight, some came up with the idea that so-called "saving faith" must produce good works. Others maintain that without a "genuine faith" one cannot be saved.

These assertions, we realize, were done in all honesty, with a pure heart and good intention. But they are wrong and have led to many false teachings that have no bearing whatsoever to what James is saying.

Chaos and confusion over this verse prompted me to carefully examine a great number of commentaries on James. To my great surprise, only a few clearly unveiled the truth of our passage. Among these, Dr. James Orr makes a noteworthy observation. He observes in James 2:14 that "*pistis* 'faith,' appears in the sense of 'creed' the truth, or body of truth, which is trusted, or which justifies trust."[90] He goes on to say that the riddle of apparent contradiction to Pauline dicta "is solved by observing that the writer uses 'faith' in the sense of creed, orthodox or belief.[91] " His insightfulness sheds more light: "This is clear from verse 19, where the 'faith' in question is illustrated: 'Thou believest that God is one.' This is the creedal confession of the orthodox Jew."[92]

Another renowned scholar, Martin Dibelius, concurs that "James is not speaking of any particular brand of faith."[94] Equally enlightening is the commentary of Earl D. Radmacher, the general editor of the NKJV:

> But the major theological issue in James is faith and works (2:14-26). Many contend that James is talking about true faith versus false faith. But it seems apparent that James is not questioning whether the recipients were genuinely believers; he repeatedly calls them "brethren" "my brethren" or "my beloved" (2:1, 14)."[94] Elsewhere, he affirms, the word "saved (Gk. Sozo) is used five times in James (1:21; 2:14; 4:12, 5:15; 5:20). Each time it refers to the saving of temporal life, not saving from the penalty of sin (5:15).[95]

Again, James is not talking about faith in relation to salvation. To help us understand this we need to approach our passage logically. For example, on the one hand, if James' major premise in 2:14 is salvation from the lake of fire, then salvation would equally be his minor premises in verses 17 and 21 respectively. *"Even so faith, if it has no works, is dead [useless], being by itself"* (v. 17). *"Was not Abraham our father justified by works when he offered up Isaac his son on the altar?"* (v. 21).

On the other hand, if salvation from the lake of fire is the main thrust of 2:14, then verses 14, 17 and 21 should logically lead us to James' conclusion: *"For just as the body without the spirit is dead, so also faith without works is dead"* (2:26). To reason otherwise would be illogical. We ask again, is the issue in our passage salvation? Obviously, the answer is no.

## Role of Works

At this juncture, open your Bible, pause, pray and take a deep breath as we objectively work through the entire message of our passage. In doing so, we factor in James 2:21. *"Was not Abraham our father justified by works when he offered up Isaac his son on the altar?"* (James 2:21).

This verse is *critical* because James uses Abraham's justification to support his major premise of "faith without works."

We ask this important question: "Was Abraham saved from the lake of fire when he offered Isaac on the altar?" *No!* He was saved when he placed his faith in Yahweh alone, long before Isaac's birth (Genesis 15:6; cf. Romans 4:9-10). If Abraham had died before the birth of Isaac, would he have gone to heaven? Yes! The *big question* then is, If James is not talking about salvation in 2:21, what is he talking about?

We thank God the Holy Spirit for His unsurpassed wisdom! Had He guided James to use Moses or David instead of Abraham in verse 21, the riddle of this passage would have been nearly impossible to solve. We do not know when either Moses or David were saved. For instance, what if James had asked, "Was not David justified by works when he killed Goliath?" Think of the confusion such a passage would have generated! Rather, James used someone who was already saved according to Scripture. The real question arises, what kind of justification is James talking about? Which bring us to the issue of dual justification.

## Dual Justification

John Calvin, our beloved brother, came extremely close to solving this riddle when he uncovered double justification. He wrote, "Primarily, justification is acceptance before God through the imputation of righteousness. This comes by faith [confidence] alone."[96] He was right! Faith alone in Christ alone (Romans 3:28; cf. 5:1)! However, he clouded the issue by adding, "Secondarily and in consequence, however, justification is the declaration or manifestation before men of the righteousness of faith. This is justification by works."[97] He missed the real meaning by mixing justification by works for reward with justification for salvation. That was an honest attempt. He came very close but failed to accurately interpret the verse. It seems that he somehow read "being born incrementally" into the text.

The Bible tells us that new birth occurs, once and for all eternity, at the moment we anchor our trust in Christ alone (Hebrews 10:10; cf. Romans 5:1; 1 John 5:1). God does not wait for us to manifest work "before men" before He can declare us justified. That is inconsistent with Scripture. The Bible is emphatic: "*Whoever believes that Jesus is the*

*Christ is [instantly] born of God [Greek tense implies once and for all]"* (1 John 5:1a). There's nothing in Scripture to suggest otherwise. Once a son, always a son!

Our mistake is that we often overlook some important teachings of the Bible. For example, anyone, regardless of age, who anchors his trust in Christ is considered a newborn in God's family (1 Peter 2:2). The baby must obey the command *"grow in the grace"* (2 Peter 3:18) to advance to spiritual maturity. If he ignores this command he will never grow up.

A baby believer, although he is saved *"once for all,"* (Hebrews 10:10), is incapable of manifesting the life of Christ. Similarly, a back-slidden believer, although he is saved once and for all, is incapable of manifesting the life of Christ until his spiritual life is restored.

A believer in carnality cannot be differentiated from an unbeliever. King David's sin of adultery and murder illustrates this point perfectly (2 Samuel 11:2-17; 12:9), not to mention King Saul's intense anger, hatred, envy and animosity against David and other sins that led to his premature death (1 Chronicles 10:13-14).

With this said, let us examine the call to practical Christianity and the justification that was the focus of James' epistle.

---

## SIXTEEN

## James 2:15-26

# A Call to Practical Christianity

We have seen that our knowledge of God's Word alone *cannot* save us from premature physical death if what we know is not applied. Confidence in Christ results in the gift of eternal life, but an arsenal of unapplied biblical truth (faith) can not save us from divine discipline. James gave a perfect example:

> "*If a brother or sister is without clothing and in need of daily food, and one of you says to them, 'Go in peace, be warmed and be filled,' and yet you do not give them what is necessary for their body, what use is that?*" (**James 2:15-16**).

James is not the only one who stressed practical love. The apostle John underscored the same truth. "*But whoever has the world's goods, and sees his brother in need and closes his heart against him, how does the love of God abide in him? Little children, let us not love with word or with tongue, but in deed and truth*" (1 John 3:17-18).

The apostle did not imply that lack of compassion for the needy is a sign that the individual is not saved but is rather an expression of lack of practical love, or at best an indication of babyhood! The characteristics of babyhood in the human arena are evident, self-centeredness, hoarding, no sense of sharing and more. In the same way, born again believers in perpetual carnality or those who remain in spiritual babyhood cannot but display the traits of immaturity (Hebrews 5:13; 1 Corinthians 3:1-3).

Having indicted his Christian readers for not taking care of the needy among them, even though they knew what the Bible teaches about that (Deuteronomy 15:7), he elaborated upon his indictment of 2:15 with the following passage:

*"Even so faith [biblical truth, creed, belief], if it has no works [if it's not applied], is dead [stagnant, 'barren' useless], being by itself"* (James 2:17).

James knew his audience very well. He knew that they were too emotional, slow to hear and quick to respond. He had already told them to refrain from such (James 1:19). He paused and applied an ancient debaters' technique: assume the question your opponent will ask you, beat him to it by asking it first, and provide the answer before he has an opportunity. This is exactly what James did. He took a would-be question from someone's mouth and asked it first:

*"But someone may well say, 'You have faith [biblical truth] and I have works; show me your faith [biblical truth] without the works [application], and I will show you my faith [biblical truth] by my works"* (James 2:18).

Heavenly Father, we pause to offer You an overflowing basket of thanksgiving for the unsurpassed mentorship of Your Holy Spirit. Thank You for bringing us this far in our study. We are again at the crossroads of a difficult passage. Father-God, we humbly ask You to throw Your beam of light on this passage, and guide us to the path of accurate interpretation, in Christ's name. Amen.

*"You believe that God is one You do well; the demons also believe, and shudder"* (James 2:19).

Beloved of God, it's my conviction that the words of James 2:18-19, were not altogether the objector's. Many scholars agree. Those who take the opposing view, obviously compound the difficulty in its interpretation. Although there's no objector per se, James simply thought of how a careless Christian in his audience might wrongly react to his message. So he conversely dealt with the objector's would-be response beforehand. We need to settle the issue as to why I believe that verse 19:

*"You believe that God is one. You do well; [but remember] the demons also believe and shudder"* was not part of the objector's comments.

Here's what we imply if we take verse 19 to be the objector's: in essence, the objector would be saying,

> "James: your claim that an accumulation of biblical truth/doctrine **will** always manifest itself in good works is false. Let me prove you wrong: look at the demons; they had so much biblical truth/doctrine more than any of us. Let me demonstrate this with an obvious biblical truth/doctrine common to all of us: *'God is one.'* James, you know this doctrine. Ah, the demons know it too. That's their belief. In fact, they believe this doctrine long before man was created. But you see; their belief was not parallel to their evil works. Their knowledge of this truth never produced good works. In spite of their knowledge, that God is one, they rebelled against His authority with eternal ramification."

Oh, the objector would have been *dead* wrong. He would have demonstrated his ignorance to James' message. Hear me: Neither James nor any writer of Scripture for that matter ever implied nor claimed that an accumulation of biblical truth/doctrine **will** *always* manifest itself in good works. Nor do they ever imply that regeneration **will** *always* manifest itself in good works. The sublime truth is that *"God created [us] in Christ Jesus for good works"* (Ephesians 2:10); but He never said anywhere that good works is a proof of the genuineness of our new birth. We have a roadblock, the Sin Nature that indwells us (Romans 7:15-18). It makes our new life a spiritual battleground. The reality is that some believers take their new life seriously; others do not. The former are prudent in their walk with the Savior; these build *"with gold, silver, [and] precious stones"* (1 Corinthians 3:12). While the carnal ones build with garbage, *"wood, hay, [and] straw"* (1 Corinthians 3:12). Perpetual carnality marks their lifestyle, and often they are removed prematurely (11:30; cf. 1 John 5:16), but still are eternally saved (**1 Corinthians 3:15**). However, they will arrive in heaven empty handed (1 Corinthians 3:15). But those who have taken their new life seriously and built with gold, silver and precious stones will arrive in heaven with enormous rewards (2 Corinthians 5:10; Revelation 3:11, 22:12). This is the teaching of God's Word!

My beloved, listen; we cannot stress these essential points enough:

- James' epistle was addressed to a Christian audience (James 2:1).
- James never implied that faith and works are inseparably united. That's to say, he never implied that one cannot have faith without works.
- James' concern was not the eternal destiny of his Christian readers; rather their temporal judgment in time (1:13-15, 21, 5:19-20).
- James never implied that faith without works negates the believer's salvation from the lake of fire.
- James never implied that good works are evidence of regeneration.

---

**The thrust of James' message is simply this: a Christian who knows Scripture, but does not do what it says will soon face the Supreme Court of heaven head-on.**

---

Repeat: spiritual life is not automatic. It's an uphill battle; some make it to the top victoriously (1 Corinthians 3:14; cf. 2 Timothy 4:7-8) and others arrive in heaven as losers (1 Corinthians 3:15). The thrust of James' message is simply this: a Christian who knows Scripture, but does not do what it says will soon face the Supreme Court of heaven head-on, *"For if **we** [the author plus his Christian readers] go on sinning willfully after receiving the knowledge of the truth [doctrine], there no longer remains a sacrifice for sins [Jesus Christ will never be re-crucified as a sin offering, nor do we need to trust in Christ anew after each sinful failure; we simply confess our sins for restoration {1 John 1:9}], but a terrifying expectation of judgment and THE FURY OF A FIRE [INTENSIVE DISCIPLINE] WHICH WILL CONSUME THE ADVERSARIES [CARNAL BELIEVERS IN TIME]. Anyone [for instance,] who has set aside the Law of Moses dies without mercy on the testimony of two or three witnesses. How much severer punishment do you [Christians, including James' audience] think he [a born again believer] will deserve who has trampled under foot the Son of God, **and has regarded as unclean the blood of the covenant by which he [believer] was sanctified [once and*** *forever, Hebrews 10:10, 14) and has insulted the Spirit of grace?"* (Hebrews 10:26-29; cf. I Corinthians 5:1-5; 11:30; Proverbs 10:27).

What can be more terrifying? What the author of the book of Hebrews is saying is, "Though, we are eternally saved (Hebrews 10:10, 14), we cannot escape severe divine discipline in time, if we take our spiritual life for granted" (2:2-3). James endeavored to hammer the same message home. He pointed his audience to the result of an improper application of God's Word by the fallen angels, the demons, *"You believe that God is one. You do well; [but you shouldn't rely on this alone; remember] the demons also believe and shudder"* (James 2:19).

Having demonstrated that the words of James 2:19, were James', we return to the passage for more scrutiny: *"But someone may well say, 'You have faith and I have works; show me your faith without the works, and I will show you my faith by my works'"* (2:18). *"You believe that God is one. You do well; [but remember] the demons also believe and shudder"* (James 2:19).

Let it be known that James was not advocating brands of faith. He was not saying that demons had fake or non-saving faith. Because many had misunderstood our passage they coined the phrase *saving faith*. We have said it before; but it's worth repeating, there's no such thing as *saving faith*. Faith is faith. You apply it or you don't. Anyone who accepts (faith/trust) the substitutionary work of Christ on the cross to be absolutely true is saved instantly (John 20:31; Acts 4:4, 10:42-44). We have to follow James' logic in order to comprehend what he was trying to communicate. Throughout, his message had been directed to believers (James 2:1), *"the called and justified ones"* (2:7; cf. Romans 8:29). He had made it clear that faith (biblical truth) without application is useless. Through a rigorous examination of our passage, we have established the fact that the *"faith"* and the *"believe"* of James 2:18-19 were a reference to doctrine or biblical truth. We noted that great scholars, such men as Dibelius, James Orr, Zane Hodges, and Gaebelein, just to name a few, agreed. "The faith or belief is intellectual orthodoxy [i.e. doctrine]."[98] Consequently, James took a position of a-would be objector and handled the believer's objection accordingly, *"But someone may well say, 'You have faith and I have works; show me your faith without the works, and I will show you my faith by my works'"* (2:18).

This is a difficult passage. This every scholar agrees. Professor Hodges noted, "The exact extent and the meaning of the objector's words have long been a problem to commentators."[99] The good news, as Dr. Mitton points out, is that it does "not greatly affect our understanding of the main teaching of the passage."[100] As a result, he refused to "consider them in any great detail."[101] I concur with him. We must focus on the main teaching of the passage. Nevertheless, the objector seemed to hold a position that one can have faith and not have works, *"You have faith and I have works; show me your faith without the works, and I will show you my faith by my work."* In other words, the objector in essence was saying, "James, don't bother us with your lesson on works. Just because we are not manifesting any good works does not mean we don't know any doctrine." The objector, by stating this, showed that he had missed the thrust of James' message: a Christian who knows Scripture, but does not do what it says will soon face the Supreme Court of heaven head-on!

> *"For if we [the author plus his Christian readers] go on sinning willfully after receiving the knowledge of the truth [doctrine], there no longer remains a sacrifice for sins [Jesus Christ will never be re-crucified as a sacrifice, nor do we need to trust in Christ anew after each sinful failure; we simply confess our sins for restoration {1 John 1:9}], but a terrifying expectation of judgment and THE FURY OF A FIRE [INTENSIVE DISCIPLINE] WHICH WILL CONSUME THE ADVERSARIES [CARNAL BELIEVERS IN TIME..."* (Hebrews 10:26-29).

Because, the objector missed the main thrust of James' epistle, James replied, *"You believe that God is one. You do well; [but remember] the demons also believe and shudder"* (James 2:19). We concede; we do not know exactly what transpired in heaven between God and the host of the angelic beings. What we do know is that one third of all angelic creatures were sentenced to the lake of fire (Matthew 25:41). We ask, "Did God offer them the opportunity to accept Him as their Sovereign God, and a third rejected Him?" The Bible is silent on this. But what's clear is that Satan and a third of these creatures rebelled against God's authority with eternal ramifications (Isaiah 14:12-14; cf. Revelation 12:3-9; Matthew 25:41).

On the other hand, we can examine Scripture, and make an intelligent deduction. We know that God is *"eternal life"* (I John 5:20), and that His *"life"* is a prerequisite for spending eternity with Him (John 3:36; cf. I John 5:13). We also know that eternal life, by its very definition, is everlasting; it cannot be lost or shortened. No circumstance can shorten God's life. Based on this premise one can deduce that God gave His life to the angels who did not rebel against Him. This grace gift guaranteed them eternity in heaven. You ask, "How did you arrive at this conclusion?" Creation! Like Adam and Eve, Angels were created beings (Colossians 1:16). Adam and Eve did not have eternal life at creation. This is why the LORD simultaneously condemned and offered both a redemption solution for their sin-problem (Genesis 3:15). Had they possessed *eternal life* at the moment of creation, they would not have been condemned, let alone be offered salvation. The same would have been true of Satan. Had he possessed eternal life at creation, his rebellion would not have caused him to lose the life, which is everlasting.

## Responsibility of Practical Christianity

We ask, "What do believers and angels have in common?" Biblical truth or doctrine! For example James' audience and the host of the angelic beings know the doctrine of the oneness of God. We ask yet another question, "Since James did not have eternal salvation in mind, why did he compare his Christian audience with the demons?" He did so in order to point them to the consequences of misapplication of God's Word, and of trampling *"under foot the Son of God"* (Hebrews 10:29). He wanted his Christian readers not to have the illusion that knowledge without proper application can safeguard them from severe punishment. On this sobering truth, James recalled their memory to what happened to the demons: They believe in the doctrine of the oneness of God: *"God is one,"* but sadly, their belief did not prevent a third of these creatures from rebelling against God's authority with an eternal price. It's on this catastrophic note that James drew a vivid picture for his Christian audience to see: *"You believe that God is one. You do well; [but remember] the demons also believe and shudder"* (James 2:19).

Recapping (James 2:19), demons are versed in God's Word. They are also masters in distortion (Psalm 91:11; cf. Matthew 4:1-4)! They knew the phenomenal truth that *"God is one"*, long before man was created. Instead of worshiping the only God, in arrogance they wanted to be gods and for this they paid dearly (Isaiah 14:12-14; cf. Revelation 12:3-9). On this, James drew parallel lines to his Christian readers: "You do well. You are to be commended for grasping this biblical truth of monotheism. But remember, the demons also knew this truth; however it did not keep them from becoming arrogant. Hence, you too cannot be shielded from severe discipline in time (not in the eternal state, Romans 8:1, 37-39), if you failed to accurately apply the reservoir of biblical truth to your life's exigencies."

Why did James refer to demons in this passage? What do they have to do with his admonition? The truth of the matter is that the feeding of James' thoughts to employ this analogy is entirely the work of the Holy Spirit.

He did this for at least two reasons.

1. To let his readers hear the echo of James 2:14 loud and clear. The direct parallel of verse 2:14 with 2:24 is most interesting.
2. So that his audience may think twice before they trample God's Word under their feet.

Irresponsibility to God's Word carries with it severe punishment,

*For if the word spoken through angels [Mosaic Law, Acts 7:53] proved unalterable, and every transgression and disobedience received a just penalty [the right amount of punishment], how will we [believers in Christ, expect to] escape [same fate that befell the people of old] if we neglect so great a salvation?* (Hebrews 2:2-3).

---

**Irresponsibility to God's Word carries with it severe punishment.**

---

Having clarified the issue of God's justice in dealing with man, James continues the answer to the hypothetical question presented in verse 2:18.

214

*"But are you willing to recognize, you foolish fellow [now he is sarcastic], that faith [implanted word or creed] without works is useless?"* (James 2:20).

It cannot do you any good. Here in verse 20, he says, *"Faith without works is useless."* But when he gets to verse 26, he will substitute the word *dead* for the word *useless*: *"Faith without works is dead."* Same concept! Of course, the faith in question is biblical truth and not the so-called "saving faith." Simply, biblical truth without application is useless!

## Example of Practical Christianity

Let us take the next three verses together.

*Was not Abraham our father justified [experientially for reward] by works when he offered up Isaac his son on the altar? You see that faith was working with his works, and as a result of the works, faith was perfected; and the Scripture was fulfilled which says, "AND ABRAHAM BELIEVED GOD, AND IT WAS RECKONED TO HIM AS RIGHTEOUSNESS," and he was called the friend of God* (James 2:21-23).

We have already established the fact that salvation is not what James had in mind when he asked, *"Was not Abraham...justified by works...?"* Instead, what he had in mind was justification for a reward. Dibelius concurs: "Abraham is not considered a 'justified' sinner, but a righteous man who is recognized and rewarded by God."[102] Furthermore, Abraham's work was not the work of morality. It was a work of application of "the biblical truth" in his soul. You see, the work James is emphasizing is not the work of morality, which the apostle Paul maintains cannot save anyone (Galatians 2:16). Rather, it is synthesizing God's Word in our souls and applying it to every exigency of life.

## Application is Divine Works

It's fair to say that God considers our application of His Word as works! Divine work is superior to running around, sweating and doing the so-called "great things for Jesus" in the energy of the flesh, fueled by selfish ambition, egocentrism, competition and approbation lust.

Divine work is anything done under the influence of the Holy Spirit. It's right thinking, mixing the biblical truth in our souls with our actions to the praise of His glory! It's an action that's guided by the inward ministry of the Holy Spirit. Once more, James is in no way in conflict with the apostle Paul, who declared, "*By the works of the Law [morality] no flesh will be justified*" (Galatians 2:16).

We saw the perfect harmony that exists between James and Paul in chapter 1. But here in our passage, though in agreement in all matters of truth, they were on different topics, handling two types of justification. The apostle Paul is talking about works of morality being useless for salvation, and James speaks about works of application of "*the word implanted*" [biblical truth] for reward. Totally different concepts!

To solidify his dissertation, James goes on to say that Abraham's "faith was perfected." What does he mean? Was his initial faith (confidence) weak? If faith as small as a mustard seed can move a mountain, what faith are we talking about here? My beloved, James is simply saying, "The biblical truth in Abraham's soul was demonstrated to the maximum!" He applied what he knew about God to the highest level. As a result, he received an unsurpassed reward, a title that no one else has ever received, "*the friend of God.*"

## Dual Justification Revisited

In view of this, James goes on to explain the two kinds of justification.

> "*You see then that a man is [also] justified [experientially] by works [for reward], and not by faith [confidence in Christ for salvation] only*" (James 2:24, NKJV).

Here James reaches out with a heart of compassion and love to let his Christian audience know that there's more than just being saved from the eternal penalty of sin. In other words, salvation from the lake of fire is just one side of God's plan; reward is the other side! Basically, he is saying, "Look, my brethren, you need to get your spiritual act together so that you can realize to the fullest measure of God's plan for your life, namely super-abundant rewards" (cf. 1 Corinthians 2:9).

This amounts to double justification: *positional* for salvation, and *experiential* for reward! What James was saying to his readers is "My beloved brethren, do not forfeit experiential justification for reward!" So James and Paul did not even come close to contradicting one another. Again, Paul emphasized salvation, and James emphasized reward after salvation.

Recapping, what James is saying is this: "Listen, believers, no matter how you have failed, the potential for you to be a winner abounds. You can still be an exceptional believer like Abraham and Rahab. You too can have a special standing with God and receive an exceptional reward, like Abraham, who was called a 'friend of God'!"

James reminded his readers about Abraham, but he also wrote about Rahab's justification for reward, saying,

> "*In the same way, was not Rahab the harlot also justified [experientially] by works when she received the messengers and sent them out by another way?*" (James 2:25).

In contrast to Rahab's reward for great application, James in the following verse addresses the exact opposite—no application at all.

> "*For just as the body without the spirit is dead [useless], so also faith [biblical truth] without works [application] is dead [or useless]*" (James 2:26).

Let us review the following points as summary.

1. James' epistle is addressed to believers (James 2:1). We know this because James addressed his audience as family members, "*brethren*" or "*my beloved brethren,*" about fifteen times.

2. James' epistle focuses on practical and applied Christianity and its eternal ramifications—rewards or lack thereof.

3. James' epistle is not a dissertation on salvation, but rather on reward. James, like Paul, believes that salvation is a grace gift appropriated through grace (James 1:17-18; cf. Romans 6:23; Ephesians 2:8-9).

4. James is not saying that the so-called "saving faith" or "genuine faith" must produce works. We come to this conclusion in light of the fact that his audience were already saved but in prolonged carnality (James 2:1-3; 14-16; 4:1-4).

5. James is saying that though one is justified positionally by faith (confidence) alone for salvation, one can equally be justified experientially by works for an ultimate reward (James 2:24).

6. James warns that premature physical death is likely for a willful believer in a prolonged state of carnality (James 1:13-15; cf. 5:19-20).

7. James is teaching and exhorting believers to get engaged in applying all their knowledge of biblical truth into basic practical Christianity, as "actions speak louder than words."

No doubt about it! God's desire is for us to be fruitful. He wants us to be conformed to the image of His Son, representing Him in all His glory. That's His plan! This is the message James wants to convey to his readers. So my beloved, it's my heartfelt prayer that the truth delineated so far would impact your theology and life's experiences.

"[James'] teaching is a greatly needed corrective to the unreal, verbalistic kind of religion that claims allegiance to high doctrine but issues in living on a low and selfish level."[103] This clear biblical insight wraps up James chapter 2. Before we leave let us look at two examples of Exceptional Reward.

SEVENTEEN

# Exceptional Reward for the Exceptional Believer

God's justice plays a role both in our salvation and reward. This is the sublime truth James was seeking to communicate.

- The sinner is declared righteous upon his faith alone in Christ alone (Romans 5:1).

- The believer is justified or declared worthy of reward, both in time and in eternity, when he grows spiritually and applies the Word of God to the maximum.

Theologically, this can be referred to as *experiential justification*. This is where James' references to Abraham's justification fits perfectly: *"Was not Abraham our father justified by works [for a reward] when he offered up Isaac his son on the altar?"* (James 2:21).

The Bibles gives us examples of those who received justification for reward. Here we examine two exceptional believers, Abraham and Rahab, who received exceptional rewards..

## Abraham

Remember, this is not the only test Abraham had as a believer. There were other tests worthy of our consideration. Abraham had at least three obvious tests in his life, as we saw in chapter 9. As a baby believer, he failed to properly handle two of these tests, as we noted. The backdrop for the first test is in Genesis 12:1-3 where God promised to make him a great nation and bless all on earth through him. Soon afterward, there was a famine in his land, so he headed to

Egypt for food. En route, being a baby believer, he told his wife to lie, to say that she was his sister, for fear of his own life (12:11-13). Fear was the source of his failure! He was an immature believer. The apostle John tells us, "*There is no fear in love; but perfect love [a reference to maturity] casts out fear, because fear involves punishment, and the one who fears is not perfected in love [is not yet matured]*" (1 John 4:18).

As a baby believer, Abraham was unable to properly process and synthesize God's promise to him. He was unable to come to the conclusion that God would not let go of him until He had fulfilled His promise to him (Genesis 28:15; cf. Acts 13:36). He should have concluded, "Look; God had made a promise to me, which, because of who and what He is, must be fulfilled no matter what!"

On another occasion, God promised Abraham a son directly from Sarah. But Abraham could not wait—he succumbed to the sin of impatience. He literally tried to help God fulfill His promise; He slept with Hagar, Sarah's maid (Genesis 16:2-4). We ask, what kind of work are the sins of fear and impatience? Was Abraham not genuinely saved then? Of course he was saved! "*Then he believed in the LORD [Yahweh]; and He reckoned it to him as righteousness*" (Genesis 15:6).

Finally came the testing that James alluded to in our passage. It was an ultimate test tailored for an extraordinary believer who had reached spiritual maturity. God told Abraham to go to Mount Moriah and offer his precious son as a sacrifice to Him. Remember, the Lord had made a promise to Abraham that the world would be blessed through Isaac (Genesis 21:12). En route, his son asked his father a heartbreaking question: "*[Dad], behold, the fire and the wood, but where is the lamb for the burnt offering?*" (Genesis 22:7).

With absolute confidence, his father replied, "*God will provide*" (22:8). What a mature believer!

At the base of the mount, Abraham told his servants, "*Stay here with the donkey, and I and the lad will go over there; and **we will worship and return to you**"* (Genesis 22:5). In essence Abraham was saying, "Young men, wait for us here. I will offer my son as God commanded, but when I am finished, we [Abraham and his resuscitated son] will return!" Here is Abraham's magnificent display of faith; the biblical truth in his soul, or, as James calls it, the word implanted, is revealed for everyone to see!

Just like Job demonstrated the power of the Word in his own soul when he was tested, so did Abraham. Once matured, Abraham became confident *"that what God had promised, He was able also to perform"* (Romans 4:21).

How do we know Abraham's state of mind when he lifted his knife to plunge it into his son Isaac? The author of Hebrews reveals,

> *By faith [by means of biblical truth residence in his soul] Abraham, when he was tested, offered up Isaac, and he who had received the promises was offering up his only begotten son; it was he to whom it was said, "IN ISAAC YOUR DESCENDANTS SHALL BE CALLED." He considered that God is able to raise people even from the dead, from which he also received him back as a type* (Hebrews 11:17-19).

What an application of *"the word implanted"*! Abraham was totally convinced that God would not let go of his son Isaac until He had fulfilled the promise made through him! It was at this juncture that he was justified experientially to be awarded an extraordinary honor, the ultimate title *"the friend of God"* (James 2:23).

Because of his promotion, Abraham received the super-abundant blessings that accompany his title. But it took time for Abraham to reach the height of spiritual maturity.

> *Then the angel of the LORD [Yahweh] called to Abraham a second time from heaven, and said, "...because you have done this thing [applied My Word to the maximum] and have not withheld your son, your only son, indeed I will greatly bless you, and I will greatly multiply your seed as the stars of the heavens and as the sand which is on the seashore; and your seed shall possess the gate of their enemies"* (Genesis 22:15-17).

Abraham is not the only example the Bible offers. To make sure his intended message was clear, James gave one more example.

## Rahab

James wanted to illustrate that, while salvation delivers us from the eternal penalty of sin, there is more that follows. God wants to transfer rewards, held in His estate, to us as an inheritance. But we must be justified experientially, by maximum application of His Word, before we receive them.

James presented Rahab as more evidence to prove his case for reward after salvation. *"In the same way, was not Rahab the harlot also justified by works when she received the messengers and sent them out by another way?"* (James 2:25)

To settle any ambiguity about which Rahab he was referring to, James qualified her as *"the harlot."* This establishes her as the Rahab of the city of Jericho in the Old Testament. There were a number of women in the Old Testament who applied the Word of God in a remarkable way, for example, Esther and Deborah. But why did the Holy Spirit impress upon James to use Rahab? He did so for at least two reasons:

- To emphasize the grace of God
- To demonstrate reward resulting from application of biblical knowledge

The story of Rahab (in Joshua 2:1-13) highlights the grace of God. James was telling his readers, "Listen; no matter how we have failed in life, past and present, if we respond to God, His grace can, and will, overcome our failures." Imagine! Rahab, a well-known prostitute, experienced God's grace in two areas: positional justification by confidence alone in Yahweh alone for eternal life, and experiential justification[104] by application of the "word implanted" in her soul. God rewarded her immeasurably. She and her family were spared when the Jews destroyed their city (Joshua 6:22-25) because she honored the Lord by demonstrating the power of application of God's Word. He made her royalty. Think of it! She was in the lineage of the King of kings, our Savior Jesus Christ (Matthew 1:5). Talk about grace!

So James asks, *"In the same way, was not Rahab the harlot also justified [experientially] by works...?"* What type of justification is James talking about? And what kind of work? We know that Rahab was not justified for salvation by works, because that would make Galatians 2:16 null and void: "*By the works of the Law no flesh will be justified.*" Rahab, like Abraham, had already placed her faith (confidence) in Yahweh and thus was clothed with God's righteousness (Genesis 15:6; cf. Romans 3:22). Read her testimony: "*For we have heard how the LORD [Yahweh] dried up the water of the Red Sea before you when you came out of Egypt [faith comes by hearing, Romans 10:17]...for the LORD your God, He [alone] is God in heaven above and on earth beneath [her faith/trust switched to on mode toward Yahweh]*" (Joshua 2:10-11, cf. 1 John 5:1).

We have the expression of her faith (confidence) even before the spies sent by Joshua came to her house. Later she expressed her loyalty to God and risked her life by hiding the spies. "*Even the righteousness of God through faith in Jesus Christ [Yahweh] for all those who believe; for there is no distinction*" (Romans 3:22; cf. 1 John 5:1).

Rahab also shows what application of God's Word implanted can accomplish. Reward! Her experiential justification then was based on her "works" of application of the "word implanted" in her soul.

My beloved, listen carefully: If she had not applied what she knew with regard to the omnipotent, sovereign God and had not hidden those spies, regrettably the "implanted word" in her soul, though impressive, would not have saved her from the calamity that fell upon her city.

Her salvation, in James' mind, is *not* from the lake of fire but from the immediate danger from the destruction of her city. With this illumination, read afresh James 2:14: "*What use is it, my brethren, if someone says he has faith [biblical truth] but he has no works [application]? Can that faith [literally 'the faith,' i.e., accumulated biblical truth] save him [from premature physical death]?*" (James 2:14). Herein is the truth.

May the spiritual life and biblical application of both Abraham and Rahab be an encouragement to us all.

\* \* \*

Beloved, let's pause here and review all the critical points we have learned so far. We have seen how James' love, concern and passion for his brethren was expressed in the first two chapters of his epistle.

- The importance of patience in suffering (James 1:2-4)
- Sin and its consequences (James 1:13-15)
- Restoration to fellowship (James 1:21)
- Study and application of the Word of God (James 1:22)
- The evil of showing favoritism to the rich (James 2:1-6)
- Biblical knowledge without application bringing discipline (James 2:14-16)
- Extraordinary reward for maximum application of God's Word (James 2:17, 21-26)

James then began another topic that he felt strongly about: the use of the tongue. Why did James choose this particular topic? To steer his readers away from the eternal bar of justice for misuse of their tongues. This principle is most important for us to understand today.

James knew that God's judgment for the improper use of our tongues can be swift and decisive: "*Death and life are in the power of the tongue*" (Proverbs 18:21). "*Who is the man who desires life And loves length of days that he may see good? Keep your tongue from evil And your lips from speaking deceit. Depart from evil and do good; Seek peace and pursue it*" (Psalm 34:12-14).

James probably realized that most of the unbearable suffering his readers were going through might have been linked to misuse of their tongues. This insight could have intensified his heartfelt anguish for his brethren, who were becoming casualties on the spiritual battleground.

All along, James had been so concerned with their lack of fruit bearing "*to the praise of His glory*," knowing much of their tremendous suffering was self-induced. His concern was so great that it is the over-arching theme of the entire epistle. For example:

Chapter 1: James alerted his readers that habitual sinning can lead a believer to premature physical death (1:13-15).

Chapter 2: James cautioned them that knowledge of God's Word without application cannot save anyone from judgment of premature physical death (2:14).

Chapter 3: James chastised them on the issue of an uncontrollable tongue and its consequences.

Chapter 4: James reprimanded them for their infidelity to God (4:1-4) and urge them to turn back to Him by means of acknowledgment of their sins to God. He pled with them earnestly to rebuild the bridge of their relationship with God through the study and application of His Word (4:7-10).

Chapter 5: James passion, love and concern for his brethren came in full force. He closed his dissertation with a message of hope for those who have failed. "*My brethren, if any among you strays from the truth [backslides] and one turns him back [helps him to recover], let him know that he who turns a sinner from the error of his way will save his soul [life] from [premature physical] death and will cover a multitude of sins*" (James 5:19-20).

In that passage he strongly urged a few who were spiritually on course to help those who were not avoid the imminent judgment that would result in an untimely death (Proverbs 10:27).

No doubt the Holy Spirit guided James in choosing his next subject: the tongue. This is not a coincidence, for there is no coincidence or accident in God's plan. This topic was pertinent to James' audience and to those in every age, for premature death shortens one's life. "*The fear of the LORD prolongs life, But the years of the wicked will be shortened*" (Proverbs 10:27).

## EIGHTEEN

James 3:1-12
# The Power of the Tongue

*Let not many of you become teachers, my brethren, knowing that as such we will incur a stricter judgment [literally "greater condemnation"]. For we all stumble in many ways. If anyone does not stumble in what he says, he is a perfect man, able to bridle the whole body as well. Now if we put the bits into the horses' mouths so that they will obey us, we direct their entire body as well. Look at the ships also, though they are so great and are driven by strong winds, are still directed by a very small rudder wherever the inclination of the pilot desires. So also the tongue is a small part of the body, and yet it boasts of great things. See how great a forest is set aflame by such a small fire! And the tongue is a fire, the very world of iniquity; the tongue is set among our members as that which defiles the entire body, and sets on fire the course of our life, and is set on fire by hell* (James 3:1-6).

A misuse of our tongues is one of the causes for premature physical death: "*Death and life are in the power of the tongue, And those who love it will eat its fruit*" (Proverbs 18:21). "*A soothing tongue is a tree of life, But perversion in it crushes the spirit*" (Proverbs 15:4; cf. Proverbs 13:3; Psalm 39:1; Proverbs 12:13).

As we look into our passage we will rely entirely on the Holy Spirit for enlightenment, for as you can see, it's very difficult to link the ending of James 2, "*Faith without works is dead*" with the beginning of James 3, "*Let not many of you become teachers.*"

Though some scholars believe chapter 3 is a continuation of James' previous work in chapter 2, Dibelius disagrees: "There is no indication of connection between this section and the preceding treatise."[105] Hence, the attempt to establish a connection in spite of everything inevitably leads to an artificiality in the exegesis."[106]

The main issue in the epistle of James is a warning against indifference to the application of the Word of God. To underscore the gravity of our topic, in six verses alone (James 3:1-6) James alluded to Old Testament Scripture at least seven times (Psalm 32:9; 12:3; 73:8; 120:2, 3; Proverbs 16:27; 26:20) and to our Lord's teachings four times (Matthew 12:36; 15:11, 18; 5:22).

Make no mistake, my beloved; sin is sin before God, no matter how little. Nonetheless, there are certain sins that have greater ramifications than others. The sin of the tongue is one of these. The punishment for this sin is impending and often swift! This is because the sin of the tongue destroys not only us but also others. A venomous tongue has enough poison to destroy an entire assembly of believers. This is one reason why the sin of the tongue made the list of the seven sins that God abhors. As Solomon wrote, "*There are...seven [sins] which are an abomination to [God]: Haughty eyes, a lying tongue*" (Proverbs 6:16-17).

Maybe this is why the Holy Spirit, in His infinite wisdom, brought this subject into focus for James' readers. His readers are already guilty of spiritual infidelity (James 4:4). It makes sense to infer that they must also be guilty of the sins of the tongue. These James admonished, "*My brethren, these things [sins of tongue] ought not to be this way*" (James 3:10).

This brings us to the first increment of James chapter 3.

## Impact of False Teaching

James was a genius and a disciplined Bible teacher. As a skillful communicator, he knew the implication of the subject at hand, and he understood that if the issue of the tongue was not handled with great care and wisdom, the hearts of his readers could be hardened, making them even more callous and indifferent to God. Therefore he tactically took the first issue, "teachers," and tackles it head-on: "*Let not many of you become teachers, my brethren, knowing that as such we will incur a stricter judgment [literally 'greater condemnation']*" (James 3:1).

James addressed teachers because they have the potential to shape man's ideology and direction. We have all seen the influential power of a teacher. We have some examples to share.

There are over one billion followers of Islam in the world today. This is because of the philosophy of one man, Mohammed. There are millions of Mormons across the globe; this is the result of the influence of one teacher, Joseph Smith. The same is true of Jehovah's Witnesses. These are just a few in the area of religion; what about the sphere of secularism? What about the daunting impact of Charles Darwin's theory of evolution? The list could go on.

Simply, teachers have the potential to influence how one thinks. This explains why James wasted no time introducing the subject of teachers.

When we read "*Let not many of you become teachers,*" it appears as if James was giving them a mandate to not take teaching positions if they didn't have that spiritual gift or if they were ill prepared. Though it does encompass that idea, it is much stronger, because a careful examination of the text shows they were already engaged in teaching. With regard to the Greek construction of this passage, Dr. Arnold Fruchtenbaum remarks, "A negative imperative in the present tense, *be not* implies that there was movement by many to become teachers, this must now be stopped."[107]

In essence, James is saying to these believers, "Stop the ongoing ambition and practice of everyone wanting an audience of listeners in your local assemblies!"

James' concern for his audience of fellow believers is in view. He wants to ensure the salvation of both the teachers and their hearers. By salvation, or *soteria* in the Greek, we do not mean salvation from eternal damnation, but from the judgment of premature physical death. That's how the apostle Paul used the word in his exhortation to Timothy: "*Pay close attention to yourself and to your teaching [he is talking to a fellow believer]; persevere in these things, for as you do this you will ensure salvation [from judgment in time] both **for yourself** and for **those who hear you**"* (1 Timothy 4:16 emphasis added).

What we teach, if inaccurate, can result in stricter judgment for ourselves and less for our hearers (Revelation 2:19-25; cf. Luke 12:47-48).

Recall, his readers were already involved in lifestyles unworthy of their spiritual birth. As a concerned shepherd and teacher, James sought to correct this. He wished to lead them away from a lifestyle of carnality and thus save them from severe discipline from the Supreme Court of Heaven, as we shall see in James 5:19-20.

We cannot overemphasize the impact of false teaching in a local church. No doubt about that! We see this all the time! One example of this is seen in our Lord's chastisement of the church at Thyatira. To this church our Lord, through the apostle John, charges,

> *"I know your deeds, and your love and faith and service and perseverance, and that your deeds of late are greater than at first. But I have this against you [as My church], that you tolerate the woman Jezebel, who calls herself a prophetess, and she teaches and leads My bond-servants [ministers] astray so that they commit acts of immorality and eat things sacrificed to idols. I gave her time to repent, and she does not want to repent of her immorality. Behold, I will throw her on a bed of sickness, and those who commit adultery with her into great tribulation, unless they repent of her deeds [grace before judgment]. And I will kill her children [believers who have subscribed to her teachings] with pestilence [literally 'death'],[108] and all the churches will know that I am He who searches the minds and hearts; and I will give to each one of you according to your deeds. But I say to you, the rest who are in Thyatira, who do not hold this teaching, who have not known the deep things of Satan, as they call them—I place no other burden on you. Nevertheless what you have, hold fast until I come"* (Revelation 2:19-25).

Question: Are the recipients of the above passage born-again believers? Absolutely, yes! The church of Thyatira consisted of members of the Royal Family of God! Another question: Was Jezebel a believer? Yes! She was!

> *"But I have this against you, that you tolerate the woman Jezebel [a believer], who calls herself a prophetess, and she teaches and*

*leads My bond-servants astray so that they commit acts of immorality and eat things sacrificed to idols. I gave her time to repent, and she does not want to repent of her immorality"* (Revelation 2:20-21).

Note: The Lord's call to her was not for her to "*repent*" (change her mind) and "*believe*" in Christ, as in Mark 1:15, but "*to repent of her immorality.*" We know that salvation is not based on one's repentance from immorality but rather by faith alone in Christ alone (Romans 3:28). Furthermore, the Lord never referred to her as a daughter of "*perdition*" (John 17:12), which would indicate an unsaved one.

"*Behold, I will throw her on a bed of sickness [severe discipline], and those [other believers] who commit adultery with her into great tribulation, unless they repent of her deeds [change their minds and attitudes]*" (Revelation 2:22). Her punishment would be on the basis of her false teaching! "*Let not many of you become teachers, my brethren, knowing that as such we will incur a stricter judgment [literally 'greater condemnation']*" (James 3:1).

As we have seen, a believer can be immoral to the core! The sooner we are settled with this biblical truth, the better positioned we shall be to understand James' epistle in its entirety.

Just as our Lord charged the church at Thyatira, the apostle Paul had earlier rebuked the Corinthian believers:

*It is actually reported that there is immorality among you, and immorality of such a kind as does not exist even among the Gentiles [unbelievers], that someone [a believer] has his father's wife. You have become arrogant and have not mourned instead [an indictment], so that the one who had done this deed would be removed from your midst* (1 Corinthians 5:1-2).

We see both the Lord's and Paul's indictments were directed to believers in Christ. As for the incestuous man, the apostle used his apostolic authority to hand him over "*to Satan for the destruction of his flesh, that his spirit may be saved in the day of the Lord Jesus*" (1 Corinthians 5:5).

In view of the apostle's certainty of the incestuous man's ultimate salvation, one concludes that his eternal destiny was not in question. This individual, at the point of his faith in Christ (1 John 5:1), was saved *"once for all"* (Hebrews 10:10). His failure, as Paul indicated, can only call for maximum discipline for his flesh, not his soul! This, my beloved, is a sound biblical teaching! We ought to check our preconceived notions at the doors of our souls. We must accept Scripture for what it is: God's Word and not ours!

You see, the question is not if believers live in extreme carnality, because they can and often do, as the epistle of James reveals. The real question is, does God ignore this? Does He look the other way? The answer is emphatically *No!* But He exhibits His judgment in grace:

- First, God pursues those in prolonged carnality with warning discipline. He sent messengers again and again (2 Chronicles, 36:15-16 cf. Hebrews 12:6; I Corinthians 11:30a; Revelation 3:19).

- Second, if God's grace warning is ignored, ultimately a premature physical death comes as His last resort. *"For this reason [prolonged carnality] many [born-again believers] among you are weak and sick, and a number sleep [untimely death].* ***But if we judged ourselves rightly [1 John 1:9], we would not be judged [grace highlighted]"*** (1 Corinthians 11:30-31; cf. Proverbs 29:1; 2 Chronicles 36:16).

This prepares us to take up another issue for examination.

## A Stricter Judgment

James, in our passage, is not trying to discourage believers from sharing their faith on a one-to-one basis. In fact, teaching is part of the Great Commission: *"Go therefore and make disciples...teaching them to observe all that I commanded you"* (Matthew 28:19-20). Based on this, every believer-ambassador should make it a point of duty to master basic truths so he can share his faith with others (1 Peter 3:15; cf. Hebrews 5:12). What James was warning against is untrained, ungifted teachers who lack the filling of the Holy Spirit mounting podiums wherever there is an audience, their motive is often to bring glory to self, not to God.

James is not alone; the apostle Paul charged, *"For some men, straying from these things [biblical truth], have turned aside to fruitless discussion, wanting to be teachers of the Law, even though they do not understand either what they are saying or the matters about which they make confident assertions"* (1 Timothy 1:6-7).

The apostle Peter also refers to these impulsive teachers as *"untaught and unstable"* (2 Peter 3:16). In view of this, he warned believers to be on guard, *"so that you are not carried away by the error of unprincipled men and fall from your own steadfastness"* (2 Peter 3:17).

So James exhorted, *"Let not many of you become teachers, my brethren, knowing that as such we will incur a stricter judgment"* (James 3:1). Here he stated his reason why his hearers, if they had no spiritual gift of communication and were untrained for the task, should have avoided the temptation of mounting a podium. This is a warning for all communicators, trained or untrained, for every teacher who interprets God's Word incorrectly will incur *"a stricter judgment."* God holds teachers to a higher standard regarding the correct interpretation of Scripture, because their words influence the spiritual life of all who hear them.

With reference to this *"stricter judgment,"* Arnold Fruchtenbaum takes the position that the judgment in question "will occur at the Judgment Seat of Christ."[109] This is the position taken by many citing James' use of present tense. Present tense can be tomorrow or a thousand years to come, but there is nothing in the text to suggest that the judgment would be deferred until the Judgment Seat of Christ, where the believer will be evaluated for reward or lack of it.

But more than that, what weighed heavily on James' mind was judgment in time. Remember, there is no pain in the eternal state (Revelation 21:4). All discipline, suffering and pain are for time and will terminate when we are face-to-face with the King of glory. So God will deal with carnal believers severely here and now and not later. The author of Hebrews painted this picture vividly:

*For if the word spoken through angels [Mosaic Law, Acts 7:53] proved unalterable, and every transgression and disobedience received a just penalty, how will we escape if we neglect so great a*

233

*salvation? After it was at the first spoken through the Lord, it was confirmed to us by those who heard* (Hebrews 2:2-3).

This is what the author of Hebrews is saying: "If the offenders of the Mosaic Law received severe punishment in time, how do we, as Christians, think we can escape judgment in time if we trample under feet the Word of Christ passed unto us through the apostles?" There is no escaping! With this in mind, we can read afresh the words of our Lord: "*I gave her time to repent, and she does not want to repent of her immorality. Behold, I will throw her on a bed of sickness [imminent judgment in time], and those who commit adultery with her into great tribulation, unless they repent of her deeds [grace before judgment]*" (Revelation 2:21-22).

We can't say this enough: Discipline for believers is on planet Earth. That explains why the apostle Paul voiced his concern regarding believers who no longer subscribe to sound teaching. To Timothy he said these had "*suffered shipwreck in regard to their faith*" (1 Timothy 1:19). Is that all? No, with his apostolic authority he pronounced judgment: "*Among these are Hymenaeus and Alexander, whom I have handed over to Satan, so that they will be taught not to blaspheme*" (1 Timothy 1:20).

The apostle Peter used the same authority in sending Ananias and Sapphira to an early grave (Acts 5:1-10). Their lies against The Holy Spirit sent them to an instant death. Chilling is indeed the right word for their fates! So, James' concern is for judgment in time as well as loss of reward at the Judgment Seat of Christ.

## Controlling the Tongue

"*For we all stumble in many ways. If anyone does not stumble in what he says, he is a perfect [mature] man, able to bridle the whole body as well*" (James 3:2). Here James highlights man's imperfection: "*For we all stumble in many ways.*" When he includes himself in the list of those who still stumble, he further underscores the fact that there's no such thing as sinless perfection! Mitton concurs: "Complete mastery over evil and total freedom from sin is not found in human life. If sin cannot work its way in by any other means it can gain entry into a man's spoken words. That at any rate is James' experience."[110]

James does not condone habitual sinning. One of the hallmarks of spiritual maturity is one's ability to control his tongue in such a way that it does not do harm to both himself and others. Dr. Fruchtenbaum says that James "refers to an individual who consistently does not stumble in word as one who has reached a goal of spiritual maturity."[111]

James now goes all out, painting a graphic picture of the power of tongue and its poisonous ramifications. Let's hang the painted picture of our passage where everyone can see it clearly:

> *For we all stumble in many ways. If anyone does not stumble in what he says, he is a perfect man, able to bridle the whole body as well. Now if we put the bits into the horses' mouths so that they will obey us, we direct their entire body as well. Look at the ships also, though they are so great and are driven by strong winds, are still directed by a very small rudder wherever the inclination of the pilot desires. So also the tongue is a small part of the body, and yet it boasts of great things. See how great a forest is set aflame by such a small fire! And the tongue is a fire, the very world of iniquity; the tongue is set among our members as that which defiles the entire body, and sets on fire the course of our life, and is set on fire by hell. For every species of beasts and birds, of reptiles and creatures of the sea, is tamed and has been tamed by the human race. But no one can tame the tongue; it is a restless evil and full of deadly poison* (James 3:2-8).

We would be remiss if we failed to acknowledge the great work of theological scholars who, for centuries, worked to cast light on this passage. However, the difficulties that many good Bible teachers had in interpreting this should be noted. Its interpretation has not been straightforward. We want to back up a bit and begin with a pair of new eyes to look closely at our subject and carefully analyze James' work from top to bottom and back again.

Let us keep this question in mind as we go along: What is the heart of James' message to his readers? With this question in front of us, we read afresh James' words, "*For we all stumble in many ways. If anyone does not stumble in what he says, he is a perfect [mature] man, able to bri-*

*dle the whole body as well"* (James 3:2). We have noted that one's ability to consistently control one's tongue is a true mark of spiritual maturity. But then comes what seems to be an apparent contradiction:

*"But no one can tame the tongue; it is a restless evil and full of deadly poison"* (**James 3:8**).

No human being has the ability to control the tongue. Mitton says, "It [the tongue] is always liable to break out."[112] Tasker agrees, "It is never sufficiently at rest for it to be brought fully under control."[113] So, can a believer control his tongue? Yes! But it takes the power of the Holy Spirit.

How long can a person control his tongue? It depends on one's level of spiritual growth. James' audience had the indwelling of the Holy Spirit (James 4:5). They had the power necessary to control the tongue. To clarify his point James employs two superb analogies: *"Now if we put the bits into the horses' mouths so that they will obey us, we direct their entire body as well. Look at the ships also, though they are so great and are driven by strong winds, are still directed by a very small rudder wherever the inclination of the pilot desires"* (James 3:3-4).

What is the essence of these two parallelisms, if James thought the tongue was uncontrollable? What James is saying is simply this: "What bits are to horses and rudders are to ships—that is what the Holy Spirit is to the believer who submits to His controlling power!" On the other hand, if left uncontrolled, *"the tongue is a fire," "a restless evil and full of deadly poison."* It burns; it poisons and is a bullet used to destroy!

Every believer has God-given power to control their tongue; consequently, God, in His justice, holds everyone accountable who misuses it as a deadly instrument. In view of this, the Psalmist asked, *"Who is the man who desires life And loves length of days that he may see good? Keep your tongue from evil, And your lips from speaking deceit. Depart from evil and do good; Seek peace and pursue it"* (Psalm 34:12-14).

King Solomon added, *"Death and life are in the power of the tongue, And those who love it will eat its fruit"* (Proverbs 18:21).

God mandates, *"Keep your tongue from evil,"* which means that the believer has the enabling power to control his tongue. Obviously, God does expect us to do what is not doable. He has provided us with the power to bridle our tongues. He expects us to use it.

One must appreciate James' message, having witnessed the spiritual life of his audience. They were already on the path of perpetual carnality, as we saw earlier from James' series of indictments. His readers were no longer "*a fragrance of Christ to God among those who are being saved and among those who are perishing*" (2 Corinthians 2:15). Their tongues had become as deadly poison, to themselves, to other members of the body of Christ, and to their community at large.

"*The tongue is set among our members as that which defiles the entire body, and sets on fire the course of our life, and is set on fire by hell*" (James 3:6). The detrimental effects of a misused tongue are terrifying! Many churches have been ruined by judging, maligning, gossiping and slandering members. The truth is, God will hold you and me responsible for the destructive words we utter. Our Lord was emphatic: "*I tell you, on the day of judgment men will render account for every careless word they utter; for by your words you will be justified, and by your words you will be condemned*" (Matthew 12:36-37 RSV).

Solomon compared one who gossips to wood; what wood is to a fire, a gossiper is to an assembly: "*For lack of wood the fire goes out; and where there is no whisperer [gossiper], quarreling ceases*" (Proverbs 26:20, RSV).

The next time you find yourself in the midst of a quarrel, stop and ask yourself, "Am I the one fueling this discord by being involved in gossip, backbiting and such?" If so, cease, before God lowers His boom of judgment.

Unfortunately, the believers to whom James was writing had become hearers only, who deluded themselves. James uses a series of analogies to illustrate that the misuse of their tongues was inconsistent with their status as believers.

"*Does a fountain send out from the same opening both fresh and bitter water? Can a fig tree, my brethren, produce olives, or a vine produce figs? Nor can salt water produce fresh*" (**James 3:11-12**).

There has been more debate on what this passage really means. One raises a question, "Does it mean that the tongue of a born-again believer can never say anything unholy?" Hardly! That's not what James was saying.

We should factor in his inclusion of himself as one of those who occasionally stumbles: "*For we [James plus other believers] all stumble in many ways*" (James 3:2). No one can doubt for a moment that James was born again. Nor can we say that he had a "head belief," based on his admission of faults. What's more, James was aware of Old Testament Scripture: "*Indeed, there is not a righteous man on earth who continually does good and who never sins*" (Ecclesiastes 7:20).

We ask, "If James is not advocating sinless perfection, what then does he mean by these analogies? A fountain cannot simultaneously send out fresh and bitter water. In fact, the Greek construction of James' question demands a negative answer: No, it cannot.

Even James himself occasionally faltered. So, what then is he talking about? Not to demean the needful work of grammatical syntax, but no amount of syntax of this verse alone can cast light on what James is saying. One has to honestly and humbly submit to the Author of Scripture, the Holy Spirit, for an illumination of His Word. To understand James, we must go outside our passage and consider the whole realm of the Word of God. In light of this, we shall examine the two natures that characterize a born-again believer.

## Two Natures

What James is saying can be explained. Every believer has two natures, one inherited at birth, and the other imputed at the point of regeneration. The apostle Paul calls the first "*the old self*" (Ephesians 4:22) and the latter "*the new self*" (Ephesians 4:24). It is equally critical to our study to know that every believer is controlled by two independent, influential powers: the sin nature or the Holy Spirit. When a believer is under the control of the sin nature, the believer can only exhibit the work of the flesh in all its ugliness (Galatians 5:19-21). But when he is under the influence of the Holy Spirit, the individual can only reflect the character of God. Based on this illumination, we can confidently say that there are two fountains, per James' analogy, indwelling or built into every believer, one bitter and poisonous—the old sin nature (Romans 7:17) and the other life-giving and life-refreshing—the Holy Spirit (James 4:5).

This is how the system works: The sin nature is the source of personal sins, including sins of the tongue. Hence when a believer fails, his sin automatically shuts off the power of the Holy Spirit. In other words, sin ruptures our fellowship with God and shuts off the influential, awesome power of the Holy Spirit in our souls. At this point our soul is controlled by the sin nature. Fellowship or filling of the Holy Spirit is restored when we acknowledge our sin to God (1 John 1:9). What James is saying in a nutshell is this: "One cannot be under the influence of the Holy Spirit and at the same time say nor do things unpleasing to God. Impossible!" That's what the apostle John had in mind when he affirmed, "*No one who abides in Him [is controlled by the Holy Spirit] sins*" (1 John 3:6). Our Lord sets the tone: "*He who abides in Me and I in him [fellowship], he bears much fruit*" (John 15:5). In other words, once a believer is under the influence of the Holy Spirit, the fruit of the Holy Spirit blossoms: "*love, joy, peace, patience, kindness, goodness, faithfulness, gentleness, self-control; against such things there is no law*" (Galatians 5:22-23).

Alternatively, in order for one to serve Satan's agenda—with his mind, actions or tongue—one has to temporarily lose or shut off the influential power of the Holy Spirit in his soul through sin. Sadly, this is the condition of many of the recipients of James' epistle, whom he labeled "*adulteresses*" (James 4:4). They had shut off the power of the Holy Spirit in their lives. Through unconfessed sin they had grieved (Ephesians 4:30) and quenched the Holy Spirit (1 Thessalonians 5:19) and had remained in a state of prolonged carnality. Even though they gathered for worship, their worship fit our Lord's indictment perfectly: "*THIS PEOPLE HONORS ME WITH THEIR LIPS, BUT THEIR HEART IS FAR AWAY FROM ME. BUT IN VAIN DO THEY WORSHIP ME*" (Mark 7:6-7).

\* \* \*

With this insight, James ends his dissertation on their tongues and thus appeals to his readers' consciences:

*"With it we bless our Lord and Father, and with it we curse men, who have been made in the likeness of God; from the same mouth come both blessing and cursing. My brethren, these things ought not to be this way"* (**James 3:9-10**).

Now we can see the irony of James' message, *"My brethren, these things ought not to be this way."* In essence, he is saying, "My beloved brethren, no one would deny the fact that both fountains within us, holy and unholy, converge in our tongue. We should be consistent in running the water of the fountain of life, whereby the fruit of the Holy Spirit abounds." Reduced to ABCs, James is saying, "Grow up spiritually! Be consistent in maintaining the filling of the Holy Spirit by consistently confessing your sins (1 John 1:9). Learn the Word and obey. This is the path to spiritual maturity."

*"If anyone does not stumble in what he says, he is a perfect [mature] man, able to bridle [control] the whole body as well"* (James 3:2). Therein is James' message! This biblical insight opens another gateway to more scrutiny of James' message to his Christian audience in the next chapter.

## NINETEEN

James 3:13-18

# Overview of Wisdom

*Who among you is wise and understanding? Let him show by his good behavior his deeds in the gentleness of wisdom. But if you have bitter jealousy and selfish ambition in your heart, do not be arrogant and so lie against the truth. This wisdom is not that which comes down from above, but is earthly, natural, demonic. For where jealousy and selfish ambition exist, there is disorder and every evil thing. But the wisdom from above is first pure, then peaceable, gentle, reasonable, full of mercy and good fruits, unwavering, without hypocrisy. And the seed whose fruit is righteousness is sown in peace by those who make peace* (James 3:13-18).

Now we come to the last segment of James' exposition of chapter 3, the dualism of wisdom. Look carefully at the last sentence, "*And the seed whose fruit is righteousness is sown in peace by those who make peace.*" This is where we will begin and work back to the rest of the verses.

Many wonderful men of God have done an injustice to this magnificent text by linking it to the idea that a so-called "genuinely saved" person *must* produce good works. A good number of commentators stand on this platform. Among these is R.V.G. Tasker, who comments, "James is insistent that religion must show itself in works. In this he is wholly true to his Master's words 'By their fruits ye shall know them' (Mt. vii. 20)."[114]

## Knowing Them By Their Fruits

Repetition is the secret to reception, retention, and recall—the 3Rs. In light of this, we revisit our previous study of Matthew 7:20, in order to resolve the misconception and misinterpretation of the beautiful message our Lord communicated therein.

---

**Context is critical to
biblical interpretation.**

---

We know that relying on morality and good works to determine if one is a child of God can be misleading. This is because anyone (believer and unbeliever alike) can be moral. In fact, some unbelievers are more moral than some born-again believers. This was true of the religious Pharisees of our Lord's day. They were moral, self-righteous to the core, so much so that the Lord described them as *"whitewashed tombs"* (Matthew 23:27).

Although we had touched on this passage (Matthew 7:20) in chapter 1, it is very important that we revisit it briefly. The Lord is not saying that regeneration *must* manifest itself in good works. Remember that context is critical to biblical interpretation. So, let's take a step back to Matthew 7:15. *"Watch out for false prophets. **They come to you in sheep's clothing**, [deception highlighted], **but inwardly they are ferocious wolves"*** (Matthew 7:15 NIV). Our Lord's message is that false prophets, namely unbelievers, come camouflaged, often using good works as their cover, as we saw in Matthew 7:21-23.

You see, at the Great White Throne Judgment (last judgment of unbelievers), these wolves in sheep's clothing will lay hold to good works. *"Lord, Lord, did we not prophesy in Your name, and in Your name cast out demons, and in Your name perform many miracles?"* (Matthew 7:22). Make no mistake; their claims of their spectacular acts are genuine! On that day, the Lord will not dispute their claims, but He will dispute their relationship with Him. *"Not everyone who says to Me, 'Lord, Lord,' will enter the kingdom of heaven, but he who does the will of My Father who is in heaven will enter"* (Matthew 7:21). We know that *"by the works of the Law no flesh will be justified"*

(Galatians 2:16) and that He "*saved us...not according to our [good] works*" (2 Timothy 1:9).

Question: What is "*the will of My Father*"?

Is it good works? Not according to Scripture (Galatians 2:16). Elsewhere, the Lord provides this answer: "*For this is the will of my Father, that every one who sees the Son and believes in him should have eternal life; and I will raise him up at the last day*" (John 6:40 RSV).

These false prophets will be damned forever, not because they weren't moral enough or did not duplicate the miraculous work of the apostolic era, but because they did not anchor their faith in Christ alone for eternal life.

You may ask: "What then did the Lord mean, '*you will know them by their fruits*' (Matthew 7:20)?" He answered this question:

> "*Whoever speaks a word against the Son of Man, it shall be forgiven him; but whoever speaks against the Holy Spirit, it shall not be forgiven him, either in this age or in the age to come. Either make the tree good and its fruit good, or make the tree bad and its fruit bad; **for the tree is known by its fruit**. You brood of vipers, how can you, being evil, **speak what is good? For the mouth speaks out of that which fills the heart**. The good man brings out of his good treasure what is good; and the evil man brings out of his evil treasure what is evil. But I tell you that every careless word that people speak, they shall give an accounting for it in the day of judgment. **For by your words you will be justified, and by your words you will be condemned**" (Matthew 12:32-37, emphasis added).

---

**A wolf camouflaged in sheep's clothing can only be differentiated from the true sheep when he eventually barks!**

---

It's crystal clear that the reference to fruit, in context of the passage, is words, and *not* works, "*for the tree is known by its fruit...For by your words you will be justified.*" A wolf camouflaged in sheep's clothing can only be differentiated from the true sheep when he eventually barks! Similarly, an unbeliever is known, not through works, but through *words*. When one engages someone in conversation, it will be evident whether the individual is saved or not.

Let us now dispel the misconception that a saved individual could be known by his "fruit," namely, outward manifestation. We owe it to ourselves, our audience and, above all, to our great God to stand on the side of truth. So let's honestly reevaluate our position by asking and answering the following questions:

Q: By what means does one obtain eternal life?
A: You are right! Faith alone in Christ alone: "*He who believes in the Son has eternal life*" (John 3:36; cf. Romans 3:28).

Q: Is it possible for one who has truly believed and is truly saved to "backslide" or fall away?
A: Right, again; yes, it's possible: "*My brethren [saved ones], if any among you strays [backslides, falls away] from the truth and one turns him back*" (James 5:19-20).

Q: Can a believer who has fallen away and is now in prolonged spiritual decline exhibit the life of Christ?
A: No, he cannot, for he has lost fellowship, lost the filling of the Holy Spirit, lost the power supply necessary to exhibit the life of Christ. "*For apart from Me [i.e., fellowship, filling of the Spirit], you can do nothing*" (John 15:5). The lifestyle of such a one who has been disconnected from the life of Christ cannot be differentiated from that of "*mere men*," the unbelievers (1 Corinthians 3:3).

Q: Has a believer in spiritual carnality lost his salvation?
A: No, he has not. Eternal means eternal! The very definition of eternal life confirms everlasting life (John 10:27-29; cf. Hebrews 10:10). Some might say, "One who is truly saved and has the life of Christ would not remain in a carnal lifestyle for too long." How long is too long? Two days, two weeks? Two years? Twenty years?

Let us not infuse into Scripture that which is not there. The truth of the matter is that a believer, truly saved, can fall away and forget that he was once "cleansed." I strongly believe that such a condition is what the apostle Peter had in mind when he wrote,

> *For by these He has granted to us His precious and magnificent promises, so that by them you may become partakers of the divine nature, having escaped the corruption that is in the world by lust. Now for this very reason also, applying all diligence, in your faith supply moral excellence, and in your moral excellence, knowledge, and in your knowledge, self control, and in your self control, perseverance, and in your perseverance, godliness, and in your godliness, brotherly kindness, and in your brotherly kindness, love. For if these qualities are yours and are increasing, they render you [a believer] neither useless [dead] nor unfruitful in the true knowledge of our Lord Jesus Christ. For [but] he who lacks these qualities [though still saved] is blind or short-sighted [renders his life ineffectual], having forgotten his purification from his former sins* (2 Peter 1:4-9).

The apostle Peter reminded the believer of the abundant life and the spiritual victory available through the pursuit of moral excellence, experiential knowledge, self-control, perseverance, godliness, brotherly kindness and love. He was concerned that the individual believer had forgotten he was once purified *"from his former sins,"* and therefore he warned about the consequences of indifference. Peter knew that the lifestyle of a believer who fails or "backslides" often imitates that of an unbeliever. Therein is the truth of God's Word! With this clarification, we reject outright the misinterpretation of Matthew 7:20, which says *"you will know them by their fruits"* means a saved person *must* produce good works.

Now back to James 3:13-16.

## Earthly Wisdom

*"Who among you is wise and understanding? Let him show by his good behavior his deeds in the gentleness of wisdom"* (James 3:13). James, a spiritual father, teacher and leader, challenged his audience, *"Who*

*among you is wise and understanding?"* Dr. Arnold Fruchtenbaum remarks, "this query was issued and intended as a call for self examination."[115] It's a call for soul-searching and reflection. According to Mitton, "In the Bible the word "wise" (sophos) described someone who has moral insight and skill in advising on practical issues of conduct rather than an academic knowledge of theoretical problems and their solutions."[116]

Everyone can talk, but not everyone can deliver results. Talk is cheap. We see this frequently in the political arena: one promise after another, with little or no delivery. But actions speak louder than words. So what James is saying is simple: "As a believer, do you consider yourself to be wise and as one who has mastery in spiritual knowledge, one who has moral insight and skill in advising others on practical issues of conduct? If so, show this by your conduct." Dr. D.J. Moo makes a striking remark regarding good conduct: "It is our acts of obedience to God, performed consistently day after day, that make up the good conduct of the wise person."[117]

---

**"Our acts of obedience to God, performed consistently day after day...make up the good conduct of the wise person."**

---

James goes on to say, *"But if you have bitter jealousy and selfish ambition in your heart, do not be arrogant and so lie against the truth. This wisdom is not that which comes down from above, but is earthly, natural, demonic. For where jealousy and selfish ambition exist, there is disorder and every evil thing"* (James 3:14-16).

Now we are drilling deeper into our study. All along we have maintained that James' epistle was addressed to believers already in a spiritual quagmire (James 4:4). The preceding passage is more evidence to support this claim. Verse 14 cannot be overlooked! The NASB starts it with the phrase *"But if you have bitter jealousy."* Translating it this way gives one the impression that James is unsure of his assertion *"if you have bitter jealousy."* However, it is not a matter of doubt. There are no "ifs" about it. James assumes the indictment to be a fact—"if, and it's true!"

When he gets to his next chapter, James shows his readers that their prayers are hindered because of a carnal lifestyle (James 4:1-3). In view of this, Dr. Donald Burdick casts light: "Apparently some of James' readers were harboring "bitter envy and selfish ambition" in their hearts. The Greek simple conditional sentence assumes the existence of the situation described."[118]

Every layer we uncover points to the intent of James' epistle, to steer his Christian audience, who were in prolonged state of carnality, back to a vibrant spiritual life. Basically James said: "The incubation of "bitter jealousy and selfish ambition" in your heart makes you a liar to your claim of possessing wisdom from above. Cease and desist this practice! Let your actions be consistent with your spiritual life!

He went on to describe the negative impact of jealousy and selfish ambition among the brethren, namely, *"disorder and every evil thing"*! That is the reason for the admonition of James 2:14.

We can see why James made the assertion *"What use is it, my brethren, if someone says he has faith [biblical truth, creed] but he has no works [application]? Can that faith [literally 'the faith,'* [119] *i.e., accumulated biblical truth] save him [from premature physical death]?"* (James 2:14). In other words, in James 3:14-16 he is saying, "What defense against divine discipline is this, if you claim to possess sound biblical knowledge (wisdom) and yet your life is marked with jealousy, selfish ambition and brewing of discord among brethren, can your claim of possessing sound biblical knowledge (wisdom) save you or protect you from judgment?"

Moving on, James correctly credits the source of their wisdom, *"This wisdom is not that which comes down from above, but is earthly, natural, demonic"* (James 3:15). That's to say, that their wisdom is not for the praise of the One who called them, but for Satan (James 4:4). Then James quickly contrasts this demonic wisdom with that which is from above, heavenly wisdom.

## Wisdom from Above

*"But the wisdom from above is first pure, then peaceable, gentle, reasonable, full of mercy and good fruits, unwavering, without hypocrisy. And*

247

*the seed whose fruit is righteousness is sown in peace by those who make peace"* (James 3:17-18).

James begins his contrast in this section with the word *but.* Technically, the word *but* is like a speed bump on which we should slow down and observe the reason for the bump. Here, *but* contrasts earthly wisdom with God's wisdom.

Let us examine the Greek *sophia* for "wisdom." *Wisdom,* in layman's terms, is superior knowledge unique to God, implanted in the believer's soul through learning the Word of God. King Solomon called God's Word "*wisdom*" (Proverbs 8).

James speaks about the ability to apply this wisdom or knowledge to the exigencies of life. Such ability or wisdom belongs to God and can only come from Him! (We need not confuse James 1:5, a prayer for wisdom, with the preceding definition.) The wisdom of God is contained in His holy Word, which He has graciously given to us. It has everything we need for instruction and righteous living. First is the acquisition of wisdom, then the application.

Now James is going to use eight attributes to display this awesome wisdom from above: "*But the wisdom from above is first pure, then peaceable, gentle, reasonable, full of mercy and good fruits, unwavering, without hypocrisy.*" C.L. Mitton said,

> God's wisdom as bestowed on man reveals itself in conduct which is PURE (hagne). This means that it is free from self-interest and selfish ambition. It is single-minded (Matt. 6:22, Luke 11:34; cf. Acts 2:46; Eph. 6:5; Col. 3:22)…It means that one who claims to be serving God is wholly serving Him and not, at the same time, seeking to further some private interest of his own; if he aims to render some service to his fellow man, he does so without ulterior thoughts of the praise and approval that will come to him as a result.[120]

These divine axioms are what God desires in full measure for James' readers and from all His children. This is what James labored to communicate to his fellow believers in Christ.

James is not saying that a believer cannot falter, because he, himself, occasionally did (James 3:2). But, his message is crystal clear: "Brethren, we have been called to bear fruit; God has lavished His grace upon our lives that we may bring forth honor and glory to His name. So, let's cast aside those things that would keep us from bearing fruit (Hebrews 12:1) and go on to bear good fruit, because we have been called for this purpose. Let's bear fruit, not because of rewards associated with fruit bearing (James 2:21-26) but because of our unsurpassed love for the One who "first loved us" (1 John 4:19) and offered Himself unconditionally as a sacrificial offering to God on our behalf."

James is saying the same thing the apostle Paul said: "*Conduct yourselves with wisdom toward outsiders, making the most of the opportunity. Let your speech always be with grace, as though seasoned with salt, so that you will know how you should respond to each person*" (Colossians 4:5-6).

God has called on us to bear fruit; that is His divine purpose for us (Ephesians 2:10). Let us learn how to control our tongues so that we may bear fruit for His glory. Let's apply the truth in our souls, not from the source of pride, ego, or selfish ambition, but from the source of sound judgment, grace, love and peace. Peter agrees: "*Whoever speaks, is to do so as one who is speaking the utterances of God; whoever serves is to do so as one who is serving by the strength which God supplies; so that in all things God may be glorified through Jesus Christ, to whom belongs the glory and dominion forever and ever. Amen*" (1 Peter 4:11).

A beautiful example of Scripture agreeing with Scripture. This clears the way for the next installment, James chapter 4.

## TWENTY

## James 4:1-5

# The Power of the Old Sin Nature

*What is the source of quarrels and conflicts among you? Is not the source your pleasures that wage war in your members? You lust and do not have; so you commit murder. You are envious and cannot obtain; so you fight and quarrel. You do not have because you do not ask. You ask and do not receive, because you ask with wrong motives, so that you may spend it on your pleasures. You adulteresses, do you not know that friendship with the world is hostility toward God? Therefore whoever wishes to be a friend of the world makes himself an enemy of God. Or do you think that the Scripture speaks to no purpose: "He jealously desires the Spirit which He has made to dwell in us"?* (**James 4:1-5**).

Previously, James appeared to have been somewhat soft-spoken with his Christian audience. But in this chapter, he got very personal and strongly alerted his readers to the dangers ahead in verse 4. He calls their attention to the detrimental ever-present power of the old sin nature.[121] Yes, we all (even believers) have a sin nature.

Beloved, whether we are aware of it or not, denial is our number one enemy when it comes to analyzing the meaning of sinful acts in the life of a believer in perpetual carnality. In the Christian community, we often overlook or downplay the injurious power of the old sin nature. We have heard those who don't understand what the Bible teaches say, "One cannot be a believer in Christ and commit this or that sin." Nothing can be farther from the truth! There's no sinful act too atrocious for a believer

251

under the influential power of the sin nature. We wear the mask of self-deception when we think otherwise.

The apostle Paul compares its influential power to that of drunkenness (Ephesians 5:18). That is to say, a person under its control cannot think rationally. The individual experiences a state where human conscience is temporarily suppressed! Yes, in this state, a believer can commit even the most deplorable acts.

With this in mind, James begins this chapter with two sobering questions: "*What is the source of quarrels and conflicts among you? Is not the source your pleasures that wage war in your members? You lust and do not have; so you commit murder.*"

The word *murder* grabs our attention. This is because many believers, both laymen and academics, cannot imagine that those who have been positionally washed, justified, and sanctified in Christ can experientially engage in murder. This is also true of a great number of scholars, who for centuries have had a hard time grasping the idea that James' indictment is against actual physical murder. The truth of the matter is that believers do commit murder, and did even in Bible times.

Mitton asserts that the phrase "*among you*" "need not be taken to mean Christians, even though the letter is addressed to Christians."[122] We reject this view, because there is no textual evidence that James had any community other than believers in mind. The apostle Paul tells us that we have no business "*judging outsiders*" (1 Corinthians 5:12). Based on this, we affirm that the phrase *among you* is a reference to those who have experienced the indwelling presence of the Holy Spirit (James 4:5) but whose spiritual life is now stuck in perpetual carnality.

Until we see this from James' vantage point, it will be difficult for us to comprehend this passage. More than that, it will be hard for us to deal with the reality of our own personal sins, let alone help others (James 5:19-20). The truth is that a believer out of fellowship with God can do just about anything! That's a biblical fact! So we take up the first component.

## Pursuit of Pleasure

James points to "*pleasures*" as the source of their spiritual chaos. The Greek word *hedonai* is correctly translated "pleasure" in our passage. Mitton quotes Ropes, who interprets it as "the pursuit of pleasure."[123] Our Lord invokes the same word in Luke 8:14, *"pleasures of this life,"* which helped to choke the good seed of God after it has been sown in human's heart.[124] It occurs also in Titus 3:3 for the "pleasures" that can enslave a man.[125]

Tasker remarks,

> These pleasures, says James, war in your members. He does not say specifically, as Peter says of lusts ( 1 Pet. ii. 11), that they 'war against the soul'; though that is implied; for so long as they have the upper hand, man is prevented from doing what he was originally created to do—acknowledge and render obedience to the will of God…[What James] asserts is that the human personality has, as it were, been invaded by an alien army which is always campaigning within it. The Greek verb strateuomenon implies that these pleasures are permanently on active service; and expression 'in your members' means that there is no part in the human frame that does not afford them a battleground.[126]

---

### What's your yardstick, materialism-induced pleasure or constant fellowship with God?

---

Men and women pour enormous amounts of time, effort, and money on the altar of pleasure. It is staggering! What James diagnosed 2,000 years ago is still true of us today. We are all guilty of doing whatever it takes to satisfy the demands of pleasures at one time or another.

Let me get personal here: As a believer in the Lord Jesus Christ, what's your yardstick, materialism-induced pleasure or constant fellowship with God? The answer to this question is a matter between you and God. As for James' audience, materialism had the upper hand!

My beloved, there's no better way to communicate this truth. We should resist the lure of the pursuit of pleasure once we realize that it is like a disease with enormous ability to consume us. Think of it. It was pleasure that ruined the spiritual life of the wisest man who ever lived. *"When Solomon was old, his [foreign] wives turned his heart away after*

*other gods; and his heart was not wholly devoted to the LORD his God*
(1 Kings 11:4).

Pleasure temporarily crippled the spiritual life of David, Israel's
finest king. After indulging himself in the pleasure of an affair with
Bathsheba and the murder of her husband, he cried, "*Restore to me [not
salvation but] the joy of Your salvation*" (Psalm 51:12).

The truth is that a believer in carnality can go to any length to satisfy the demands of pleasure, including murder. That's biblical truth:
"*You lust and do not have [the demands of your pleasure]; so you [brethren,
believers] commit murder*" (James 4:2).

If we are still doubtful, beloved of God, doubt no more. King
David was a perfect example of what catering to the demands of pleasure can do to a believer. No one can, with good conscience, argue
scripturally that David was not a believer. He was not only a believer
but also "*a man after [God's] own heart*" (1 Samuel 13:14). Think of
it—it was David's intense craving for pleasure that sent Uriah the
Hittite to his early grave (2 Samuel 12:9).

That's not all! What about Naboth? Was not lust the bedrock of
pleasure that cut his life short by the hands of Ahab and Jezebel (1
Kings 21:6-15)? And Moses who murdered the Egyptian (Exodus
2:12)? Are believers capable of ending other people's lives? Joseph's
brothers came very close to killing him, but he was spared by God's
providential protection.

We can go on and on! The truth we wish to emphasize is that
believers, even today, do (directly or indirectly) commit murder. We
should not allow personal feelings and notions to explain away the
obvious truth that James communicates: Believers in carnality can commit murder. When their desires are not satisfied, as Mitton points out,
they often "use every available means to seize forcefully what [they]
want, or remove the offending person."[127] In fact, there was an instance
where a pastor hired a killer to kill another pastor who was a hindrance
to his pleasurable way of life. Ah, one may say, "That pastor was not
really saved!" Is that necessarily so? If so, then what about David?

## Praying in Carnality

"*You are envious and cannot obtain; so you fight and quarrel. You do not have because you do not ask. You ask and do not receive, because you ask with wrong motives, so that you may spend it on your pleasures*" (James 4:2-3). Beloved of God, do not be deceived: a prayer offered by a believer who does not take God's Word seriously is an abomination to the Holiness of God.

"*He who turns away his ear from listening to the law [he who is indifferent to learning and applying God's Word], Even his prayer is an abomination*" (Proverbs 28:9). Indifference to His Word blocks access to the throne room of His grace; personal sin does the same.

"*If I regard [harbor] wickedness [sin] in my heart, The Lord will not hear [my prayer]*" (Psalm 66:18).

"*Then they [carnal believers] will cry out to the LORD [in prayer], But He will not answer them. Instead, He will hide His face from them at that time Because they have practiced evil deeds*" (Micah 3:4; cf. Isaiah 1:15).

In other words, we can agonize in the closet all day long or fast until we pass out, but if our spiritual life is not pleasing to God, our prayers are mere words.

The opposite is true for an obedient child of God, "*Beloved, if our heart does not condemn us [if our conscience is clear], we have confidence before God; and whatever we ask we receive from Him, because we keep His commandments and do the things that are pleasing in His sight*" (1 John 3:21-22). This is good news for believers who are on course!

James awakened his readers with a paradox. He opened with "*You do not have because you do not ask.*" Reading this, one is tempted to draw the conclusion that perhaps his audience of fellow believers was no longer using the vehicle of prayer. But not so fast! For soon after his remarks, he rebutted: "*You ask and do not receive, because you ask with wrong motives, so that you may spend it on your pleasures.*" Their problem was not lack of prayer; rather, the issue was that their priorities were out of balance. Essentially James was saying, "Brethren, look at yourselves; your prayers are no longer effective because of your poor spiritual condition!" To be specific, "Pleasure consumes your mind to the point you have become completely self-absorbed, even in your prayer requests."

We know that prayer is a privilege and prerogative of a Father-son relationship. Scripture is clear about that "*God does not hear [the prayers of] sinners [unbelievers]*" (John 9:31). So James' mention of prayer in our passage is yet another proof that his readers were born-again believers.

Unbelievers may have occasionally shown up in a congregation of the early Church, but their presence never drew the attention of any writer of the New Testament epistles. In other words, the authors never addressed both believers and unbelievers in the same epistle. We must read Scripture carefully! Consequently, the attempt to divide James' epistle, saying that it is for both genuinely saved believers and the unsaved, is futile at best! At worst it is an attempt to corrupt or abate the truth therein.

James finally reached the boiling point in his castigation:

> *You adulteresses [believers in perpetual carnality], do you not know that friendship with the world is hostility toward God? Therefore whoever wishes to be a friend of the world makes himself an enemy of God. Or do you think that the Scripture speaks to no purpose: "He jealously desires the Spirit which He has made to dwell in us"?* (James 4:4-5)

James addressed his readers in spiritual adultery, a subject worthy of thorough dissection.

## Spiritual Adultery

Right away the word *adulteresses* (v. 4) raises an eyebrow of the student of God's Word. Scholars have debated about James' employment of such an emphatic word in his epistle. Perplexed by this, the editors of the King James Version went as far as adding the word *adulterers* to the passage in order to balance the text. They wondered why James left men out of his indictment of sexual immorality. But the translators missed the mark. Most scholars agree that James is not talking about sexual misconduct but spiritual infidelity. The Greek word *moichalides* used by James, as Douglas Moo points out, "is actually feminine."[128] It occurs as singular in the original text. James used the word deliberately. A failure to correctly understand the definition will lead to a false conclusion, such as, how can James indict the women alone for sexual immorality and not the men equally? This riddle is solved when one considers two factors.

The readers were all Jewish Christians (James 1:1).
James was aware of their Old Testament reference to a sacred marriage between God and His people.

While we may be disturbed by James' use of the word *adulteresses*, his readers were not. Familiar with the Old Testament, they were concretely aware of the seriousness of James' condemnation. His indictment underscored their spiritual failure. James was *not* talking about physical adultery, but spiritual. Nonetheless, the effects of both weigh the same.

Adultery, as we know it, is a heinous sin in that it affects one's body. To this, the apostle Paul posed a serious question:

*Do you not know that your bodies are members of Christ? Shall I then take away the members of Christ and make them members of a prostitute? May it never be! Or do you not know that the one who joins himself to a prostitute is one body with her? For He says, "THE TWO SHALL BECOME ONE FLESH." But the one who joins himself to the Lord is one spirit with Him* (1 Corinthians 6:15-17).

On the subject he exclaimed, "*Flee from sexual immorality. All other sins a man commits are outside his body, but he who sins sexually sins against his own body. Do you not know that your body is a temple of the Holy Spirit, who is in you, whom you have received from God [the Father]?*" (1 Corinthians 6:18-19 NIV).

Paul later reminded the Corinthians of the same thing James taught his audience: the presence of the indwelling Holy Spirit (James 4:5; cf. 1 Corinthians 6:19). Understanding the ramifications of physical infidelity would help shed light on the interpretation of the phrase "*He jealously desires the Spirit which He has made to dwell in us*" (James 4:5). In view of infidelity, we can appreciate the author of Hebrews' bluntness.

*"Marriage is to be held in honor among all, and the marriage bed is to be undefiled; for fornicators and adulterers God will judge"* (Hebrews 13:4). Adultery is so repugnant to God that under His permissive will He grants it as the only basis for divorce (Matthew 5:32). Of course He Himself hates divorce (Malachi 2:16), This divorce is in the human realm. In the spiritual realm God *cannot* divorce the believer and cancel his salvation, no matter what (2 Timothy 2:11; cf., Romans 8:38-39). God will very severely discipline those who commits the sin of unfaithfulness, in either the physical or spiritual realm.

James uses the word *adulteresses* in a metaphorical sense. We see the marriage relationship referred to elsewhere in Scripture. For example, in the Old Testament, the people of Israel are called the "bride" or "wife" of God (Deuteronomy 31:16; Isaiah 54:5; Jeremiah 3:20), and within the context of this metaphor any disloyalty on the part of Israel to their covenant with God could be described as "adultery."[129]

Hosea spoke on the same subject: "Those who by their disobedience thus 'forsook God,' in spite of their pledged covenant with Him, may be said to be 'playing the harlot' against Him (Hos. 9:1)."[130]

This is where James' indictment comes fully into focus, *"You adulteresses."* What is true in regard to the relationship between God and the people of Israel in the Old Testament is equally true between believers and the Lord Jesus Christ in all generations. We are in a marriage relationship with Him (Revelation 19:7).

For instance, John the Baptist referred to the Lord as the *"bridegroom"* (John 3:29), and the apostle Paul referred to the church as the bride (2 Corinthians 11:2). The apostle spoke of the relationship between the believer and Christ in terms of a union, *"joined to another"* (Romans 7:4). Furthermore, he qualifies the "church" with the feminine word "her," arguing our relationship with Christ in terms of marriage (Ephesians 5:22-32). John the apostle, on the other hand, uses the metaphor of *"bridegroom and bride"* (Revelation 18:23) to underscore our marriage relationship with Christ. The list can go on endlessly; but that's unnecessary, for the truth has been established.

James goes one step further to explain his indictment: *"Do you not know that friendship with the world is hostility toward God? Therefore whoever wishes to be a friend of the world makes himself an enemy of God"* (James 4:4)

This paints a vivid picture of "pleasure" for all to see. It is friendship with the world! You cannot be on both sides at the same time, God's side and pleasure. Which side are you? James' audience was on the side of pleasure as a priority, which put them on the opposing side of God and made them the *"an enemy of God."*

You and I cannot afford to be God's enemy. Regrettably, that's what we unintentionally do when we put a premium on anything above God, be it marriage, business, work, or materialism and pursuit of wealth. James is not alone. Later, the apostle John wrote, *"Do not love the world nor the things in the world If anyone loves the world, the love of the Father is not in him. For all that is in the world, the lust of the flesh and the lust of the eyes and the boastful pride of life, is not from the Father, but is from the world"* (1 John 2:15-16).

---

**We commit spiritual adultery, the worst kind of sin against Him, when our love for this world exceeds our love for God.**

---

We commit spiritual adultery, the worst kind of sin against Him, when our love for this world exceeds our love for God. Is there anything that comes between you and your fellowship with God?

As an example, if a friend invited you to a party that coincides with Bible study, which one would you attend? Your answer is a matter between you and the Lord. But, to the point that party takes precedence over Bible study (Hebrews 10:25), you have just demonstrated that *"the love of the Father is not in [you]."* You may ask, "What's the big deal?" Huge! Such behavior is a clear demonstration of one's indifference to the things of God! This indifference is what James was seeking to help his readers understand and avoid. This may sound extreme, but it is the truth of God's Word!

Trying to bring his audience to face their ways, James asked, *"Or do you think that the Scripture speaks to no purpose: 'He jealously desires the Spirit which He has made to dwell in us'?"* (James 4:5).

Scholars, great and small, have had many heated debates as to which "spirit" James had in mind, the human spirit or the Holy Spirit. Particularly troubling to many is the phrase "*He jealously desires the Spirit.*" In regeneration, the Bible always talks of spiritual rebirth and never indwelling, therefore James must have been referring to the Holy Spirit rather than the human spirit. "*That which is born of the flesh is flesh [a reference to physical birth], and that which is born of the [Holy] Spirit is [human] spirit*" (John 3:6).

Zane Hodges holds the same opinion.

[The] text translated by the NKJV (and supported by a large majority of manuscripts), the reference to the Holy Spirit is even more probable. The aorist form [of the Greek] katoikesin is a past tense and almost means something like "has taken up residence" in us. Such a form of expression would be strange if used of the human spirit, but quite natural if used of the Holy Spirit who "took up residence" in us at the moment of salvation.[131]

James wants them to realize that God does not accept infidelity with indifference. Thus he reminds them that it is not in vain that the Scripture says God's Spirit is jealous over us. This is surely the meaning of this text.[132]

Dibelius agrees: "The Holy Spirit, which God [the Father] allows to dwell within a person, is the 'good identity' of the person."[133]

Considering Paul's commentary on sexual immorality (1 Corinthians 6:18, a sin to the body that God's Spirit inhabits), it makes sense that God would manifest righteous jealousy (Exodus 20:5; 34:14; Zechariah 8:2). After all, His ultimate purpose in creation is His glory (Isaiah 43:7), and that is equally true in regeneration, "*to the praise of His glory*" (Ephesians 1:12). Sooner or later God's justice will catch up with us when we abuse His grace. This is the explanation of "*Or do you think that the Scripture speaks to no purpose [or in vain]: 'He jealously desires the Spirit which He has made to dwell in us?'*" (James 4:5).

Zane Hodges concurs. He says, "In fact, the word vain coupled with strong assertion of God's Spirit, hint at the possibility of some kind of retribution if the Spirit yearning over them is ignored."[134]

Martin Dibelius is of the same opinion, affirming that the

indwelling Holy Spirit "must assert itself in opposition to an "evil identity."[135] On this ground, James, a man of passion, knew his Christian audience was heading to God's judgment swiftly. He wished to steer them onto the right course before it was too late.

Next, we will examine the words James used to turn his hearers from their path of spiritual infidelity and redirect them Godward—for blessing in both time and eternity.

Until then, it's my heartfelt prayer that God would make this teaching real to you.

## TWENTY-ONE

James 4:6-17

# The Road to Spiritual Recovery

*But He gives a greater grace Therefore it says, "GOD IS OPPOSED TO THE PROUD, BUT GIVES GRACE TO THE HUMBLE." Submit therefore to God Resist the devil and he will flee from you. Draw near to God and He will draw near to you Cleanse your hands, you sinners; and purify your hearts, you double-minded. Be miserable and mourn and weep; let your laughter be turned into mourning and your joy to gloom. Humble yourselves in the presence of the Lord, and He will exalt you* (James 4:6-10).

We cannot say this enough, James was a well-rounded, Spirit-filled Bible teacher. He masterfully combined the elements of rebuke with a message of hope. This is an amazing picture of grace-orientation and ingenuity—compassion garnished with love. What is more, he emulated our Lord, who chewed out the religious crowd of His day with these condemning words: *"An evil and adulterous generation"* (Matthew 12:39). But with an unfailing love, Jesus had invited the same audience to *"Come to Me, all who are weary and heavy-laden, and I will give you rest"* (Matthew 11:28).

In the same manner James followed in our Lord's footsteps. On one hand he lambasted his Christian readers, *"You adulteresses."* On the other hand, with passion, grace-thinking and love, he stated, *"But He gives a greater grace. Therefore it says, 'GOD IS OPPOSED TO THE PROUD, BUT GIVES GRACE TO THE HUMBLE'"* (James 4:6).

James reminded them that there's no failure too *great* for the awesome grace of God. He wanted them to know that they could still avoid severe discipline. This phenomenal truth is revealed in the Old Testament. "*Let the wicked forsake his way And the unrighteous man his thoughts; And let him return to the LORD, And He will have compassion on him, And to our God, For He will abundantly pardon*" (Isaiah 55:7).

Let's not forget, James was admonishing his brethren in Christ who for a prolonged period had been consumed with pleasure, egocentrism, self-sufficiency and arrogance. To these he exhorted, "*Draw near to God and...Cleanse your hands...and purify your hearts*" (James 4:8).

James' choice of words is intriguing: *resist, flee, draw, cleanse, purify, mourn, weep*, and *humble*. We can examine those words and clearly understand that James' epistle was addressed to believers. Sadly, some teachers still misinterpret those words. For example, John MacArthur, in his book *The Gospel According to Jesus*, calls this passage, specifically vv. 7-10, "perhaps the most comprehensive invitation to salvation in the epistles. [He went on to say] While James addresses most of his epistle to genuine believers, it is also evident that he is concerned about those who are not genuine."[136]

To this assertion Zane Hodges replies, "But what is there in this passage that reflects James' concern with 'those who are not genuine'?...Nothing at all. Such an idea is being read into a text that neither says this nor implies it."[137]

Make no mistake; the Gospel of the apostle John is the most comprehensive gospel message in the Bible. Not once does it refer to the words *resist, flee, draw, cleanse, purify, mourn, weep*, or *humble* in our passage as a condition for eternal life. John gave the gospel so clearly and so simply: "*But these have been written so that you may believe that Jesus is the Christ, the Son of God; and that believing [alone] you may have life in His name*" (John 20:31).

It is beyond my comprehension why other human writers add anything else to salvation. Only the human authors confuse salvation. It is simple: faith alone in Christ alone.

Oh, how we cloud the gospel of our Lord! Jesus Christ Himself compared salvation to the simple act of drinking water when one is thirsty (John 4:13-14); The prophet of the Old Testament gave a similar invitation: *"Ho! Every one who thirsts, come to the waters; And you who have no money come, buy and eat. Come, buy wine and milk Without money and without cost"* (Isaiah 55:1).

Salvation comes with no strings attached. No commitment, no evidence of good works. It's a free gift (Romans 6:23), offered in grace and appropriated in a non-meritorious way! That's grace (Ephesians 2:8-9)!

---

**It is man's pride and self-deception that make him think that he can enjoy life outside of fellowship with God.**

---

On the topic of grace James goes on to underscore the most critical element in the spiritual life—humility.

## Importance of Humility

*"But He gives a greater grace. Therefore it says, 'GOD IS OPPOSED TO THE PROUD, BUT GIVES GRACE TO THE HUMBLE"* (James 4:6).

There can be no restoration for the fallen believer until he deals with the issue of pride in his life. It is man's pride and self-deception that make him think that he can enjoy life outside of fellowship with God. More seriously, it is the ultimate in arrogance to think that worldly pleasure has more to offer than an intimate relationship with God.

What James is saying is this: a believer who has been in extended carnality and wishes to be restored must be willing to recognize, in his soul, that enjoyment outside of God is a manifestation of extreme arrogance. James is not saying that remorse is a prerequisite for forgiveness of one's sins. One's decision to return to God begins with a change of mind, and arrogance is replaced with humility, whether he is aware or not. For example, the Prodigal Son never mentions the word humility in his decision to come back to his father, but it is obvious.

Remember, the story of the Prodigal Son is not about salvation but restoration to fellowship. *"But when he came to his senses [cloud of arrogance cleared], he said, 'How many of my father's hired men have more than enough bread, but I am dying here with hunger! I will get up and go to my father [humility highlighted], and will say to him, "Father, I have sinned against heaven, and in your sight"""* (Luke 15:17-18).

*"Submit therefore to God. Resist the devil and he will flee from you. Draw near to God and He will draw near to you. Cleanse your hands, you sinners; and purify your hearts, you double-minded"* (James 4:7-8).

James recognizes that a decision to jump-start one's spiritual life will be met with strong opposition. This is because Satan enjoys the imprisonment of carnal believers. His audience was no exception. So James shows them the way back: *"Submit therefore to God. Resist the devil and he will flee from you."*

In essence, James is saying, "Submit yourself daily to the teaching and authority of God's Word. Use it as the Lord did in His defense when He was tempted by Satan (Matthew 4:1-4). What's more, the truth of Scripture is your defense against Satan's attempt to lure you back into the world or make your resolve of commitment to God null and void."

*Resist* simply means to defend your ground by articulating His Word in your soul on a consistent basis. Following that, James makes a powerful promise, *"he will flee from you."* Additionally, the call to *"draw near to God"* and the promise that *"He will draw near to you"* is simply a call to fellowship. The question is, how can a carnal believer achieve this? James gives the answer: *"Cleanse your hands, you sinners; and purify your hearts."*

Moving on, we know the recipients of James' epistle were no strangers to the mandate *"Cleanse your hands, you sinners."* They understood James' plea because they were familiar with the Old Testament, where God mandated the provision of a basin of water for the priests.

*"You shall also make a laver of bronze, with its base of bronze, for washing; and you shall put it between the tent of meeting and the altar, and you shall put water in it. Aaron and his sons shall wash their hands and their feet from it; when they enter the tent of meeting, they shall wash with water, so that they will not die; or when they approach the altar to minister, by offering up in smoke a fire sacrifice to the LORD. So they shall wash their hands and their feet, so that they will not die; and it shall be a perpetual*

*statute for them, for Aaron and his descendants throughout their generations"* (Exodus 30:18-21).

This washing symbolized confession and restoration to fellowship. The procedure was simple. The priests, prior to approaching the altar, dipped their hands in the designated basin of water. In so doing they recognized, like the prophet Isaiah, that God is holy and that they were soiled by sin (Isaiah 6:5). Washing then highlighted confession done in humility.

The good news today is that we need not wash our hands or feet to be restored. We simply admit our sins before a Holy God, who knows us inside and out. *"If we confess our sins, He is faithful and righteous to forgive us our sins and to cleanse us from all unrighteousness"* (1 John 1:9).

In fact, the problem with Christians in every generation is that we do not take sin as seriously as God does. James told his audience to *"mourn and weep"* over the detrimental effects of sin. Obviously, the mandate to *"Be miserable and mourn and weep; let your laughter be turned into mourning and your joy to gloom"* does not in any way imply that one must have great remorse before one's sins can be forgiven. These are metaphorical words calling for his hearers to sit down and consider the effects of sin in their lives. Remember his audience. They were spiritual adulteresses. They had been in carnality for so long. Therefore James wanted them to reflect on God's grace upon their lives. He wanted them to reflect on how they had trampled God's grace underfoot. Such reflection, when honestly done, often induces tears (2 Chronicles 34:19, 27; Nehemiah 8:1-9).

He wanted his fellow believers to reflect on the seriousness of sin and the magnitude of God's judgment of it on the Cross of Calvary. They were to do this, not in the sense of holding a "mourning and weeping" camp meeting or mourning with lighted candles. Rather, a believer should individually seriously reflect upon the effect of sin in his own life. He should consider how sin robbed Adam and Eve of blessing intended for them in the Garden. He should reflect on what it did to King David when it enticed him to commit adultery and murder. The outcome of such reflection should results in inward or outward tears for the believer sensitive to God and His mercy.

267

Those are some examples from the past. But what about today? We have all known high-ranking government officials and celebrities or famous sports stars whose achievements have been overshadowed by scandal. They have been removed from high positions and their faces erased from endorsements. No one is immune to failure, not even King David! There are many heart-wrenching examples of the horrendous effects of sin. Anyone can fall prey to his old sin nature. The real issue of any misconduct is not the gratification of the lust pattern of the flesh but the consequences generated by that gratification. That was James' message!

Above all, James wanted his audience to dwell on the agony and tortured scream of the Son of God on the Cross when He came in contact with all our sins: "*'ELI, ELI, LAMA SABACHTHANI?' that is, 'MY GOD, MY GOD, WHY HAVE YOU FORSAKEN ME?'*" (Matthew 27:46; cf. Psalm 22:1-3). He was screaming, not because of any sinful act on His part, but because "*He made Him who knew no sin to be sin on our behalf*" (2 Corinthians 5:21). In other words the perfect Son of God was there, for the first and only time in history, carrying the entire burden of the sins of the whole world. James wanted his audience, who had drifted from their spiritual life, to stop and reflect upon this.

---

**Humility—the key to everything
in the spiritual realm.**

---

James added, "*Humble yourselves in the presence of the Lord, and He will exalt you.*" There is no better way of saying it: Humility is the key to everything in the spiritual realm. It's the key to exaltation! The command "*humble*" is in the passive voice, which means it is not self-effacing. It simply means, under the mentorship of the Holy Spirit, the believer is to allow the biblical truth in his soul to alter his thinking—a thought system that realizes that all we are is a matter of God's grace.

This brings the next portion of James' message for discussion.

## Avoid the Temptation of Judging Others

*Do not speak against one another, brethren. He who speaks against a brother or judges his brother, speaks against the law and judges the law; but if you judge the law, you are not a doer of the law but a judge of it. There is only one Lawgiver and Judge [God], the One who is able to save and to destroy; but who are you who judge your neighbor?* (James 4:11-12).

Arrogance is so subtle. It wears a thousand and one disguises, which makes it very difficult to detect. It deceives us into thinking that we are better than others. This evil thought is at the root of usurping God's prerogative in judgment. Joseph B. Mayor said it beautifully in his commentary:

> What St. James means is that we are not to indulge in the habit of fault-finding from the mere love of it, where duty does not call us to it, for the sake of showing off acuteness and pulling down others by way of exalting ourselves…There is no fault which brings about its own punishment more certainly than the love of fault-finding. While we become quick to see the mote in a brother's eye, the beam is still growing in our own.[138]

How true is Mayor's commentary! King David, when confronted by the prophet Nathan, could not see the beam in his own eye but clearly saw the mote in another's: *"Then David's anger burned greatly against the man, and he said to Nathan, 'As the LORD lives, surely the man who has done this deserves to die. He must make restitution for the lamb fourfold, because he did this thing and had no compassion"* (2 Samuel 12:5-6).

See who is angry? David! *"As the LORD lives, surely the man who has done this deserves to die."* David's reason for his outrageous judgment: *"because he did this thing and had no compassion."* David, in his self-righteousness, had the nerve to judge and indict another for lack of compassion. But the moment Nathan said to him *"You are the man!"* (2 Samuel 12:7), David sought God's compassion! (2 Samuel 12:13). That's human nature, always wanting to be the recipient of compassion and not the giver.

This is the blind side of arrogance. We are righteous; the other person is evil. We have no faults; the other person is full of faults. We deserve mercy; the other person must be buried alive. This is nothing but a sign of lack of grace-orientation,[139] a disease of the heart!

---

**Human nature always wants to be the recipient of compassion and not the giver.**

---

Through James, God strictly mandates that we cease and desist from judging others: *"Do not speak against one another, brethren."* We are always short of facts. On the surface it appears as if James is exhorting his readers to avoid the temptation of judging others. But more than that, according to the Greek text, it's a sharp rebuke to cease and desist from the habit of passing judgment on other believers. Basically, James is saying, "Right now! Stop your habit of fault-finding!"

You may ask, "Why the mandate?" Because judging is demeaning others, which is tantamount to destruction. The danger is that once one engages in the act of judging another, one inevitably slides into the mire of gossip, criticizing, maligning, backbiting and slander (harmful words to ruin one's reputation). In so doing we engage in a more serious sin: destroying believers *"for whom Christ died"* (Romans 14:15). In addition the Bible tells us that judgment belongs to God. *"Never take your own revenge, beloved, but leave room for the wrath of God, for it is written, 'VENGEANCE IS MINE, I WILL REPAY,' says the Lord."*

We must not become so casual that we are not thinking about what we are doing. None of us is capable of withstanding the swiftness of God's justice for injuring the members of the body of Christ. God loves His Son and every believer who is part of that Body!

Saul of Tarsus couldn't withstand the light of God's judgment. He fell flat on the ground and was blinded for several days (Acts 9:1-9). No one who tears down any part of the body of Christ can escape God's wrath! We are commanded to encourage one another! This is the reason why the Holy Spirit inspired James to address the issue of passing judgment on others. God abhors the act and from His justice severely disciplines those who take part. We need to stop and think hard about what we do to others when we cut them to pieces in a judgmental way. Just remember, it is a portion of Christ's body that you are cutting. To this effect, consider Paul's exhortations: "*Therefore let us not judge one another anymore, but rather determine this—not to put an obstacle or a stumbling block in a brother's way*" (Romans 14:13). "*Therefore encourage one another and build up one another, just as you also are doing*" (1 Thessalonians 5:11).

James then moved quickly to deflate another balloon of pride, making plans without any regard for God's sovereignty.

## Don't Take God's Sovereignty for Granted

*Come now, you who say, "Today or tomorrow we will go to such and such a city, and spend a year there and engage in business and make a profit." Yet you do not know what your life will be like tomorrow. You are just a vapor that appears for a little while and then vanishes away. Instead, you ought to say, "If the Lord wills, we will live and also do this or that." But as it is, you boast in your arrogance; all such boasting is evil. Therefore, to one who knows the right thing to do and does not do it, to him it is sin* (James 4:13-17).

James chastised his readers, who no longer lived their lives or did business with any acknowledgment that their "*times [were] in [God's] hand*" (Psalm 31:15). They were moving about recklessly with no regard to the sovereignty of God. That's arrogance! So he, reiterating the admonition of the Lord Himself, sought to inject reality into the thinking of his audience. James' message replicates the Lord's:

*Then He [Jesus] said to them, Beware, and be on your guard against every form of greed; for not even when one has an abundance does his life consist of his possessions." And He told them a parable, saying, "The land of a rich man was very productive. And he began reasoning to himself, saying, 'What shall I do, since I have no place to store my crops?' Then he said, 'This is what I will do: I will tear down my barns and build larger ones, and there I will store all my grain and my goods. And I will say to my soul, "Soul, you have many goods laid up for many years to come; take your ease, eat, drink and be merry."' But God said to him, 'You fool! This very night your soul is required of you; and now who will own what you have prepared?' So is the man who stores up treasure for himself, and is not rich toward God"* (Luke 12:15-21).

There we have it in black and white. So beloved, whatever we do, we should be mindful that our lives are *"just a vapor that appears for a little while and then vanishes away"* (James 4:14). We should live our lives with the view that whatever we are now or will attain in the future is a matter of the greatness of His grace. That's the epitome of humility orientation.

With this in mind, James concludes this section with a word of admonition: *"Therefore, to one who knows the right thing to do and does not do it, to him it is sin"* (James 4:17)

James underscores the infallible truth. Sin is not just doing the wrong thing. Sin is equally knowing the right thing and not doing it. Let us ponder this before proceeding to the next chapter.

## TWENTY-TWO

James 5:1-6

# Misuse of Riches

*Come now, you rich, weep and howl for your miseries which are coming upon you. Your riches have rotted and your garments have become moth-eaten. Your gold and your silver have rusted; and their rust will be a witness against you and will consume your flesh like fire. It is in the last days that you have stored up your treasure! Behold, the pay of the laborers who mowed your fields, and which has been withheld by you, cries out against you; and the outcry of those who did the harvesting has reached the ears of the Lord of Sabaoth. You have lived luxuriously on the earth and led a life of wanton pleasure; you have fattened your hearts in a day of slaughter. You have condemned and put to death the righteous man; he does not resist you* (James 5:1-6).

The opening words of this passage don't exactly sound spiritual, do they? "*Come now* ["*Now listen,*" *NIV*],[140] *you rich, weep and howl for your miseries which are coming upon you.*" Every honest teacher of God's Word knows it is unpopular to speak the truth without compromise. However, God's obedient servants are unsettled within until they declare nothing but the whole realm of truth.

Mayor echoes this: "Wherever sin is rampant, wherever oppression and cruelty prevail, where the denunciation of the evil-doer is a dangerous and unpopular service, there the heart of the prophet will still burn within him, till at the last he speaks with his tongue."[141]

In the beginning, James was very gentle in his exhortations and admonitions, addressing his readers most often with saintly phrases, such as "brethren," "my brethren" and even "my beloved brethren." He saved his stern warning for the last. The time for the introduction, "*James, a bond-servant of God*" (James 1:1) had come and gone. The time for exhortation, "*Consider it all joy, my brethren, when you encounter various trials*" (1:2), had come and gone. The time for admonition, "*Do not speak against one another*" (4:11), had come and gone. Then came time for denouncement: "*Your riches have rotted and your garments have become moth-eaten. Your gold and your silver have rusted; and their rust will be a witness against you and will consume your flesh like fire*" (James 5:2-3).

James sharply lambasted the well-to-do and the rich, those arrogant believers, stiff-necked Christians, in his audience who thought they were on top of the world. Who was James addressing when he said "*your riches*"? Tasker states,

> It is clear from i.10 [James 1:10] that there were rich men known to the writer who professed the Christian faith, and that some of them may have been oppressing their less well-to-do brethren. In this section…in effect [James is] holding up as a warning to all Christians, who may be tempted to worldliness, the divine judgment that awaits those who, in one way another, misuse the gift of wealth.[142]

Remember, James' readers were *believers*. There is no shred of evidence in the text that he ever addressed the unbelievers. Why would he? This spiritual failure was a family matter and needed to receive an in-house rebuke.

To this same end, the apostle Paul later asked, "*For what have I to do with judging outsiders [non-Christians]? Do you not judge those who are within the church?*" (1 Corinthians 5:12). Good question! In other words, why should James waste his ink and energy denouncing those who might never read his epistle? Keep in mind, James' epistle is not like the Sermon on the Mount, where the audience was mixed. On the contrary, his epistle was directed to the first group of Church Age *believers*: "*the twelve tribes who are dispersed abro*ad" (James 1:1).

What seems to perplex some scholars is James' change of tone. This is not an exhortation as before but an announcement of the impending judgment their carnal lifestyle would bring. As Dibelius points out, "[Verse 1] is not to be understood as a kind of admonition to repent for but rather as a proclamation: In the future affliction, it will come to pass that you will weep and wail."[143]

It is prophetic! On this scholars agree. My beloved, God is not joking around; His judgment will be swift and certain.

In this passage James did not issue a call to repentance. It was unnecessary, because his readers (believers) understood God's character. It is similar to what the Prophet Isaiah declared to Hezekiah: "*Thus says the LORD, 'Set your house in order, for you shall die and not live'*" (2 Kings 20:1). That's a proclamation, "*you shall die*"! At face value, one would think this prophecy was certain; after all, there was no call to repentance. But the outcome depended on Hezekiah's response. Even though there was no call to repentance, Hezekiah knew God was all merciful, and therefore "*he turned his face to the wall and prayed to the LORD...wept bitterly*" (2 Kings 20:2-3). Consequently, God, the Author of compassion, had mercy on him: "*I have heard your prayer, I have seen your tears; behold, I will heal you*" (2 Kings 20:5).

One errs if one concludes that, because James did not call them to repent from their sin, his message must have been for unsaved wealthy individuals. Remember, his audience was all Jewish believers. They knew about God's mercies from the failures of their forefathers in the wilderness, ranging from God's move to obliterate them from history (Exodus 32:10) to Moses' entreaty (Exodus 32:11-13) and "*the LORD changed His mind*" (Exodus 32:14). They were familiar with all this! What's more; we belittle the monstrous power of the old sin nature when we think that a rich believer is not prone to the same arrogance complex of self-sufficiency that marks unbelievers. If you think otherwise, consider our Lord's rebuke of the church at Laodicea, "*Because you are lukewarm...I will spit you out of My mouth. Because you say, 'I am rich, and have become wealthy, and have need of nothing,' and you do not know that you are wretched and miserable and poor and blind and naked*" (Revelation 3:16-17). Impending judgment is underscored in this verse.

## Impending Judgment

The tragedy in Christianity today is that many do not grasp the truth of Scripture that we are simply God's stewards (1 Peter 4:10). Many have failed to realize that they are God's employees.

Even James begins his letter "*James, a bond-servant [slave] of God.*" Slaves don't own property—they take care of it for others. We are employed to manage and disburse God's wealth for the praise of His glory. Our failure to latch on to this axiom is the source of hoarding, greed, love for money, and "*all sorts of evil, and some [of us] by longing for it [money] have wandered away from the faith [biblical truth] and pierced themselves with many griefs*" (1 Timothy 6:10).

Solomon made a similar remark: "*He who loves money will not be satisfied with money, nor he who loves abundance with its income. This too is vanity*" (Ecclesiastes 5:10).

How often do we erroneously think that abundance in life consists of the possession of things (Luke 12:15)! In contrast, the apostle Paul assured God's faithful stewards,

> And God is able to make all grace abound to you, so that always having all sufficiency in everything, you may have **an abundance for every good deed**...He...will supply and multiply your seed for sowing and increase the harvest of your righteousness; you will be enriched in everything for all liberality, which through us is producing thanksgiving to God. For the ministry of this service is not only fully supplying the needs of the saints, but is also overflowing through many thanksgivings to God (2 Corinthians 9:8-12, emphasis added).

God's surplus is for His plan and purpose, not for our pleasure and hoarding. This may sound extreme, but consider James 5:1: "*Come now, you rich, weep and howl for your miseries which are coming upon you.*"

We ask, "Is being rich sinful?" Tasker replies, "Neither here nor elsewhere in the New Testament are the rich denounced merely for being rich, but rather for yielding so readily to the temptations to which the rich are prone."[144] "Some rich men in their eagerness to get more and more goods have blinded themselves to the obvious fact that such goods, if not used, do and must deteriorate."[145]

James is not denouncing rich believers, for that would contradict the rest of Scripture. Abraham was "*very rich*" beyond measure (Genesis 13:2) and so was Job, "*the greatest of all the men of the east*" (Job 1:3), to name just two. These men, though exceedingly rich, glorified God to the maximum. For instance, Job was constantly on the look out for the needy in every respect (Job 29:12-17). What James is denouncing is the believers' stubbornness in hoarding and refusing to disburse God's wealth to the glory of God, who claims, "*The silver is Mine and the gold is Mine*" (Haggai 2:8).

Was this surprising to James' audience? Not really. We know, as believers, they were spiritually in carnality (James 4:1-4). They, particularly the rich, were living in arrogance like the church at Laodicea: "*I am rich, and have become wealthy, and have need of nothing*" (Revelation 3:17). They had a total disregard for God. These rich brethren were wasting God's money (as if they were not stewards) and, like the Corinthian believers, were suing and defrauding their fellow believers, even to the point of committing murder (1 Corinthians 6:1-7; cf. James 4:1-3; 5:1-5).

God judges those who squander His wealth. Think of it. At the time of James' writing, believers were in unbearable hardship, the poor hit even harder. But God had blessed some of James' Christian audience to benefit the less fortunate. Instead, they hoarded God's resources.

Let's look at it in another way. Today, as in every generation in the Church Age, there are many believers who often worship under conditions of duress, such as under a tree because they can not afford a church building. There are believers who can hardly put food on the table. Many missionary organizations have folded for lack of funding, and willing workers lack resources in corners of the world where many are perishing without hearing of Christ and His saving work. These situations prevail while some believers blessed by God use their wealth instead to improve their lifestyles. Some churches do the same, building newer, more elaborate structures while failing to focus on those around the world who are in great need of the gospel.

These are just a few examples. Sad, is it not? There are a good number of believers whom God has showered with blessings beyond their wildest imagination. God has blessed them with *"an abundance for every good deed"* (2 Corinthians 9:8). But many of these, seeing their fellow believers in horrible conditions, look the other way. They close their pockets as they hear debilitating stories of what missionaries go through to make ends meet or what Christians suffer in general. The response to such an action may be "That's *their* money; *they* can do whatever they wish." But the Bible reminds us, "'*The silver is Mine and the gold is Mine,' declares the LORD of hosts*'" (Haggai 2:8). Hence, James' denouncement, *"Come now, you rich, weep and howl for your miseries which are coming upon you"* (James 5:1).

Considering the shame that awaits the believer at the Judgment Seat of Christ, James said, *"Their rust will be a witness against you and will consume your flesh like fire"* (James 5:3). Essentially, what James is saying is this: "On that day, the Lord will point to a heap of our hoarded unused treasures and then turn His attention to us, His plan for the treasures entrusted to us unfinished because of our greed."

Beloved of God, such a thought calls to mind the apostle John's warning. In his epistle we read, *"Now, little children, abide in Him, so that when He appears, we may have confidence and not shrink away from Him in shame at His coming"* (1 John 2:28).

And we can appreciate the teaching of Jesus as James did. *"Do not store up for yourselves treasures on earth, where moth and rust destroy…But store up for yourselves treasures in heaven, where neither moth nor rust destroys"* (Matthew 6:19-20).

This brings us to another symptom of greed, withholding wages from laborers when due.

## Indictment of Withholding Wages

*"Behold, the pay of the laborers who mowed your fields, and which has been withheld by you, cries out against you; and the outcry of those who did the harvesting has reached the ears of the Lord of Sabaoth"* (James 5:4).

Tasker makes this concept lucid:

James draws attention to what is perhaps the most inhumane of all its manifestations—the withholding from the labourer the payment that is due. In the Mosaic law the divine prohibition of this offense is clear and specific ["The wages of a hired servant shall not remain with you all night until morning" (Lev. 19:13)]. "Thou shalt not oppress an hired servant that is poor and needy...At his day thou shalt give him his hire, neither shall the sun go down upon it; for he is poor, and settteth his heart upon it: lest he cry against thee unto the Lord, and it be sin unto thee' (Dt. Xxiv. 14, 15, brackets added).[146]

Moreover, the labourers, specified by James, whose hire is of you kept back by fraud, are none other than the men who have reaped down your fields: and as Calvin commented, 'What can be more base than that they, who supply us with bread by their labour, should be pinned through want? And yet this monstrous thing is common; for there are many of such a tyrannical disposition that they think that the rest of mankind live only for their benefit.'[147]

Once a believer is carnal, the poison of carnality affects all aspects of his life. He becomes greedy—even to the point of withholding wages. This action of withholding from one whose wage is due begs for severe divine punishment (Malachi 3:5). "So in verses 4-6 James rebuked the rich for breaking this just law of God by failing to make daily payments, and by using the delay in payment to defraud worker of his due."[148]

"'The outcry of those who did the harvesting has reached the ears of the Lord of Sabaoth,' which begs for swift judgment. The "expression 'God of Sabaoth' is one of the most majestic of all titles of God in the Old Testament, drawing attention, as it does, to His sovereign omnipotence."[149]

James goes on to say that these carnal, callous believers "*have lived luxuriously on the earth and led a life of wanton pleasure; you have fattened your hearts in a day of slaughter.*" In other words, these are not to anticipate escaping God's judgment in time, as Tasker points out:

> Assuming their unrepentance...he [James] announces, in the spirit of the Old Testament prophets, the inevitable doom that confronts them. And the inference he would wish his Christian readers to draw from this denunciation is the folly of setting a high value upon wealth, or of envying those who possess it.[150]

The last phrase in this segment of our study is chilling: "*You have condemned and put to death [by your greed] the righteous man; he does not resist you.*"

It is true that a believer in perpetual carnality can do just about anything. He can cheat, he can lie, and he can commit adultery, and yes, even murder, like David. Hence James' indictment: "*You have condemned and put to death the righteous man; he does not resist you.*" The righteous man is no other than a fellow believer in Christ. The rich man used his wealth to get his way. He bribed judges and caused them to twist justice. We all hear the familiar saying "money talks"! Yes. For those callous, rich believers who misused their funds or their wealth, money did indeed talk. But as for the poor believer, he had no means of defense.

The horror that awaits a lifestyle without any regard for God or His commands is worthy of our attention: "*It is a terrifying thing to fall into the hands of the living God*" (Hebrews 10:31). This we must pause and reflect. *Premature physical death* and *no blessings* in all of eternity will be the judgment of a believer that doesn't "get right with God!"

## Reflection

Beloved of God, before we examine another passage, let's reevaluate ourselves. We human beings are buck-passers. We rarely point to ourselves, rarely accept accountability, and rarely accept responsibility but often pass blame to others. Adam passed the buck of his disobedience back to God for creating a woman in the first place. Eve passed the buck to Satan, and ever since, the buck-passing game continues. It is always someone else. That was true of David. He looked past himself when Nathan confronted him for his adultery and murder. Unaware that Nathan was referring to him, David angrily shouted, "*As the LORD lives, surely the man who has done this deserves to die*" (2 Samuel 12:5). David was so blinded, he could not see that *he* was the man.

So, as we come to the end of this chapter. We must ask ourselves a question: "How is my spiritual life? As God's steward, am I using His wealth, no matter how little, in the manner that honors Him?" "Am I living for pleasure or for His Kingdom, "for the praise of His glory"? The answers to these questions are a matter between you and your Savior-God. But in all this, remember: "*But just as it is written, 'THINGS WHICH EYE HAS NOT SEEN AND EAR HAS NOT HEARD, AND which HAVE NOT ENTERED THE HEART OF MAN, ALL THAT GOD HAS PREPARED FOR THOSE WHO LOVE HIM*'" (1 Corinthians 2:9).

In contrast to this good news of reward for the faithful believer, information on the eternal state of those who fail God in time has been withheld by God the Holy Spirit. Scripture only gives sporadic warnings about eternal ramifications of spiritual failure (1 Corinthians 3:11-15). James' epistle was a call for his hearers to return to faithfulness so they would receive great rewards.

His message is just as timely and pertinent for us today.

## TWENTY-THREE

James 5:7-12

# Exhortation for Patience

*Therefore be patient, brethren, until the coming of the Lord. The farmer waits for the precious produce of the soil, being patient about it, until it gets the early and late rains. You too be patient; strengthen your hearts, for the coming of the Lord is near. Do not complain, brethren, against one another, so that you yourselves may not be judged; behold, the Judge is standing right at the door. As an example, brethren, of suffering and patience, take the prophets who spoke in the name of the Lord. We count those blessed who endured. You have heard of the endurance of Job and have seen the outcome of the Lord's dealings, that the Lord is full of compassion and is merciful. But above all, my brethren, do not swear, either by heaven or by earth or with any other oath; but your yes is to be yes, and your no, no, so that you may not fall under judgment* (**James 5:7-12**).

Patience is a virtue. It is the monopoly of the Holy Spirit: "*the fruit of the Spirit is...patience*" (Galatians 5:22). It is the enduring devotion and courage of the believer under overwhelming pressure, both from within and without. Patience is critical in realizing the full measure of the eternal hope that is set before us. Dr. Vine agrees: "Patience perfects Christian character, Jas. 1:4, and fellowship in the patience of Christ is therefore the condition upon which believers are to be admitted to reign with Him, 2 Tim. 2:12; Rev. 1:19."[151]

The author of Hebrews instructed, "*Let us run with endurance the race that is set before us, fixing our eyes on Jesus, the author and perfecter of faith, who for the joy set before Him endured the cross, despising the shame, and has sat down at the right hand of the throne of God"* (Hebrews 12:1-2). James similarly instructed his beloved in 5:7, *"Therefore be patient, brethren, until the coming of the Lord."*

James addressed believers who might be the objects of unfair treatment from their fellow believers or others. He wanted them to know that the road of Christian experience is paved with injustice and unfairness and without regard for God. We are reminded that Christ Himself was the first to set foot on this road. He forewarned, *"If the world hates you, you know that it has hated Me before it hated you"* (John 15:18). He was a perfect man, yet He experienced unfair treatment and human injustice. He perfected this walk for us (Hebrews 2:14-18). For instance, He was ridiculed, slandered, spat upon, beaten mercilessly and sent to His death for something He did not do. My beloved, that's injustice at the height of its cruelty.

---

**Patience is a virtue…the fruit
of the Holy Spirit.**

---

The apostle Peter later highlighted this:

*If when you do what is right and suffer for it you patiently endure it, this finds favor with God. For you have been called for this purpose, since Christ also suffered for you, leaving you an example for you to follow in His steps, WHO COMMITTED NO SIN, NOR WAS ANY DECEIT FOUND IN HIS MOUTH; and while being reviled, He did not revile in return; while suffering, He uttered no threats, but kept entrusting Himself to Him who judges righteously* (1 Peter 2:20-23).

So James urged his brethren to not take matters into their own hands but rather leave retaliation to God, who says, *"VENGEANCE IS MINE, I WILL REPAY"* (Romans 12:19).

Furthermore, James' audience and everyone else for that matter, should realize that God, in His omniscience, knows all that is knowable.

He has all the facts and will, in His perfect timing (not ours), render judgment in accordance with His justice. We must pause and reflect on the God-Man and learn from Him. He went through the terror of injustice and "*while being reviled, He did not revile in return; while suffering, He uttered no threats, but kept entrusting Himself to Him who judges righteously.*" Spiritual life depends entirely on "*the strength of His might*" (Ephesians 6:10). Similarly, patience, the fruit of the Holy Spirit (Galatians 5:22) comes through Him, and can be experienced only by those who are born again. In other words, believers must maintain a constant fellowship with God through confession of sin when they are aware of it (1 John 1:9). James says, "*Be patient, brethren, until the coming of the Lord*" when every believer's work will be made manifest (1 Corinthians 3:11-15; cf. 2 Corinthians 5:10; Romans 14:10-12).

---

**God knows when, and how, to punish wrongdoers. If we get in His way, God will pardon the wrongdoer and deal with us.**

---

James goes on to exhort, "*Do not complain, brethren, against one another, so that you yourselves may not be judged; behold, the Judge is standing right at the door*" (James 5:9). There is only one judge, God! He never needs our assistance in determining the time, place or manner of dealing with the guilty ones. He knows when, and how, to punish the wrongdoers. If we get in His way, God will pardon the wrongdoer and deal with us.

We often ignore this principle of Scripture. I am sure James was familiar with Solomon's writing: "*Do not rejoice when your enemy falls, And do not let your heart be glad when he stumbles; Or the LORD will see it and be displeased, And turn His anger away from him*" (Proverbs 24:17-18). Yes, you read it correctly! God can forgo the discipline due the one that has wronged you and turn the discipline to you instead because of your impatience or joy at the pain of one who has wronged you.

Simply put, dare not get even with the one who has ill-treated you! It is not worth it! This brings up another topic.

## The Patience of Job

*"As an example, brethren, of suffering and patience, take the prophets who spoke in the name of the Lord. We count those blessed who endured. You have heard of the endurance of Job and have seen the outcome of the Lord's dealings, that the Lord is full of compassion and is merciful"* (James 5:10-11). What a remarkable and excellent Bible communicator James was! He knew when and how to use illustrations or examples to drive his point home. He used Abraham and Rahab to prove that believers can be justified positionally, not only for salvation from the lake of fire, but also experientially for an immeasurable reward in both time and eternity future (James 2:14-26).

Now he turns to Job, the master of patience, to encourage them and to emphasize his point. He shows that God rewards the believer who, in spite of even satanic assaults, demonstrates both in words and actions the power of God's Word in his life.

Obviously, we cannot appreciate Job's patience without looking into his spiritual life. With careful scrutiny one concludes that Job's knowledge of God's character guided him throughout his ordeal. He realized that God was omniscient and sovereign and therefore knew what He was doing: *"But He knows the way I take; When He has tried me, I shall come forth as gold"* (Job 23:10).

It's one thing to give a testimony of how the Lord delivered you from the pressure of testing; it's another thing altogether to assure a friend, without any doubt in your mind, that you "believe God" will see you through your predicament (Acts 27:25). Remember, Job was still inside the furnace of testing when he declared, *"I shall come forth as gold."*

James in his masterpiece now seeks to underscore his earlier exhortation when he told them to *"Consider it all joy, my brethren, when you encounter various trials, knowing that the testing of your faith [biblical truth] produces endurance. And let endurance have its perfect result [literally, work], so that you may be perfect [mature] and complete, lacking in nothing"* (James 1:2-4).

James reminded his readers that God had a purpose in Job's suffering, and likewise He has a purpose in whatever dilemma a believer might find himself. What is the solution for suffering? Patience! We are commanded to wait. "*Be still before the LORD, and wait patiently for him*" (Psalm 37:7, RSV). More than that, patience is self-assurance that "*The LORD will accomplish what concerns me*" (Psalm 138:8). So James affirmed, "*We count those blessed who endured. You have heard of the endurance of Job and have seen the outcome of the Lord's dealings, that the Lord is full of compassion and is merciful*" (James 5:11).

James reminded them of "*the outcome of the Lord's dealings*" with Job. Every thorough student of God's Word knows the outcome of Job's testing and patience. God blessed him beyond measure because through the trials Job developed superior capacity for superior abundant blessings. This too is the message of James!

This brings up another element.

## Speak the Truth

"*But above all, my brethren, do not swear, either by heaven or by earth or with any other oath; but your yes is to be yes, and your no, no, so that you may not fall under judgment*" (**James 5:12**). James returns to a subject on which he clearly feels very deeply—the evil that so easily finds its way into speech and conversation. He has already dealt with some aspects of this "restless evil," as he calls the tongue.[152]

We have studied the tongue previously, but James has reason to return to this topic. As Mitton remarks, "So low had ordinary standards of truthfulness sunk that a statement or a promise was felt to be valueless unless it was supported by a solemn oath."[153] This is heartbreaking, a sad picture of the Christian readers of James' epistle. James is warning them about a prohibition with which they were all too familiar.

"*You shall not take the name of the LORD your God in vain, for the LORD will not leave him unpunished who takes His name in vain*" (Exodus 20:7). Taking the name of the Lord in vain is more than swearing or worse, using God's name as a curse word. It also encompasses using the name of Jesus or God to falsely endorse something that He absolutely does not subscribe to. When we invoke the phrase "In Jesus' name," we must be sure we correctly represent His position as we find it in the Bible.

We observe that in James' exhortations and admonitions, he has been careful in selecting some of the sins that often beg for immediate divine discipline. One of these is the sin of the tongue, one of the seven sins that God hates (Proverbs 6:16-19). The Psalmist asks, "*Who is the man who desires life And loves length of days that he may see good? Keep your tongue from evil And your lips from speaking deceit. Depart from evil and do good; Seek peace and pursue it*" (Psalm 34:12-14).

Under the mentorship of the Holy Spirit, James reaches into the pile of their spiritual failures and grabs the sin of using the name of the Lord in vain. It appears that believers were no longer taking other believers' word at face value unless it carried the signature of God's name. This our Lord speaks against: "*I say to you, make no oath at all...let your statement be 'Yes, yes' or 'No, no'; and anything beyond this is evil*" (Matthew 5:34-37).

The Lord is saying, "Be truthful!" The apostle Paul also said, "*Therefore, laying aside falsehood, SPEAK TRUTH EACH ONE of you WITH HIS NEIGHBOR, for we are members of one another*" (Ephesians 4:25).

This is a hallmark of Christianity, holding high the banner of truth, in both words and actions.

We now pause to examine another pivotal passage of James chapter 5.

## TWENTY-FOUR

James 5:13-18

# The Fervent Prayer of the Believer-Priest

*Is anyone among you suffering? Then he must pray. Is anyone cheerful? He is to sing praises. Is anyone among you sick? Then he must call for the elders of the church and they are to pray over him, anointing him with oil in the name of the Lord; and the prayer offered in faith will restore the one who is sick, and the Lord will raise him up, and if he has committed sins, they will be forgiven him. Therefore, confess your sins to one another, and pray for one another so that you may be healed. The effective prayer of a righteous man can accomplish much. Elijah was a man with a nature like ours, and he prayed earnestly that it would not rain, and it did not rain on the earth for three years and six months. Then he prayed again, and the sky poured rain and the earth produced its fruit* (**James 5:13-18**).

Beloved of God, as you can see, we are nearing the end of our biblical study. We can't thank God enough for His unsurpassed faithfulness. His Spirit has been so faithful in mentoring us in uncovering the truth in this powerful epistle.

James 5:13-18 has for centuries been a battleground for scholars and interpreters of the infallible Word of God. The ramifications of its misinterpretation are too deep for measurement. There has been much confusion in churches today on various issues, ranging from praying for the sick to the use of anointing oil. For instance, some pastors have made fortunes marketing so-called "prayer cloths" and "anointing oil" to their congregations. They base their tradition of anointing oil on our passage. Our task is to untangle the misconceptions surrounding James' message.

There is little or no disagreement among scholars about the first half of this passage, "*Is anyone among you suffering? Then he must pray Is anyone cheerful? He is to sing praises*" (James 5:13).

---

**The believer must be in fellowship and his spiritual life pleasing to God for prayer to be effective.**

---

Prayer is so vital in every area of our lives, we should use it more often: when we are troubled (Psalm 50:15), distressed or suffering (James 5:13), seeking for wisdom (James 1:5) or bombarded with the storm of anxiety (Philippians 4:6-7). Although we have been called to petition the throne of His grace, we should never forget that prayer is a condition-based weapon (1 John 3:18-22). In other words, the believer needs to have certain things in order before he begins to pray. The believer must be in fellowship (1 John 1:9) and his spiritual life pleasing to God (Psalm 66:18) for prayer to be effective. With this in mind, we dive straight into this challenging section.

## A Call to Compassion

"*Is anyone among you sick? Then he must call for the elders of the church and they are to pray over him, anointing him with oil in the name of the Lord*" (**James 5:14**). Who can argue that James has not shown his readers what compassion is all about? Over and over again, he has succinctly applied this principle of Scripture. Even Paul wrote on this topic: "*Brethren, even if anyone is caught in any trespass, **you who are spiritual, restore such a one in a spirit of gentleness; each one looking to yourself, so that you too will not be tempted*" (Galatians 6:1).

As a spiritual believer, in James 1:22 James exhorts, "*Prove yourselves doers of the word, and not merely hearers.*" Who can argue that James had not lived up to his own exhortation? His reproof, rebuke and exhortation have all been done in the spirit of humility, with compassion and the love of Christ.

As he comes to the end of his epistle, James turns his attention to those who might be going through difficult times, emotionally or physically. To these, in reference to the degree of their suffering, he asks, "*Is anyone among you sick? Then he must call for the elders of the church and they are to pray over him, anointing him with oil in the name of the Lord*" (James 5:14).

I know of a young man who tells of his experience in a medical preparatory program. One of the crucial lessons they learned in patient care was the importance of compassion in caring for those in pain. This was often exhibited by touching the patient and making eye contact. In other words, let patients know that physicians share in their pain and suffering. If this is expected of caregivers in the secular world, how much more in the spiritual realm?

The annals of Scripture are filled with compassionate deeds. Examples abound! Consider the testimony of a blind man to whom the Lord showed compassion: "*The man who is called Jesus made clay, and anointed my eyes, and said to me, 'Go to Siloam and wash'; so I went away and washed, and I received sight*" (John 9:11).

We are talking about the Creator Himself, who "*said, 'Let there be light'; and there was light*" (Genesis 1:3; cf. Colossians 1:16). He could have, without a touch, commanded, "Receive your sight!" and the blind man would have received his sight instantly! After all, He called Lazarus out from the grave, "*Lazarus, come forth*" (John 11:43), and "*The man who had died came forth*" (v. 44). But, instead, "*He spat on the ground, and made clay of the spittle, and applied the clay to his eyes*" (John 9:6).

What's the underlying message of this miracle? You are right: compassion! Our Lord took time to work the clay and apply it. Such a gesture sends the message of love, care and compassion! What is more, He even touched an outcast with the disease of leprosy! "*He stretched out His hand and touched him, saying, 'I am willing; be cleansed.' And immediately the leprosy left him*" (Luke 5:13).

He likewise touched children with a hand of compassion (Luke 18:15). The citations are endless!

James' underlying message is compassion. It is the main thrust, and in 1 Peter 2:21 we are commanded to "*follow in His steps.*" We noted three elements of compassion in James exhortation:

- The sufferer makes a compassionate plea
- A compassionate gesture from the elders
- An expectation of compassion from the "God of Compassion"

Many of us read the Scripture so hastily that often we miss, or add to, what the writer had in mind. The fact is that one cannot properly interpret a passage until one has a firm grip on what the author is saying. Before I researched how scholars interpreted this passage, I went through the passage and made some observations.

The first observation is very crucial to our interpretation: The sick person was asked to "*call for the elders.*" Why? Because the sick person couldn't walk to the elders. This is important! Dr. Fruchtenbaum underscores that observation. He says that the Greek word James uses for "sick" in our passage means "to be without strength…It refers to an incapacitated sickness…the weakness produced by sickness…This deterioration…causes one to become incapable of working and it can even lead to death…In John 4:46-47, the word is used of one who was about to die."[154]

This explains why the sick person is mandated to "*call for the elders of the church.*" He is to call the elders because of his weakened condition. For a reason known to God alone, this invitation to pray is to be done once. Dr. Spiros Zodhiates, a Greek scholar, comments, "The aorist tense indicates that this is not a repeated prayer but a single prayer."[155] Both the call of the sick person and the prayer of the elders are to be done once.

Perhaps this is the type of illness that defies medical help and therefore is incurable by human means. The sickness might also be as a result of divine judgment due to perpetual carnality, as verse 15 indicates: "*if he has committed sins, they will be forgiven him*" (cf. John 5:14; I Corinthians 11:24-30). If this assumption stands, that could explain why the sick person should call the elders not more than one time. In other words, God would make the final decision as to whether He would extend grace to the person by healing him and allotting him more time, as He did for Hezekiah (2 Kings 20:1-6), or call the believer home. His decision would be in response to the prayer of the saints.

This, however, does not mean that every prayer offered by the elders would receive an instantaneous "yes" answer. The answer would still be according to the will of God: "*This is the confidence which we have before Him, that, if we ask anything according to His will, He hears us*" (1 John 5:14).

Christ in His intense prayer in Gethsemane said, "*Father, if You are willing, remove this cup from Me; yet not My will, but Yours be done*" (Luke 22:42). God's will has the last word concerning all prayers, no matter how intense! Another example is the apostle Paul's "*thorn in the flesh*" (2 Corinthians 12:7). There's no doubt in my mind that even if Paul had summoned all the elders of every church to pray for him, the answer would still be the same as he received when he prayed three times: "*My grace is sufficient for you, for power is perfected in weakness*" (2 Corinthians 12:9). You see, it was the will of God for the thorn in Paul's flesh to remain for his own good and blessing (2 Corinthians 12:7). This is the beauty of God's matchless grace!

\* \* \*

Before we go any further, we need to correct some unbiblical practices that permeate some of our churches today. Read our passage again. James never instructed the sick individual to call the "faith healers." The sick individual is never asked to look for those with the gift of healing. Why is that? It is because the spectacular, miraculous gift of healing was restricted to the apostles and their delegates (Acts 5:12; cf. 2 Corinthians 12:12).

Some churches today have ignored Scripture and set up "healing camps." These are not serving God, for they are without scriptural authorization. God is not a God of confusion (1 Corinthians 14:33). If God had wanted us to practice "faith healing," James or other writers of the New Testament epistles would have so stated.[156] This brings up another important issue in our discussion: oil.

## Anoint With Oil

James' instruction continues, "*They are to pray over him, anointing him with oil in the name of the Lord*" (James 5:14).

There is a sharp division about what James meant by "*anointing him with oil.*" Those with medical experience know too well what can happen to a person who is bedridden or incapacitated. Often the person develops bedsores. This would help explain James call "*to pray over him, anointing him with oil in the name of the Lord.*"

Some have gone as far as ascribing the oil to the Holy Spirit. There's no room for such an assertion. Every believer from the day of Pentecost onward is already indwelt by the Holy Spirit from the moment of salvation, so it does not make sense for the elders to apply the Holy Spirit to the sick.

Another suggestion is that the oil would increase the faith of the elders. That too is a weak interpretation. God does not need help manifesting His omnipotent power. Besides, faith that needs a prop is not really faith. Beloved, we need to be logical in our interpretation. This we shall do in light of the facts we have before us.

---

**Faith that needs a prop
is not really faith.**

---

What do we know about this situation? First, the sick person is bedridden, therefore he probably has developed bedsores. Second, we are acutely aware of the medical significance of oil in treating these and other wounds. This practice goes back to time immemorial. Mitton points out, "The use of oil in the treatment of illness was very common in the ancient world. Mayor (p. 158) quotes evidence for this from such writers as Josephus, Philo and Pliny."[157] Mitton continues, "Galen (Med. Temp. ii) calls oil 'The best of all remedies for paralysis.'"[158] This is why James takes the pain to ensure that there is no ambiguity with regard to his instruction. He uses a Greek word, *aleipho*. It is this word that was translated "anointing" in our passage but literally means "rubbing." Aleipho, in the original, is never used in a sacramental sense. It simply means "to rub or to apply ointment."[159]

This makes sense considering the condition of the one whom the elders were visiting, one who perhaps had developed open sores because of his incapacitation. The elders were to be compassionate. They were to demonstrate love. Untreated bedsores can become infected and odorous. What should the elders do if this was the case? Pray from a distance because of an unbearable odor? No! They were to go in, clean his wounds if necessary, and then apply oil as medicine to his wounds. My beloved, such a gesture can soothe a depressed soul and bring refreshment. For the sick man, the impact of their love would be its own medicine. That's what practical Christianity is all about, care from the heart.

This is exactly the story of the Good Samaritan (Luke 10:34). Dr. Zuck agrees with our interpretation. He states,

> The word in James 5:14 is *aleipho*, which means to rub with oil. What James was referring to, then, was not a spiritual ritual. Instead it was a refreshing and encouraging act for an ill or discouraged person. (Aleipho is used in Matt. 6:17 with reference to rubbing oil on one's head [to refresh himself] and in Luke 7:46, with reference to the sinful woman rubbing perfume on Jesus' feet.)[160]

Just think about what was happening here. For one thing, the Lord was not sick; and for another thing, the one performing the act is a sinner. So rubbing can also be a gesture of love or appreciation, as it is in this case of the sinful woman rubbing perfume on Jesus' feet.

In view of the biblical command to rightly divide the word of God, we consider one of the other two words for anointing used in the New Testament Greek. That word is *chrio*. Clearly, this is the one that's "used in a religious sacramental sense."[161] Consider that James, under the guidance of the Holy Spirit, avoided the use of that word. Is this a mistake? Not at all! This is significant! It underscores the fact that James did not intend for the church to institute an anointing ministry.

This should also sound a warning to ministers who use olive oil in a sacramental manner in their church services. This practice is an introduction to idolatry. This may sound extreme. However, consider believers who carry so-called "anointing oil" in their bag, or even keep it at home as a means of keeping the evil one away. I know of a woman who anointed every car in a parking lot to keep those attending her daughter's wedding from car accidents. That's worshipping oil, not God. That's idolatry!

Sacramental use of oil is clearly prescribed in a very defined and restricted nature in Scripture:

> *"You shall make of these a holy anointing oil, a perfume mixture, the work of a perfumer; it shall be a holy anointing oil. With it you shall…anoint Aaron and his sons, and consecrate them, that they may minister as priests to Me. "You shall speak to the sons of Israel, saying, 'This shall be a holy anointing oil to Me throughout your generations. It shall not be poured on anyone's body, nor shall you make any like it in the same proportions; it is holy, and it shall be holy to you.* **Whoever shall mix any like it or whoever puts any of it on a layman shall be cut off from his people** *'"* (Exodus 30:25-33).

It is important to note that every believer in Christ already has His anointing. This is the truth of Scripture. *"And as for you, the anointing [the Holy Spirit] which you received from Him abides in you"* (1 John 2:27).

Scriptural references abound to further identify that James was referring to ordinary oil used for its medicinal value (Luke 10:34; Isaiah 1:5-6; Jeremiah 8:22; 46:11). Under the Lord's instructions His disciples went around *"anointing with oil many sick people and healing them"* (Mark 6:13). The ritual accomplished the same purpose, expression of compassion, love and care.

The question arises: "Should believers practice the same today?" The answer is yes, if we have grasped the principles behind the exhortation, namely expression of compassion and medicinal application! We can, instead of olive oil, use more advanced therapeutic oil on the sick person's wounds or sore body, such as medicated petroleum jelly. Today there are advances in many types of essential oils that are helpful in restoring a person to health. Obviously, as those who follow the heartbeat of our Savior, we do not need to wait until those who cannot come to our assembly because of their incapacitation invite us. In fact, the Lord encourages our voluntary visitation of them: "*I was sick, and you visited Me*" (Matthew 25:36). Further, our visitation should not just be one time, if the individual still needs help.

* * *

This brings us to the next verses for discussion: "*Pray over him, anointing him with oil in the name of the Lord; and the prayer offered in faith will restore the one who is sick, and the Lord will raise him up, and if he has committed sins, they will be forgiven him*" (**James 5:14-15**).

As we said at the beginning of our chapter, prayer is a wonderful thing! Certain conditions must be met before a prayer can be effective. One of the conditions is that the one offering the prayer be in fellowship (Psalm 66:18; cf. 1 John 1:9), with a lifestyle that's honoring to the Lord (1 John 3:22; cf. John 15:7). The prayer of course is to be offered in total confidence that God will respond according to what is best for the present circumstance. "*Anointing him with oil in the name of the Lord*" does not make the oil sacramental in any sense. Rather the phrase "*in the name of the Lord*" is a reference to the manner in which the believer is to render his service, as unto the Lord: "*Whatever you do in word or deed, do all in the name of the Lord Jesus, giving thanks through Him to God the Father*" (Colossians 3:17).

James said, "*The prayer offered in faith will restore the one who is sick, and the Lord will raise him up.*" James was not saying that every prayer that is offered by the elders will receive a favorable answer instantly. Remember, he had already laid a foundation of patience, using Job as a perfect example. Our prayers will not interrupt God's purpose and plan for our lives. For instance, had Job's friends offered prayer for his recovery, Job would not have recovered until the testing had run its course. That's the beauty of "*not My will, but Yours be done*" (Luke 22:42)!

We are getting close to the end of our work. James was not finished. He had yet another topic to address.

## Sin and Sickness

*And the prayer offered in faith will restore the one who is sick, and the Lord will raise him up, **and if he has committed sins, they will be forgiven him**. Therefore, confess your sins to one another, and pray for one another so that you may be healed. The effective prayer of a righteous man can accomplish much. Elijah was a man with a nature like ours, and he prayed earnestly that it would not rain, and it did not rain on the earth for three years and six months. Then he prayed again, and the sky poured rain and the earth produced its fruit* (**James 5:15-18**).

Beloved of God, how many times in our dissertation have we come across the word *sin* in connection with suffering, or even death? Here James links the possibility of severe illness to sin: "*The Lord will raise him up, and if he has committed sins, they will be forgiven him.*" With James' assumption in mind, you can read our other difficult passage one more time: "*What use is it, my brethren, if someone says he has faith [biblical truth, creed] but he has no works [application]? Can that faith [literally 'the faith,' i.e., accumulated biblical truth] save him?*" (James 2:14).

Save him from what? Divine discipline! Sin is the source of many miseries that believers frequently go through. Mitton agrees:

The connection between sickness and SIN is a problem which haunts the human mind. It appears again and again in the Bible, as men grope to discover an answer to it. In the Old Testament times it was customary to assume that sickness was caused by sin, but Jesus emphatically denied that this was always the case (John 9:3; Luke 13:1-5). He did, however, make it plain that some sickness has its origin in sin, as in Mark 2:5ff.[162]

Some of these sins could be injuries done to others that really need to be resolved on a personal basis, one-on-one with the offended parties or individuals (Matthew 5:23-24; Mark 11:24-26). Hence the exhortation, "*Therefore, confess your sins to one another.*" James is not asking that we run around or stand in front of everyone and confess our sins. That would be unreasonable and ludicrous! All sins are an offense against God—"*Against You, You only, I have sinned*" (Psalm 51:4)—and therefore all confessions are made directly to Him: "*I acknowledged my sin to You*" (Psalm 32:5; cf. 1 John 1:9). The idea of confessing our sins to human priests is a man-made one with no scriptural foundation whatsoever. After all, today *every* believer is a priest (1 Peter 2:9). Each believer priest represents himself before God, through our Great High Priest, Jesus Christ (Hebrews 2:17).

Surprising? No. James reminds them about Elijah, another hero of faith. Elijah was a man called by God, prepared by God, to confront and steer the degenerate believers of his day back to God. He was the man of the hour. "*Elijah was a man with a nature like ours, and he prayed earnestly that it would not rain, and it did not rain on the earth for three years and six months*" (James 5:17).

James, as an excellent teacher, reaches into the Old Testament and selects Elijah to encourage these elders (mature leaders) and everyone else too. Elijah was not a super man; he was simply an ordinary man who had confidence in Yahweh.

"*If we ask anything according to His will, He hears us*" (1 John 5:14). We must offer prayer in confidence, with no iota of doubt, after we have the assurance that we are not praying contrary to the known will of God according to Scripture. "*The effective prayer of a righteous man can accomplish much*" (James 5:16).

Mayor's remarks are worthy of note in concluding this section:

> The object of the passage is to encourage the exercise of those mutual spiritual aids rendered by Christians to each other, which is one of the great objects and privileges of the institution of the church. The body was to sympathize with its several members. If a man was in trouble, he was to pray; if in joy to sing hymns…St. Paul's command, "Rejoice with them that do rejoice and weep with them that weep," applies to this same sympathy…care, however, is taken to show that the virtue of their prayers arises not from their priests, but from their being Christians, and standing in the place of the whole church.[163]

It's my heartfelt prayer that the truth communicated so far will make an indelible mark, causing us to reexamine our priorities, therefore serving God with fear and trembling. We know that one day we would stand before Him to be evaluated!

We are now poised to examine the last increment, the joy shared in restoring one who has backslidden from God's plan for his spiritual life, or simply known as the "backslider's restoration."

## TWENTY-FIVE

James 5:19-20

# Sharing the Joy of a Backslider's Restoration

*My brethren, if any among you strays from the truth and one turns him back, let him know that he who turns a sinner from the error of his way will save his soul from [premature physical] death and will cover a multitude of sins* (**James 5:19-20**).

We have come to the last passage of this magnificent epistle. Our Lord spoke of joy in heaven *"over one sinner who repents"* (Luke 17:7). While Luke's account is a reference to an unsaved sinner, James here speaks of a failed or "backslidden" believer.

You say, "How do we know for sure that the sinner in our passage is a believer?" The answer is found in the context: *"My brethren, if any among you strays from the truth."* James identifies his audience with his usual family address, *"My brethren,"* meaning those who already have *"faith in our glorious Lord Jesus Christ"* (James 2:1). There can only be one interpretation of the phrase *"among you,"* those in the body of Christ.

* * *

The conclusion of this section should erase any preconceived notion anyone might have about James' ultimate purpose. It is imperative to revisit some of our previous work in order to help us totally understand the last two verses of James. It should demonstrate beyond doubt that James' epistle was written to bring those he had already labeled spiritual *"adulteresses"* (James 4:4) back to God and thus save their lives from premature physical death. This is clearly seen in his statement *"Let him know that he who turns a sinner from the error of his way will save his soul from death"* (James 5:20). Or as Zane Hodges puts it,

> In fact, anyone who turns a sinner from the error of his way (*hodos*: "road") is in reality turning him aside from a sinful path that can lead him to his [premature] physical death (see 1:15). Thus a Christian's efforts for the restoration of his brother to the pathway of obedience are life-saving in scope. If successful, he will save a soul (*psuche*: "life," "person") from [premature physical] death.164

Let's remember the word *save*, which is the bedrock of this passage. Understanding it can clear up much confusion with the entire epistle. The Greek word *sozo*, "to save," has several meanings, as we studied in our introduction (see chapter 2). But how can we determine when the word is used in reference to salvation from hell fire and when is it used to mean salvation from physical danger? The answer is a simple one: context!

James in his epistle used the word *save* five times (James 1:21; 2:14; 4:12; 5:15; 5:20). Careful analysis of these passages, according to their contexts, reveals that all refer to salvation from premature physical death or lost of life, with the exception of 4:12: *"There is only one Lawgiver and Judge, the One who is able to save [eternal soul salvation] and to destroy [a reference to eternal judgment]."*165

In 1:21, James, writing to those who had already anchored their "faith in our glorious Lord," exhorted, *"Receive the word implanted, which is able to save your souls [lives, from premature physical death]"* (James 1:21).

In 2:14, James posed a provocative question to these believers: *"What use is it, my brethren, if someone says he has faith [biblical truth, creed] but he has no works [application]? Can that faith [literally 'the faith,' i.e., accumulated biblical truth] save him [from premature physical death]?"*

In 5:15, James closed in: *"And the prayer offered in faith [confidence] will restore [same Greek word for save—from premature physical death] the one who is sick."*

In 5:20, James rested his dissertation: "*Let him know that he who turns a sinner [a backslider] from the error of his way will save his soul [life] from [premature physical] death.*"

Mayor's commentary on James' last words fits here perfectly:

"Conversion" to us already implies 'saving the soul'; but this need not have been so to the first readers of the epistle. To them the words may have meant 'However many sins the wanderer has been guilty of, still, if he turns, he will be saved from the death he has deserved, and all his sins will be forgiven.[166]

There's no doubt in James' mind that anyone who lives in perpetual carnality will eventually come to an early grave, for he was familiar with the Old Testament passage "*The years of the wicked [believer in perpetual carnality] will be shortened*" (Proverbs 10:27).

Let us make a quick recap of our study:

1. James was acutely aware of the spiritual state of his readers. He knew they were in grave danger because they were "*adulteresses.*" So he began in the first chapter of his epistle with a warning: "*When sin is accomplished, it brings forth death*" (James 1:15).

2. Realizing this, he appealed, "*[Put] aside all filthiness*" (James 1:21); and "*In humility receive the word implanted, which is able to save your souls [lives]*" (James 1:21).

3. He knew believers could be spiritually cleansed and receive God's Word but, without application, still be liable to discipline. So he further exhorts, "*Prove yourselves doers of the word*" (James 1:22).

4. Moving on, he zooms home with the all important question: "*What use is it, my brethren, if someone says he has faith [accumulation of biblical truth] but he has no works [application of the accumulated Word]? Can that faith [literally 'the*"[167] *] faith [creed, orthodox "belief"* [168]] *save him [from divine judgment and punishment]?*"

5. He reminded them about dual justification, one by faith alone for salvation from hellfire, and the other for a reward. Still passionately concerned, he expresses his loving care.

One would think that James would now rest his pen, but not yet. He goes on to exhort the remnants who are still spiritually on course: "*My brethren, if any among you strays from the truth and one turns him back, let him know that he who turns a sinner from the error of his way will save his soul [life] from [premature physical] death and will cover a multitude of sins*" (James 5:19-20).

What a servant of God! You see, James never questioned the eternal salvation of his audience. He called them brethren fifteen times. He knew they had received a free gift of eternal life (James 1:17-18; cf. Romans 6:23). What's more, from Genesis to Revelation, we cannot find a passage that suggests that the author of any book is in doubt of the salvation of those they knew had already trusted in Yahweh (Jesus Christ).

We remember those from the Old Testament who failed but were truly saved. Among them we studied the believers of the Exodus generation and King Saul and David. And in the New Testament we studied the apostle Peter and the immoral Corinthian believers. All saved!

Consider our Lord. He never questioned whether Peter's salvation was genuine; He only said to Peter, "*When once you have turned again [recovered from your spiritual failure], strengthen your brothers*" (Luke 22:32).

James' message to his hearers in 5:19,20 is like that of our Lord to Peter in Luke 22:32. They didn't question the salvation of the believers based on their poor performance in the spiritual arena. They saw the believers' sinful state and called for them to consider their state, confess their sins, learn and apply biblical truth, and encourage others around them to do the same. This message is the same for the Church today.

There's no ground for making people who have personally trusted in Christ doubt whether their faith is saving faith or to fear they only have a head belief. Such phrases cannot be found in Scripture anywhere! We err when we read James 2:14 and conclude that James had saving faith in mind. On the authority of the Word of God, that's not what he had in mind. The faith in question is not trust or confidence but rather accumulated biblical truth.

\* \* \*

**Beloved of God, only when we understand that casualties are part of war, human or spiritual, can we honestly sympathize with the wounded brethren**—those who have fallen on the wayside of the spiritual battleground. The apostle Peter understood the danger, and so he exhorted, *"Be of sober spirit, be on the alert Your adversary, the devil, prowls around like a roaring lion, seeking someone to devour"* (1 Peter 5:8). Yes, the devil can devour even great believers.

Only when this reality settles into your soul, that a believer can backslide and cease to bear fruit, can we honestly and passionately heed the impassioned exhortations of the servants of old, men like James and the apostle Paul. Consider their words:

> *My brethren, if any among you strays from the truth and one turns him back, let him know that he who turns a sinner from the error of his way will save his soul [life] from [premature physical] death and will cover a multitude of sins* (James 5:19-20).

> *Brethren, even if anyone is caught in any trespass, you who are spiritual, restore such a one in a spirit of gentleness; each one looking to yourself, so that you too will not be tempted* (Galatians 6:1).

Only when the truth dawns on us that a baby believer can only produce baby fruit (1 Corinthians 3:1) can we resist the temptation of using the idea of "saving faith" as a measuring device to determine whether a believer is truly saved. Coming to grips with this truth will help us pray fervently for those who have *"left [their] first love"* (Revelation 2:4) and *"have fallen"* on the wayside of the spiritual battleground (2:5). It is my deepest prayer that this truth, which has been presented under the mentorship of the Holy Spirit, will be a source of tremendous challenge to all of us, to the praise of His glory!

So then, it's fitting that we conclude this comprehensive study with the words of Dr. John Walvoord:

James has given clear instructions about how to achieve practical holiness and spiritual maturity. His pointed exhortations were designed to stab the consciences and stir the souls of his beloved Jewish brothers [and sisters]. Stand with confidence, serve with compassion, speak with care, submit with contrition, and share with concern. A believer should be what God wants him to be, do what God wants he to do, say what God wants him to say, sense what God wants him to sense, and share what God wants him to share. Spiritual maturity involves every aspect of life.[169]

He couldn't have said it better! Above all, what a joy we share when a fallen believer is reunited in fellowship with our Savior Jesus Christ!

## TWENTY-SIX

# Final Thoughts

So, my beloved brothers and sisters in Christ, it is obvious that we have traveled a long way together in this study. We have defined words, dissected verses and reexamined long-held ideas. I am sure along the way we all have hit some bumps in the road. No doubt many of us are suffering bruises from the long, hard journey. I stand by your side as your brother in Christ. My heart is with you, for I know we all are searching to know how to better serve God and, consequently, how to better serve our fellow brothers and sisters in Christ.

As we have come to the end of our work, I humbly ask you to be like the Bereans (Acts 17:11). My objective is not to correct you but to challenge you. My prayer is that with the guidance of the Holy Spirit you will carefully review and consider the material presented. Ask God to cast His beam of light on His Word and show you what He has for you. Let Scripture, not me, be your guide. If you encounter any correction from the Word, I pray that you will accept it as from the Lord.

As the members of the body of Christ we are all in this spiritual battle together. If the head is not feeling well, it is hard for the rest of the body to function. If the foot is hurt, how can we travel together to take the good news? **When the Church is well we can strengthen and encourage one another, and together we can reach out to those in darkness, without hope, without Christ.** Together we can represent Jesus, in both word and deed, and together we can guide the perishing to hope and eternal life through Him.

Only when the Church is strong and healthy will God bring the revival we all so desperately need and desire. The ills of the world have spiritual roots and need a spiritual solution. God, who is loving and just, will not, **in all fairness**, spark revival until there are healthy churches full of growing and mature believers. For He knows the new spiritual babies will need spiritual homes where they can "*grow in the grace and knowledge of our Lord and Savior Jesus Christ. To Him be the glory, both now and to the day of eternity. Amen*" (2 Peter 3:18).

So let us stand shoulder to shoulder in the battle as we strengthen ourselves and our brothers and sisters, encouraging each other every step of the way.

*Now to the King eternal, immortal, invisible* (1 Timothy 1:17).

*To Him who is able to keep you from stumbling, and to make you stand in the presence of His glory blameless with great joy, to the only God our Savior, through Jesus Christ our Lord, be glory, majesty, dominion and authority, before all time and now and forever. Amen* (Jude 1:24-25).

# Endnotes

[1] Zane Hodges, *The Epistle of James* (Grace Evangelical Society, 1994), 12.

[2] John A. Robinson, *Redating the New Testament* (Philadelphia: Westminster Press, 1976), 122.

[3] Author's translation.

[4] Zane Hodges, *The Epistle of James* (Grace Evangelical Society, 1994), 7.

[5] Introduction to 1 Corinthians, New American Standard Bible (1995), 1507.

[6] Ibid.

[7] Author's translation.

[8] *Agape* means supreme love, emphasizing the integrity of the subject rather than the object. It is God's love—God, who loves man unconditionally based on who and what He is, not the reverse.

[9] Millard J. Erickson, *Christian Theology* (Grand Rapids: Baker Books, 1998), 972-973.

[10] Arnold G. Fruchtenbaum, *Ariel's Bible Commentary* (San Antonio, TX: Ariel Ministries, 2005), 261.

[11] Ibid., 262.

[12] Enduement: An empowerment of the Holy Spirit in the Old Testament, experienced by only a few believers. It could be withdrawn by God due to sin. Enduement was replaced by a permanent indwelling of the Holy Spirit for all believers in the Church Age.

[13] Barbara B. Simons, *Webster's New World Dictionary* (The World Publishing Company, 1971), 399.

[14] W.E. Vine, *An Expository Dictionary of New Testament Words* (London, UK: n.p., 1940), 231.

[15] Ibid.

[16] Lewis Sperry Chafer, *Systematic Theology*, vol. 7 (Dallas, Texas: Dallas Seminary Press, 1948), 146.

[17] James 2:14, middle column, New American Standard Bible (1995).

[18] James Orr, ed., *The International Standard Bible Encyclopedia*, vol. 2 (n.p.: Hendrickson Publishers, 1956), 1087.

[19] Merrill F. Unger, *Unger's Survey of the Bible* (Eugene, Oregon: Harvest House Publishers, 1974), 355.

[20] James Orr, ed., *The International Standard Bible Encyclopedia*, vol. 2, 1087.

[21] "Lexical Aids to the Old Testament," in New American Standard Bible (1995), 1751.

[22] Author's translation.

[23] Author's translation.

[24] Craig S. Keener, *The Gospel of John* (Peabody, Massachusetts: Hendrickson Publishers, Inc., 2003), 653.

[25] Ibid.

[26] Commonly known as "If Christ is not Lord of all He is not Lord at all."

[27] C. Leslie Mitton, *The Epistle of James* (Grand Rapids, Michigan: Wm. B. Eerdmans Publishing Co., 1996), 198.

[28] Ibid.

[29] Ibid.

[30] Footnote, New American Standard Bible (1995), 1642.

[31] John F. Walvoord and Roy B. Zuck, *The Bible Knowledge Commentary* (Wheaton, IL: Victor Books, 1983), 815-816.

[32] Ibid., 815.

[33] Ibid.

34 Ibid.

35 Ibid.

36 Ibid.

37 "Lexical Aids to the New Testament," in New American Standard Bible (1995), 1827.

38 www.ericliddell.org

39 John A. Robinson, *Redating the New Testament*, 122.

40 J.C. Brumfield, *Comfort for Troubled Christians* (Chicago: Moody Publishers, 1961), 4.

41 "Lexical Aids to the New Testament," in New American Standard Bible, 1886.

42 Douglas J. Moo, *The Letter of James* (Grand Rapids, Michigan: Wm. B. Eerdmans Publishing Co., 2000), 54-55.

43 Arnold G. Fruchtenbaum, *Ariel's Bible Commentary*, 218.

44 J. Dwight Pentecost, *Designed to Be Like Him* (Grand Rapids: Kregel Publications, 1966), 60.

45 KJV Rainbow Study Bible (Illustrated Reference Edition), Rainbow Study International, EL Reno, OK, 1998, p. 1355.

46 Martin Dibelius, *James, A Commentary on the Epistle of James* (Philadelphia: Fortress, 1976), 74.

47 Peter H. Davis, *The New International Greek Testament Commentary, The Epistle of James* (Grand Rapids Michigan: Wm. B. Eerdmans Publishing Co., 1982), 69.

48 Arnold G. Fruchtenbaum, *Ariel's Bible Commentary*, 219.

49 Ibid., 220.

50 Douglas J. Moo, *The Letter of James*, 57.

51 Martin Dibelius, *James*, 79.

52 D. Edmond Hiebert, *James* (n.p.: The Moody Bible Institute of Chicago, 1992), 71.

53 Martin Dibelius, *James*, 83.

54 New American Standard Bible (1995), 1817.

55 C. Leslie Mitton, *The Epistle of James*, 152.

56 Douglas J. Moo, *The Letter of James*, 187.

57 Ibid., L.T. Johnson, "The Use of Leviticus in the Letter of James" (1982), in Douglas J. Moo, *The Letter of James*.

58 John F. Walvoord and Roy B. Zuck, *The Bible Knowledge Commentary*, 754.

59 A.T. Robertson, *Word Pictures in the New Testament*, vol. 6, *The General Epistles and the Revelation of John* (Nashville, TN: Broadman Press, 1933), 27.

60 James Orr, etc. The International Standard Bible Encyclopedia vol. II Wm. B. Eerdmans Publishing Co. 1939, 1956. p. 1088.

61 William J. Federer, *America's God and Country* (St Louis, MO: Amerisearch, Inc., 2000), back cover.

62 Martin Dibelius, *James,* 83.

63 Douglas J. Moo, *The Letter of James*, 68.

64 Arnold G. Fruchtenbaum, *Ariel's Bible Commentary,* 222.

65 Douglas J. Moo, *The Letter of James*, 71.

66 C. Leslie Mitton, *The Epistle of James*, 44.

67 "Lexical Aids to the New Testament," in New American Standard Bible, 1880: "In 1 Jn. 4:18 he tells us agape, perfect love, means the love that is not wanting, the love which accomplishes its goal. Frequently it means full growth, either of men or beasts (1 Cor. 2:6; 14:20; Eph. 4:13; Heb. 5:14)."

68 C. Leslie Mitton, *The Epistle of James*, 44-45, emphasis added.

69 Zane Hodges, *The Epistle of James*, 26.

70 Lewis, Gordon R. "God's Attributes of." *Evangelical Dictionary of Theology*. Walter A. Elwell, ed. Grand Rapids: Baker, 1984.

71 Zane Hodges, *The Epistle of James*, 29.

72 New American Standard Bible (1995), 1495.

73 Ronald F. Youngblood, in Frank E. Gaebelein, *The Expositor's Bible Commentary*, vol. 3 (Grand Rapids, Michigan: Zondervan, 1992), 1096. Kirkpatrick, *The Second Book of Samuel*, p. 223; cf. Job 1:12; 2:6-7, 10; cf. KD, 503. Archer, *Encyclopedia of Bible Difficulties,* 186-88. Kaiser, *Hard Sayings of the Old Testament*, 129-132.

[74] John F. Walvoord and Roy B. Zuck, *The Bible Knowledge Commentary*, 481.

[75] Merrill F. Unger, *Unger's Survey of the Bible*, 271.

[76] George L. Bryson, *The Five Points Of Calvinism, The Word for Today* (Costa Mesa, CA: n.p., 2006), 9-10.

[77] Moses C. Onwubiko, *Eternal Security of the Believer*.

[78] New American Standard Bible, 1995 Update (LaHabra, CA: The Lockman Foundation, 1995), James 2:14.

[79] R.V.G. Tasker, *The Tyndale New Testament Commentaries: The General Epistle of James* (Grand Rapids, Michigan: Wm. B. Eerdmans Publishing Company, 1957), 49-50. See J.H. Moulton, Grammar of New Testament Greek, vol. 2, 222.

[80] R.V.G. Tasker, *The Tyndale New Testament Commentaries*, 50.

[81] John F. Walvoord and Roy B. Zuck, *The Bible Knowledge Commentary*, 637.

[82] A.T. Robertson, *Word Pictures in the New Testament*, vol. 6, *The General Epistles and the Revelation of John* (Nashville, TN: Broadman Press, 1933), 22.

[83] R.V.G. Tasker, *The Tyndale New Testament Commentaries*, 51.

[84] The aorist participle expresses simple action, as opposed to the continuous action of the present participle. It's like a snapshot or a photograph—it freezes a moment in time, and it stays that way forever.

[85] New American Standard Bible (1995).

[86] Frank E. Gaebelein, *The Practical Epistle of James* (Great Neck, New York: Doniger and Raughley, Inc., 1955), 71.

[87] A.T. Robertson, *Word Pictures in the New Testament*, vol. 6, 27.

[88] Arnold G. Fruchtenbaum, *Ariel's Bible Commentary*, 241.

[89] New American Standard Bible (1995), 1639.

[90] James Orr, ed., *The International Standard Bible Encyclopedia*, vol. 2, 1088.

[91] Ibid.

[92] Ibid.

[93] Martin Dibelius, *James,* 152.

[94] Earl D. Radmacher, ed., New King James Version (Nashville: Thomas Nelson, 2007), 1969.

[95] Earl D. Radmacher, *Nelson's New Illustrated Bible Commentary* (Nashville: Thomas Nelson, 1999), 1667.

[96] John Calvin, in Paul Enns, *The Moody Book of Theology* (Chicago: Moody Press, 1989), 452. Bromiley, *Historical Theology,* 236.

[97] Ibid.

[98] Frank E. Gaebelein, *The Practical Epistle of James* (Great Neck, New York: Doniger and Raughley, Inc., 1955), 71.

[99] Zane C. Hodges, *The Epistle of James* (Grace Evangelical Society, 1994), 65.

[100] C. Leslie Mitton, *The Epistle of James,* (WM. B. Eerdmans Publishing Company, Grand Rapids, Michigan, 1966), p. 108

[101] Ibid. p. 108.

[102] Martin Dibelius, *James,* 162.

[103] Frank E. Gaebelein, *The Practical Epistle of James,* 73.

[104] Positional justification is that act of grace whereby a sinner who trusts in Christ alone is acquitted of all penalties against Him on the merit of the work of Jesus Christ. Experiential justification is that act whereby the justice of God declares one righteous or worthy for super-abundant blessing on the basis of one's maximum application of His Word.

[105] Martin Dibelius, *James,* 181.

[106] Ibid.

[107] Arnold G. Fruchtenbaum, *Ariel's Bible Commentary,* 76.

[108] Note, New American Standard Bible (1995), 1675.

[109] Arnold G. Fruchtenbaum, *Ariel's Bible Commentary,* 276.

[110] C. Leslie Mitton, *The Epistle of James,* 122.

[111] Arnold G. Fruchtenbaum, *Ariel's Bible Commentary,* 276.

[112] C. Leslie Mitton, *The Epistle of James,* 130.

[113] R.V.G. Tasker, *The Tyndale New Testament Commentaries,* 77.

[114] Ibid., 82.

[115] Arnold G. Fruchtenbaum, *Ariel's Bible Commentary*, 283.

[116] C. Leslie Mitton, *The Epistle of James*, 134.

[117] Douglas J. Moo, *The Letter of James*, 170.

[118] Frank E. Gaebelein, ed., *The Expositor's Bible Commentary*, vol. 12 (Grand Rapids, Michigan: Zondervan, 1981), 190.

[119] Center note, New American Standard Bible (1995).

[120] C. Leslie Mitton, *The Epistle of James*, 140.

[121] Old sin nature: sin we inherit at birth, because of its origin in Adam.

[122] C. Leslie Mitton, *The Epistle of James*, 146.

[123] Ropes, J.H.: *A Critical and Evangelical Commentary on the Epistle of St. James* (International Critical commentary, T&T Clark, Edinburgh, 1954).

[124] C. Leslie Mitton, *The Epistle of James*.

[125] Ibid.

[126] R.V.G. Tasker, *The Tyndale New Testament Commentaries*, 85.

[127] C. Leslie Mitton, *The Epistle of James*, 150.

[128] Douglas J. Moo, *The Letter of James*, 186.

[129] C. Leslie Mitton, *The Epistle of James*, 152.

[130] Ibid.

[131] Zane Hodges, *The Epistle of James*, 106.

[132] Ibid., 93.

[133] Martin Dibelius, *James*, 224.

[134] Zane Hodges, *The Epistle of James*, 94.

[135] Martin Dibelius, *James*, 224.

[136] John F. MacArthur Jr., *The Gospel According to Jesus* (Grand Rapids, Michigan: Zondervan, 1988).

[137] Zane Hodges, *The Epistle of James*, 95.

[138] Joseph B. Mayor, *The Epistle of James* (Grand Rapids, Michigan: Kregel Publications, 1990), 228, 538.

[139] Moses C. Onwubiko, *Overview of God's Grace* (Jericho Press, Nashville, TN 2010).

[140] Douglas J. Moo, *The Letter of James*, 209.

[141] Joseph B. Mayor, *The Epistle of James*, 230, 540.

[142] R.V.G. Tasker, *The Tyndale New Testament Commentaries*, 109.

[143] Martin Dibelius, *James*, 235.

[144] R.V.G. Tasker, *The Tyndale New Testament Commentaries*, 109.

[145] Ibid., 110.

[146] Ibid., 112.

[147] Ibid.

[148] C. Leslie Mitton, *The Epistle of James*, 179.

[149] Ibid., 113.

[150] Ibid., 109-110.

[151] W.E. Vine, Merrill F. Unger, and William White Jr., *Vine's Complete Expository Dictionary of Old and New Testament Words* (n.p.: Thomas Nelson Publishers, 1996), 463.

[152] C. Leslie Mitton, *The Epistle of James*, 184.

[153] Ibid., 191.

[154] Arnold G. Fruchtenbaum, *Ariel's Bible Commentary*, 308.

[155] Footnote, New American Standard Bible (1995), 1642.

[156] Moses C. Onwubiko, *Signs and Wonders* (Jericho Press, Nashville, TN 2010).

[157] C. Leslie Mitton, *The Epistle of James*, 198.

[158] C. Leslie Mitton, *The Epistle of James*, 198.

[159] Footnote, New American Standard Bible (1995), 1642.

[160] Roy B. Zuck, *Basic Bible Interpretation* (Colorado Springs, Colorado: Chariot Victor Publishing, 1991), 87.

[161] Ibid.

[162] C. Leslie Mitton, *The Epistle of James*, 201.

163 Joseph B. Mayor, *The Epistle of James,* 236, 546. *Fragment of the Church,* 44.

164 Zane Hodges, *The Epistle of James,* 120.

165 Reference, New American Standard Bible (1995), 1639.

166 Joseph B. Mayor, *The Epistle of James,* 238 (548).

167 Reference, New American Standard Bible (1995), 1639.

168 James Orr, ed., *The International Standard Bible Encyclopedia,* vol. 2, 1087.

169 John F. Walvoord and Roy B. Zuck, *The Bible Knowledge Commentary,* 835.

# Bibliography

Brumfield, J.C. *Comfort for Troubled Christians*. Chicago: Moody Publishers, 1961.

Bryson, George L. *The Five Points Of Calvinism, The Word for Today*. Costa Mesa, CA, 2006.

Chafer, Lewis Sperry. *Systematic Theology*, vol. 7. Dallas, Texas: Dallas Seminary Press, 1948.

Davis, Peter H. *The New International Greek Testament Commentary, The Epistle of James*. Grand Rapids Michigan: Wm. B. Eerdmans Publishing Co., 1982.

Dibelius, Martin. *James, A Commentary on the Epistle of James*. Philadelphia: Fortress, 1976.

Enns, Paul. *The Moody Book of Theology*. Chicago: Moody Press, 1989.

Erickson, Millard J. *Christian Theology*. Grand Rapids: Baker Books, 1998.

Federer, William J. *America's God and Country*. St Louis, MO: Amerisearch, Inc., 2000.

Fruchtenbaum, Arnold G. *Ariel's Bible Commentary*. San Antonio, TX: Ariel Ministries, 2005.

Gaebelein, Frank E. *The Expositor's Bible Commentary*, vol. 3. Grand Rapids, Michigan: Zondervan, 1992.

Gaebelein, Frank E. *The Practical Epistle of James*. Great Neck, New York: Doniger and Raughley, Inc., 1955.

Hiebert, D. Edmond. *James*. The Moody Bible Institute of Chicago, 1992.

Hodges, Zane. *The Epistle of James*. Grace Evangelical Society, 1994.

Keener, Craig S. *The Gospel of John*. Peabody, Massachusetts: Hendrickson Publishers, Inc., 2003.

*KJV Rainbow Study Bible* (Illustrated Reference Edition). Rainbow Study International, EL Reno, OK, 1998.

Lewis, Gordon R. "God's Attributes of." *Evangelical Dictionary of Theology*. Walter A. Elwell, ed. Grand Rapids: Baker, 1984.

MacArthur Jr., John F. *The Gospel According to Jesus*. Grand Rapids, Michigan: Zondervan, 1988.

Mayor, Joseph B. *The Epistle of James*. Grand Rapids, Michigan: Kregel Publications, 1990.

Mitton, C. Leslie. *The Epistle of James*. Grand Rapids, Michigan: Wm. B. Eerdmans Publishing Co., 1996.

Moo, Douglas J. *The Letter of James*. Grand Rapids, Michigan: Wm. B. Eerdmans Publishing Co., 2000.

Onwubiko, Moses C. *Eternal Security of the Believer*.

Onwubiko, Moses C. *Overview of God's Grace*. Nashville, TN: Jericho Press, 2010.

Onwubiko, Moses C. *Signs and Wonders*. Nashville, TN: Jericho Press, 2010.

Orr, James, ed. *The International Standard Bible Encyclopedia*, vol. 2.: Hendrickson Publishers, 1956.

Pentecost, J. Dwight. *Designed to Be Like Him*. Grand Rapids: Kregel Publications, 1966.

Radmacher, Earl D., ed. *New King James Version*. Nashville: Thomas Nelson, 2007.

Radmacher, Earl D. *Nelson's New Illustrated Bible Commentary*. Nashville: Thomas Nelson, 1999.

Robertson, A.T. *Word Pictures in the New Testament*, vol. 6, *The General Epistles and the Revelation of John*. Nashville, TN: Broadman Press, 1933.

Robinson, John A. *Redating the New Testament*. Philadelphia: Westminster Press, 1976.

Ropes, J.H.: *A Critical and Evangelical Commentary on the Epistle of St. James*. International Critical Commentary, T&T Clark, Edinburgh: 1954.

Simons, Barbara B. *Webster's New World Dictionary*, The World Publishing Company, 1971.

Tasker, R.V.G. *The Tyndale New Testament Commentaries: The General Epistle of James*. Grand Rapids, Michigan: Wm. B. Eerdmans Publishing Company, 1957.

Unger, Merrill F. *Unger's Survey of the Bible*. Eugene, Oregon: Harvest House Publishers, 1974.

Vine, W.E. *An Expository Dictionary of New Testament Words*. London, UK: 1940.

Vine, W.E., Merrill F. Unger, and William White Jr. *Vine's Complete Expository Dictionary of Old and New Testament Words*: Thomas Nelson Publishers, 1996.

Walvoord, John F. and Roy B. Zuck. *The Bible Knowledge Commentary*. Wheaton, IL: Victor Books, 1983.

Zuck, Roy B. *Basic Bible Interpretation*. Colorado Springs, Colorado: Chariot Victor Publishing, 1991.

# Quick Guide to Key Words in James

*Faith* wherever the word, *faith* or its cognate *believe* is used, it's ALWAYS in reference to *Biblical truth* (1:3; 2:5, 14, 17, 18, 19, 20, 22, 24, 26), (with only 4 exceptions).

• *faith* (**trust**) to mean salvation from the eternal penalty of sin.
  1) 2:1, as in "*do not hold your faith* [**trust**] *in our glorious Lord Jesus Christ with an attitude of personal favoritism*" and in
  2) 2:24, "*You see that a man is justified by works* [**application of Biblical truth for a reward**], *and not by faith* [*trust*] *alone* [for eternal salvation]"; 24b). *Two justifications are in view!*

• *faith* with reference to having *confidence* in God as regards prayer
  3) 1:6 "*But he must ask in faith without any doubting*"
  4) 5:15 "*And the prayer offered in faith will restore the one who is sick*"

*Save:* Can be used in a spiritual or physical sense. In the spiritual sense, it is ALWAYS in relation to salvation from the eternal penalty of sin. James uses it that way, only once (4:12); the rest of the times, he ALWAYS used it in relation to salvation from premature physical death (1:21; 2:14; 5:15, 20).

*Dead:* James only uses it to mean uselessness or inactive, and never uses it to reference a corpse.

*Works*: The word, *works* in James's Epistle, ALWAYS refers to *works* of application of Biblical truth (2:14, 17, 18, 20, 21, 22, 24, 25, 26; 3:13).

*Soul:* Appears only twice in James's Epistle and in both cases, they reference human life (James 1:21; 5:20).

*Fruit:* Appeared only once in the entire text, and he uses it in a metaphorical sense (James 1:18).

*Anointing oil:* Was used once by James' and is RESTRICTED ONLY to medicinal use (never for spiritual purposes). His use of *aleipho*, puts to rest any possible thought for a debate.

## PUBLICATIONS AVAILABLE FREE OF CHARGE

*Riding the Death Train*
*(A powerful tool for evangelism)*
*Montados en el Tren de la Muerte*
*(Riding the Death Train* in Spanish)
*Eternal Security of the Believer*
*Comfort in Suffering*
*God's Plan after Salvation*
*Biblical Doctrine of Salvation*
*Focus on Christian Marriage*
*Overview of God's Grace*
*Paul, a Trophy of God's Grace*
*Joseph, A Pillar of Grace*
*Signs & Wonders (A Biblical Reply to the Claims of*
*Modern Day Miracle Workers)*
*The Spiritual Gift of Tongues (A Biblical Response to*
*Modern Day Tongues)*
*Disaster: God's Warning Bell*


*Grow in the grace and knowledge of our Lord and Savior Jesus Christ. To Him be the glory, both now and To the day of eternity. Amen (2 Peter 3:18).*

To receive this or any other publication,
please write:

**In the U.S.A.**
Grace Evangelistic Ministries
P. O. Box 111999
Nashville, TN 37222-1999
U.S.A.
www.GEMworldwide.org

**In Africa**
Grace Evangelistic Ministries
P. O. Box 583
Jos, Plateau State
Nigeria
www.GEMAfrica.org

**In the U.K.**
Grace Evangelistic Ministries Europe
Mail Box 212
179 Whiteladies Road
Clifton, Bristol
BS8 2AG
United Kingdom
www.GEMEurope.org

# Notes

# Notes

**Notes**

# Notes

# Notes

**Notes**

**Notes**

# Notes

# Notes

**Notes**

# James

## Faith Without Works Is Dead

### An Urgent Call to Practical Christianity

# "Buy Truth, and do not sell it."
## Proverbs 23:23a

Are you aware that sound Bible teaching is a precious and a priceless piece of spiritual jewelry? Indeed, Church History has shown how difficult it is to come by, especially in Christianity today! So when God, from His jewel box of grace, exposes us to pearls of Truth in His infallible and inerrant Word, we ought to embrace and cherish them without reserve. Sound Bible teaching and its application are the treasures that hold our capacity to enjoy abundant life, maximum happiness, friendship, marriage, business, and the source of our unprecedented blessing for today, tomorrow and eternity. Therefore my beloved, "buy Truth" [stay rooted in sound biblical teaching], for Truth *"...is better than jewels; and all desirable things cannot compare with her [it]"* (Proverbs 8:11).